BIBLIOGRAPHY
OF
COMMONWEALTH
LAW REPORTS

BIBLIOGRAPHY OF COMMONWEALTH LAW REPORTS

Edited by
Wallace Breem
and
Sally Phillips

MANSELL

LONDON AND NEW YORK

First published 1991 by
Mansell Publishing Limited, *A Cassell Imprint*
Villiers House, 41–47 Strand, London WC2N 5JE, England
387 Park Avenue South, New York, NY 10016–8810, U.S.A.

British Library Cataloguing in Publication Data

Bibliography of Commonwealth law reports.
1. Commonwealth countries. Law
I. Breem, Wallace II. Phillips, Sally
016.34171241084

ISBN 0–7201–2023–3

Library of Congress Cataloging-in-Publication Data applied for.

This book has been printed and bound in Great Britain by
Biddles Ltd, Guildford and King's Lynn

Law librarians all over Britain were shocked by the sudden death of Wallace Breem, Librarian of the Inner Temple, London and President of the British and Irish Association of Law Librarians, on 12 March 1990—just six weeks after the corrected final proofs had been delivered to the publishers. It was in 1981, that he, as Chairman of BIALL's Standing Committee on Publications, began to plan this work and persuaded me that to act as co-editor was something I always wanted. Over the following years we worked closely together and I came to know him and appreciate his deep knowledge of bibliographical sources and meticulous scholarship. I shall always regard it as a particular and personal tragedy that he never saw the final work.

S.P.
June 1990

As Wallace would have wished, this book is dedicated

TO RIKKI

CONTENTS

THE CONTRIBUTORS

Charles Benson, M.A., Dip.Lib.Stud. Keeper of Early Printed Books, Trinity College Library, Dublin

Jean Burdzik, B.Bibl., LL.B., LL.M. (Witwatersrand), Senior Lecturer, Department of Private Law, University of South Africa

Sheila Cameron, M.A., M.Litt., A.L.A., *formerly* Assistant Librarian, Institute of Advanced Legal Studies, London

Hilary Charlton, LL.B., *formerly* Law Librarian, University of Dundee

John Dyrud, B.A., M.A., LL.B., J.D., Member of the Maryland Bar, Law Librarian and Senior Lecturer in Law, University of the West Indies

A. J. Edwards, B.Sc., Dip.N.Z.L.S., A.N.Z.L.A., Law Librarian, University of Otago, New Zealand

E. J. Glasson, LL.B., Dip.Lib., Law Librarian, Monash University, Australia

Elizabeth Gleeson, B.A., Dip.Lib., Barrister, Law Librarian, Trinity College Library, Dublin

H. C. Jain, M.A. (Eco.), LL.B., B.Lib.Sci., Librarian, Indian Law Institute, New Delhi

Oluremi Jegede, M.L.S., Barrister, Institute Librarian, Nigerian Institute of Advanced Legal Studies, Lagos

Robert G. Logan, LL.B., F.L.A., Assistant Librarian, Bodleian Law Library, Oxford

Alice G. Nkhoma-Wamunza, B.A., M.A., Senior Librarian and Head, Law Collection, University of Dar es Salaam

Sally Phillips, B.L., F.L.A., Supreme Court Librarian, London, *formerly* Librarian, Law Commission, London

Parmodh Singh, B.A., LL.B., LL.H., Deputy Librarian, Indian Law Institute, New Delhi

Nigel Smith, M.A., LL.B., A.L.A., Information Services Manager, Curtis Simpson, Leeds, *formerly* Law Librarian, University of Nottingham

Jules Winterton, B.A., LL.B., Dip.Lib., A.L.A., Law Librarian, Queen Mary College, University of London, *formerly* Assistant Librarian, Institute of Advanced Legal Studies, London

INTRODUCTION

Over fifty years have elapsed since W. H. Maxwell and C. R. Brown's *Complete list of British and colonial law reports and legal periodicals*, 3rd edition, was issued in 1937 for private circulation only. This work was described in an untitled preface as being a 'check-list' and its compilers, both in publishing, stated that 'the notes are not intended to supersede those in Soule's *Lawyer's reference manual* [of 1883]. A fifteen page supplement followed in 1946.

As was inevitable, a high proportion of Maxwell and Brown's data was drawn from secondary sources, publishers' catalogues, files and lists, as well as library catalogues; the balance from the books themselves. Their work also included schedules of English sovereigns, the Year Books, and of countries issuing legislation. The core material totalled some 1743 law report titles and *c.* 343 periodicals, of which only a proportion included either reports of or notes of cases. Included also were selected treatises containing unreported cases. The extensive notes throughout gave useful information about editions, contents, parts, collations, 'ghosts', etc. Though their work's title was always more ambitious than accurate as later research has shown, the 3rd edition is an achievement which those who follow after must acknowledge with respect. It remains still a valuable research tool for the bibliographer. The relevant text was subsequently incorporated with added material in W. H. and L. F. Maxwell's *Legal bibliography of the British Commonwealth of Nations*, 2nd edition, issued in seven volumes in 1954–64, but the alterations necessary for a differing style of presentation varied in quality and the notes were heavily excised to suit the economic discipline of a more austere publishing age.

The Maxwells' *Legal bibliography* was out of print for nearly a decade (reprinted London, John Rees, 1989–91), and though Maxwell and Brown's work was reprinted in 1974 by a Canadian publisher, the need for an updated edition or replacement has grown more urgent as this century draws towards its close. For there has developed firstly, a 'boom' in the issue of new law report titles, particularly in respect of specialist or subject reports; secondly, a need for practising lawyers to consult and cite if necessary, not only the proliferating case law of common law jurisdictions other than their own, but also notes of cases now printed in almost every professional journal whether designed in the first instance for lawyers or not. As a result it is not unreasonable to suggest that while an update of Maxwell and Maxwell remains highly desirable, a successor to Maxwell and Brown is the more essential.

This bibliography first germinated in a proposal approved by the British and Irish Association of Law Librarians' (BIALL) Standing Committee on Publications in

1981. It was agreed initially that a work of this kind could best be undertaken with the assistance of contributors outside the United Kingdom who would be responsible for collecting the information pertaining to their own jurisdictions. In the event it proved impossible to cover every jurisdiction in this way, not only for some of the smaller jurisdictions, such as The Gambia, but also for some of the larger, such as Canada.

The Contributors

A list of contributors is given at the beginning of the work. For practical reasons it is not possible to attribute individual responsibility but in general the contributor's country of residence determines their contribution. Some exceptions to this require notice. Robert Logan was responsible for pre-1865 England and Wales, Sheila Cameron and Nigel Smith for post-1865 material, Sally Phillips for Canada, Jules Winterton for Sri Lanka and a variety of small jurisdictions. The delay between receipt of the contributions and their delivery to the publisher was due partly to illness on the part of both editors but chiefly to the complexity of the work involved in editing them for publication. The difficulties of this task were sadly underestimated.

Scope

The *Bibliography of Commonwealth Law Reports* is a work of enumerative not descriptive bibliography and aims to record all published law report titles issued by Commonwealth jurisdictions, whether primary (Canada) or subordinate (Punjab), that may be cited by lawyers for professional purposes.

The term 'Commonwealth' is taken to include: (1) all sovereign jurisdictions which are or have been members of the Commonwealth (Sri Lanka, and South Africa), or formed a part of the former British Empire (Aden, now part of South Yemen; and Burma); (2) all dependent and semi-dependent jurisdictions for whose external affairs either the U.K. or another member nation is responsible (Bermuda and Gibraltar); and (3) all jurisdictions now defunct, lacking a precise successor (Bengal, the Federation of Rhodesia and Nyasaland, the Straits Settlements, and the Western Pacific High Commission) which have issued law reports. Reports of the former British North American colonies however are excluded, the major proportion having been published only by American learned societies, the whole possessing a historical rather than practical value.

The term 'published' is taken to cover material available for purchase (then or now) on the open market, reproduced in book form, microform or any information storage and retrieval system, except only the following which have in general been excluded: (1) journals, unless these issue law reports that may be separately distinguished through having either their own title page or pagination, or both; (2) tribunal reports, unless published and held citable in courts of law; (3) court records (containing cases) published by learned societies; (4) works, such as treatises, which include unreported cases, but which were not primarily published for their law report content, together with case books designed for students, the report content of which may be found elsewhere; (5) law report digests.

Editorial discretion has been exercised however, often upon a contributor's advice and greater knowledge of his own jurisdiction's practice, by the inclusion of titles in the excluded categories when in our combined views the circumstances seem to warrant an exception being made: for example the *Malayan Law Journal*, long a vehicle devoted almost exclusively to the reporting of cases (Indian law journals, identically structured, are generously represented also); digests, in instances where report publication for a particular jurisdiction is sparse and the digest adds to the coverage, not simply repeating it.

It must be stated that this *Bibliography* is not complete, even within our terms of reference. Those titles wanting fall into two categories: firstly, items known only through incomplete or imprecise references or listings, whose detail or even existence could not be ascertained; secondly, items missed through human error. As regards the latter we shall be grateful to readers who care to draw our attention to overlooked titles; these could possibly be issued in a supplement to *The Law Librarian*.

Method

Detailed procedural instructions were issued to each contributor and the basic style of the *Anglo-American Cataloguing Rules*, second edition, was followed with editorial preference being given to the modifications recommended by BIALL. Our instructions emphasized the need to refer to the work rather than to a secondary source but it was clear that no contributor would necessarily have all his jurisdiction's law reports within easy access, that time and distance alone might in the larger jurisdictions make examination impossible, and that recourse must be made to the most reliable secondary source available, whether a colleague or catalogue.

As regards Canada we naturally consulted the National Library of Canada's *Check-list of Law Reports and Statutes in Canadian Law Libraries*. A high proportion of these titles are held in United Kingdom libraries together with others which post-dated the *Check-list*. For the balance we had to rely on secondary sources and, more importantly, on the patience and good nature of individual Canadian librarians, who sent us copies of title pages and helped resolve conflicting evidence. A major exclusion requires notice. A large number of reports listed in the *Check-list* emanate from regulatory bodies, most of which appear to have been published in typescript and of these virtually none is available in the United Kingdom. We decided therefore that we would have to omit all the Canadian administrative reports and have done so.

Order of Arrangement

The *Bibliography* is arranged alphabetically by primary jurisdiction followed by subordinate jurisdiction. Within each jurisdiction the entries are arranged alphabetically by title with a second sequence listing reports which deal with particular subjects arranged under broad subject headings. We have tried to keep these headings consistent over all jurisdictions. Where the number of entries warrants this, however, the primary jurisdiction has a further sequence subdivided by courts. The alphabetical arrangement throughout is word by word, not letter by letter.

Jurisdiction

All primary jurisdictions are entered under their current official designation, for example, Malawi not Nyasaland, excepting only those now defunct, noted above, together with Palestine, subsequently divided, and Aden, absorbed by South Yemen, both being taken over by non-common law jurisdictions. The Index of Jurisdictions (p. 330) lists every jurisdiction mentioned, with references from former or variant names. Where appropriate primary jurisdictions are followed by subordinate jurisdictions. The choice of these was pragmatic, based on the material available. Some are constitutional, such as states comprising a federation, others are geographical regions, former separate territories, etc. Some have presented a more complex problem particularly those of India and Nigeria where internal constitutional changes have occurred more frequently since their independence than elsewhere. In general the same principles have been applied as in the case of primary jurisdictions. If the state or province has remained unaltered but for minor boundary changes it is recorded under the name currently in use; if however it has been split two or more ways it remains *sui generis* as regards its law report material. The schedule on the Nigerian states at page 164 of Moys' *Classification scheme for law books* (2nd ed. 1982), illustrates this procedure admirably. The genealogical/geographical development of the Indian states is even more complicated still as successor states were themselves split and absorbed by a new round of successor states. As a result few, if any, intermediate successors saw reports issued, printing the case law of their jurisdictions, and their names survive only in the short-lived coverage offered by the ubiquitous *All India Reporter*. In these circumstances it has seemed reasonable to accept as the successor state the one that has absorbed the major portion of an intermediate predecessor.

At the start of each jurisdiction we have given brief details of its political and constitutional history when this is relevant to law reporting. It should be emphasized, however, that this is not intended to be exhaustive. We have not made any attempt to include any information for jurisdictions which have no separate series of reports. Reports relating purely to a particular province or country will often also include reports from superior courts outside the jurisdiction concerned although these have not necessarily been separately noted. It is assumed that general reports of any jurisdiction will include reports from subordinate jurisdictions.

Form of Entry

In general it may be said that in the United Kingdom at least until 1865 law reports were issued only by individuals and are as a rule known best by the names of their editors, and that since that date reporting has been undertaken only commercially so that law reports are now best known by their title which may or may not have as its lead words the name of the publishing authority initiating the series.

The variants are considerable however and are as devious as human ingenuity can make them. The *Sessions Cases* of Scotland are as often cited by the names of their early editors as by the overall title of the series; Clark and Finnelly's *House of Lords Cases* is equally well known, and with better reason, by its title. Title pages can mislead the unwary for, in the first volume of two, Sabah's *Fanti Law Cases* is entitled *Fanti Customary Laws*; while in a series with a long life the popular title may be given formal recognition by appearing in print on the title page of a much later volume.

Entries appear under their title unless better known by the name of their editor or compiler, when they are so recorded with initials supplied. The title is given in 'full' but discretion has had to be exercised in extremely lengthy titles by omitting the less important parts. Such omissions are indicated by the insertion of three dots [...]. If the first words of the title are vague and insubstantial we have used the popular title as a filing title. The dates of coverage have been put at the end of the title statement.

Punctuation and Spelling

If punctuation is supplied in the title this is reproduced as it appears on the title page and is adjusted only if it makes for ambiguity; and, if not supplied on the title page, is only inserted to avoid ambiguity. Spelling has been preserved as it appears on the title page even if the spelling forms are archaic. If an editor's name however is used either as the form of entry or as an alternative and appears in two or more works under variant spellings then the most commonly used is the one adopted.

Coverage Dates

These have been given in the arabic form. If transposition has been necessary from a non-numeral form, for example, 'Mich. Term 2 Vict. to Mich. Term 17 Vict.' this form has been followed by the calendar dates in square brackets. Pairs of dates have been shown thus: 1961–69, but where the years covered are part of two calendar years they have been presented thus: 1971/2–1981/2. If a publication has stopped and started again the break has been divided by a semi-colon thus: 1919–50; 1952–to date. Open dates for live series are shown thus: 1960– .

Coverage dates as recorded on the title page do not always marry up with the coverage of the content matter within the volume(s). The difficulty in ascertaining precise coverage dates explains the discrepancies recorded in bibliographies and catalogues.

Imprint Data

The name of the publisher has only been included for entries which are still current, but all entries have the place of publication and date of publication. When there have been several editions of a title we have used the information from the latest and put the details of the earlier editions in a note.

The number of volumes issued is given in respect of completed series, but to the end of 1982 (the year in which contributors commenced work) in respect of series still in progress, regardless of whether or not the volumes themselves were actually numbered. But variations can arise in the case of both numbered and unnumbered series. In either instance, by instruction or reason of library policy, these may be bound in multiple parts that do not remain constant, creating the difficulty of knowing precisely how many published as opposed to bound volumes have actually been issued. These figures therefore should not be regarded as definitive.

Notes

Following the entry will be found a wide variety of information given in note form. This includes variations of title, details of preceding and succeeding series, the courts covered, the name of the editor and other bibliographical information which may be of value. Two of the more important are:

Reprint statement: An indication has been made, both where the work has been included in a reprint of several series of law reports and also where the reprint was an isolated event, generally fairly soon after publication. The latter is another area where information is particularly hard to find. Many major series are also available on either microfilm or microfiche. While the work was in proof stage, the editors received a copy of a microfiche catalogue from the Law Library Microform Consortium. It was too late to include in the main work details of all the volumes they have available but it includes most of the main series of English and Canadian reports. Anyone who is interested should write to the Consortium at P.O. Box 11033, Honolulu, Hawaii. In some jurisdictions, reports are available on a computerized database. For further details of these, users are referred to the publishers: LEXIS-Butterworth (Telepublishing Ltd), 6, Bell Yard, Temple Bar, London WC2A 2IR, and Q.L. Systems Ltd, 1, Gore Street, Kingston, Ontario, Canada K7L 2L1.

Changes in title: These are recorded under 'continuation of' or 'continued by' with the appropriate name(s) or title inserted. For practical reasons this form has been used not only for undisputed changes, for example the U.K. *Planning and Compensation Reports* but also (i) the continuation in 1953 of the *Times Law Reports* by the *Weekly Law Reports*, an official continuity not recorded in print, and (ii) the technical continuation of one series by another when two differently titled series, covering the same court, are linked by continuous coverage of the court in question.

Indexes

There are three separate indexes.

The Title Index lists all items under the form given in the *Bibliography*, together with the jurisdiction (if this is not apparent from the title), dates and any other information necessary for identification. It also includes the variations of title mentioned in the notes following the entry. Since the manner in which law reports are cited tends to be idiosyncratic, we have tried to include all the variants given by our contributors. We have not, however, made any attempt to include abbreviations since lists of these are already generally available to which the user is referred, the most recent being Raistrick's *Index to Legal Citations*, 1981.

The Subject Index is subdivided by jurisdictions and refers to specific topics rather than the general headings used in the main sequence.

The Index of Jurisdictions lists all jurisdictions and subordinate jurisdictions and includes references from former and variant names.

Acknowledgments

Firstly we wish to thank the contributors to the main text, all of whom were in full-time employment and gave so willingly of their time and energy to make this work possible. The majority were not members of BIALL and their assistance is the more appreciated for this simple fact.

We are indebted to the following institutions who made their resources and knowledge available to us: the Bodleian Law Library; the Canadian High Commission, London; the India Office Library; the Institut für Internationales und Ausländische Recht Und Rechtsvergleichung Frei Universität, Berlin; the Institute of Advanced Legal Studies, London; Lincoln's Inn Library; the Max Planck Institut für Ausländische und Internationales Privatrecht, Hamburg; the Middle Temple Library; the School of Oriental and African Studies Library; and the Law Library of the University of Zimbabwe.

We thank also the following for their valuable advice and assistance: Mr Ken Best, formerly Departmental Librarian to the Lord Chancellor's Department; Miss Sheila Cameron; Mr Balfour Halévy, Law Librarian, York University; Miss Susan Jackson, Director of Library Services, Department of Justice, Canada; Mr Robert Logan; Sir Orby Mootham, formerly Chief of the High Court of Judicature at Allahabad; Miss Iris O'Donnell, College of Law Library, University of Saskatchewan; Miss Daphne Parnham, Sub Librarian to the Inner Temple; the Secretary, Council for Law Reporting, Accra; and Miss Mary Jane T. Sinclair, Assistant Librarian, Supreme Court of Canada, and last but not least Veronica Higgs from Mansell Publishing Limited whose patience and understanding have been sorely tried over the past years.

End Note

The task of editing this work has occupied a considerable proportion of our time since 1981 and we feel that Dr Johnson's view that lexicographers are 'well meaning drudges' could with equal relevance be applied to bibliographers. As to whether our work will prove as useful as we hope, only time can tell.

Wallace Breem
Sally Phillips

THE BIBLIOGRAPHY

A F R I C A

SUBJECT REPORTS

Mercantile Law

1. The African law reports. Commercial series, 1964- . Oxford, Law Reports International, 1968- . 33 v.

Includes reports from all territories in Africa, Privy Council appeals to 1970. To 1973 published Dobbs Ferry, Oceana Publications.

EAST AFRICA

2. East Africa law reports ... cases in the Court of Appeal for East Africa, 1968-75. London, 1968-75. 8 v.

Continuation of: Eastern Africa law reports. Includes cases from Kenya, Tanzania and Uganda.

3. [Eastern Africa Court of Appeal reports.] Law reports of the Court of Appeal for Eastern Africa and of the ... Privy Council. 1934-56. Nairobi, 1935-57. 23 v.

Reprinted: Dobbs Ferry, Oceana Publications.

Continued by: Eastern Africa law reports. Includes cases from Kenya, Malawi, South Yemen, Tanzania and Uganda.

4. East African law reports. Cases ... in the Court of Appeal for Eastern Africa, the superior courts of the constituent territories and the Privy Council, 1957-67. London, 1957-68. 11 v.

To 1962 published in Durban. Includes cases from Somalia (to 1960), Tanzania (to 1961), Kenya, St Helena and Seychelles (to 1964), South Yemen (to 1967) and Uganda. Continuation of: Eastern Africa Court of Appeal reports. Continued by: East Africa law reports.

SOUTHERN AFRICA

5. Decisions in review and appeal cases in the Court of the Resident Commissioner of Basutoland, the Special Court of Bechuanaland Protectorate and the Special Court of Swaziland, 1935-38. Morija, 1937-39. 2 v.

6. The High Commission Territories law reports, 1926-66. Maseru, Lesotho, 1955-67. 10 v.

Continued in part by: Botswana law reports, Lesotho law reports, and Swaziland law reports. Includes cases from Botswana, Lesotho, and Swaziland.

WEST AFRICA

7. [West African Court of Appeal reports] Selected judgments of the West African Court of Appeal, 1930/33-55. London, 1936-57. 15 v.

Reprinted: London, Sweet and Maxwell, 1961-62.

Vol. 1-9 published in Accra. Includes cases from Gambia, Ghana, Nigeria and Sierra Leone; the reprint includes cases to 1960.

8. The West African law reports: cases in the Supreme Courts of the Gold Coast, Sierra Leone, Gambia, the High Court of Gambia Protectorate, West African Court of Appeal and appropriate cases in the Judicial Committee of the Privy Council, 1956-58. Achimota, 1956-61. 3 v.

Vol. 2 cases from Ghana and the Gambia; Vol. 3 cases from Ghana.

A U S T R A L I A

See also no. 316.

9. The Argus law reports, 1894-1958. Melbourne, 1895-1959. 66 v. Continued by: Australian Argus law reports.

10. Australian Argus law reports of the High Court of Australia, and Judicial Committee of the Privy Council, Federal Court of Bankruptcy, Supreme Courts of Australian Capital Territory, Northern Territory; and of matrimonial causes, 1959-72. Sydney, 1960-73. 15 v.

Continuation of: Argus law reports. Continued by: Australian law reports.

11. The Australian law journal reports, 1958/59- . Sydney, Law Book Company, 1958- . 25 v.

Microfiche: Sydney, Law Book Company.

Published as a separately paginated section of the Journal.

12. The Australian law reports being reports of judgments of the High Court of Australia, the Judicial Committee of the Privy Council,

the Federal Court of Australia, other federal courts and tribunals, state and territory supreme courts exercising federal jurisdiction, and incorporating reports of judgments of the Supreme Court of the Australian Capital Territory (revised by the judges) and authorized reports of the Supreme Court of the Northern Territory, 1973- . Sydney, Butterworths, Australia, 1974- . 43 v.

Continuation of: Australian Argus law reports.

13. The Commonwealth law reports: cases determined in the High Court of Australia, 1903/04- . Sydney, Law Book Company, 1905- . 144 v.

Microfiche: Sydney, Law Book Company.

14. The Federal law reports being reports of cases decided by the Federal Court of Australia, the Family Court of Australia and other federal courts (other than the High Court), state courts exercising federal jurisdiction, courts of territories, the Courts-Martial Appeal Tribunal, the Trade Practices Tribunal, the Copyright Tribunal and the Administrative Appeals Tribunal, 1956/60- . Sydney, Law Book Company, 1956- . 57 v.

Microfiche: Sydney, Law Book Company.

SUBJECT REPORTS

Administrative Law

See also no. 14.

15. Administrative law decisions, being the authorized reports of decisions of the Administrative Appeals Tribunal (with notes of decisions not fully reported) together with reports of cases on appeal from the Tribunal, 1976/78- . Sydney, Butterworths, Australia, 1979- . 4 v.

Criminal Law

16. The Australian criminal reports, 1979/80- . Sydney, Law Book Company, 1981- . 5 v.

Family Law

17. Australian family law cases, 1976- . North Ryde, CCH Australia, 1977- . 7 v.

18. Family law reports being reports of judgments on family law of the High Court of Australia, the Family Court of Australia, the

Family Court of Western Australia, the supreme courts of the states and territories, 1976- . Sydney, Butterworths, Australia, 1977- . 7 v.

Industrial Law

19. Commonwealth arbitration reports, 1905/07- . Canberra, Australian Government Publishing Service, 1908- . 267 v.

Microfiche.

20. Commonwealth Public Service arbitration reports. Determinations made and interpretations given during the period ... pursuant to the Public Service Arbitration Act 1920, 1921- . Canberra, Australian Government Publishing Service, 1921- . 83 v.

21. Industrial reports, 1981- . Sydney, Law Book Company, 1982- . 2 v.

Intellectual Property

22. Australian industrial & intellectual property cases, 1982- . North Ryde, CCH Australia, 1983- .

23. Intellectual property reports, 1983- . Sydney, Butterworths, Australia, 1983- .

Land Law

24. Australian & New Zealand conveyancing reports, 1979- . North Ryde, CCH Australia, 1981- . 2 v.

First vol: includes cases from 1978.

25. Australian planning appeal decisions, 1980/81- . Sydney, Law Book Company, 1983- .

Continuation, in part, of: South Australian planning appeals.

Local Government

26. The local government reports of Australia being decisions relating to local government, valuation of land, compensation and town planning throughout Australia including the authorized reports of local government cases in the N.S.W. Land and Valuation Court, 1956- . Sydney, Law Book Company, 1957- . 45 v.

Continuation, in part, of: N.S.W. local government reports.

Mercantile Law

27. Australian & New Zealand insurance cases, 1979/81- . North Ryde, CCH Australia, 1982- . 1 v.

28. Australian bankruptcy cases being reports of cases decided in the courts having jurisdiction in bankruptcy throughout Australia, 1928/29-1957/64. Sydney, 1930-65. 20 v.

29. Australian company law cases, 1971/73- . North Ryde, CCH Australia, 1971- . 6 v.

Title varies: 1977-81 Company law cases.

30. Australian company law reports, 1974/76- . Sydney, Butterworths, Australia, 1977- . 6 v.

31. Australian consumer sales and credit law reporter cases, 1978- . North Ryde, CCH Australia, 1978- . 2 v.

32. Australian securities law cases, 1971- . North Ryde, CCH Australia, 1971- . 1 v.

33. Australian trade practices reports, 1974/77- . North Ryde, CCH Australia, 1978- . 3 v.

34. Trade Practices Commission decisions and determinations, 1975/76. Sydney, 1976. 1 v.

35. Trade practices reporting service, 1974-81. Sydney, Law Book Company, 1976-81. 6 v., looseleaf.

Continued by: Trade practices reports.

36. Trade practices reports, 1974/80- . Sydney, Law Book Company, 1983- . 4 v.

Volumes not published in chronological sequence. V. 1 covers 1981-82, v. 2, 1982-83; v. 3, 1974-80; v. 4, 1978-81. Continuation of: Trade practices reporting service. Cases and decisions section.

Practice

37. Australian High Court and Federal Court practice reports, 1978- . North Ryde, CCH Australia, 1979- . 2 v.

Revenue Law

38. Australasian tax decisions being the reports of tax cases issued as the court decisions section of the Law Book Company's Taxation Service, 1943/45-1968/69. Sydney, 1945-69. 8 v.

Reprinted: Sydney: CCH Australia as part of Australian tax decisions.

Continuation of: Australian tax decisions. Continued by: Australian tax cases. Includes New Zealand cases.

39. Australasian tax reports, 1968- . Sydney, Butterworths, Australia, 1970- . 13 v.

Continuation of: Australian and New Zealand income tax reports.

40. The Australian and New Zealand income tax reports, 1936-69. Sydney, 1940-69. 10 v.

Continued by: Australasian tax reports. Title varies: v. 1-2, Australian income tax reports. From v. 3 includes New Zealand cases.

41. Australian estate and gift duty cases, 1971-80. North Ryde, 1971-80. 1 v.

42. Australian tax cases, 1969- . North Ryde, CCH Australia, 1969- . 14 v.

Continuation of: Taxation Board of Review decisions, n.s. and Australasian tax decisions. 1969-82 includes New Zealand cases.

43. Australian tax decisions being the reports of tax cases issued as the court decisions section of the Law Book Company's Taxation Service, 1930/32-1940/42. Sydney, 1932-42. 6 v.

Reprinted: Sydney, CCH Australia.

Continuation of: Income tax decisions of Australasia. Continued by: Australasian tax decisions. v. 6 has Appendix entitled New Zealand tax decisions 1931-1942.

44. Commonwealth Taxation Board of Review decision (New series), 1950- . Sydney, Butterworths, Australia, 1952- . 25 v.

Continuation of: Taxation Board of Review decisions.

45. Income tax decisions of Australasia being a compendium of reported and numerous unreported legal decisions (excepting the New South Wales Court of Review), on appeals arising under the Income Tax Assessment Acts of the Commonwealth and the states of Australia and the Dominion of New Zealand, 1891-1930. Sydney, 1928-31. 2 v.

Continued by: Australian tax decisions. Also known as: Ratcliff and McGrath's Income tax decisions. v. 1-2 contain sections of New Zealand cases, 1893-1927 and 1928 respectively from the New Zealand law reports.

46. [Taxation Board of Review decisions] Income tax assessment act. Decisions of the Board of Review, 1926-50. Canberra, 1927-51. 15 v.

Selected decisions reprinted as Commonwealth Taxation Board of Review decisions: Canberra, 1968-69.

Continued by: Taxation Board of Review decisions (n.s.) **and** Commonwealth Taxation Board of Review decisions (n.s.). Title varies: to 1942 Income Tax Board of Review decisions.

47. Taxation Board of Review decisions (New series), 1950/51-1967/68. Sydney, 1951-69. 18 v.

Continued by: Australian tax cases.

AUSTRALIAN CAPITAL TERRITORY

48. Australian Capital Territory reports, being reports of cases decided in the Supreme Court of the Australian Capital Territory, 1973- . Sydney, Butterworths, Australia, 1974- . 43 v.

Published as a separately paginated series in the Australian law reports.

NEW SOUTH WALES

49. A'Beckett, W. Reserved and equity judgments of the Supreme Court of New South Wales, 1845. Sydney, 1846. 1 v.

50. Knox, G. Cases argued and determined in the Supreme Court of New South Wales in its common law jurisdiction, 1877. Sydney, 1891. 1 v.

Microfiche: Sydney, Law Book Company.

51. Knox, G. and Linklater, F.H. Reports of cases argued and determined in the Supreme Court of New South Wales. New series, 1878-79. Sydney, 1879-80. 2 v.

Microfiche: Sydney, Law Book Company.

V. 2 has additional reporter: G.H. Fitzhardinge. Also known as Knox and Fitzhardinge's reports; New South Wales supreme court reports, n.s.

52. Legge, J.G. A selection of Supreme Court cases in New South Wales, 1825-62. Sydney, 1896. 2 v.

Microfiche: Sydney, Law Book Company.

53. New South Wales district court reports, 1952-75. Sydney, 1969-76. 3 v.

54. The New South Wales law reports, 1880-1900. Sydney, 1881-1900. 21 v.

Microfiche: Sydney, Law Book Company.

Continued by: State reports, New South Wales. Published in three series. 1 Cases at law; 2 Cases in equity; 3 Matrimonial cases.

55. The New South Wales law reports, 1971- . Sydney, Law Book Company, 1971- . 24 v.

Continuation of: State reports, New South Wales.

56. New South Wales reports: authentic law reports of the Supreme Court of New South Wales and the Land and Valuation Court, 1960-70. Sydney, 1960-71. 21 v.

Microfilm, microfiche: Sydney, Butterworths, Australia.

57. New South Wales statute law decisions. Cases decided by the courts of N.S.W., the High Court of Australia and the Privy Council, in which sections of N.S.W. statutes have been the subject of judicial interpretation, 1825/1918-1919/29. Sydney, 1919-29. 2 v.

58. [New South Wales Supreme Court reports] Reports of cases argued and determined in the Supreme Court of New South Wales, 1862-76. Sydney, 1863-93. 14 v.

Microfiche: Sydney, Law Book Company.

59. New South Wales weekly notes, 1884/85-1970. Sydney, 1885-1971. 92 v.

Microfiche: Sydney, Law Book Company.

Incorporates the New South Wales bankruptcy, company and probate cases from 1900.

60. The State reports, New South Wales, 1901-70. Sydney, 1902-72. 72 v.

Microfiche: Sydney, Law Book Company.

61. [Tarleton's term reports] Reports of cases argued and determined in the Supreme Court of New South Wales, 1881-82. Sydney, 1881-82. 2 v.

SUBJECT REPORTS

Industrial Law

62. The industrial arbitration reports New South Wales, 1902- . Sydney, Government Printer, 1902- . 79 v.

63. Industrial reports, 1981/82- . Sydney, Law Book Company, 1982- 1 v.

64. Workers' compensation reports New South Wales, 1926/27- . Sydney, Workers' Compensation Commission of New South Wales, 1928- . 52 v.

Land Law

See also no. 26.

65. Butterworths property reports being reports of decisions of the Supreme Court of New South Wales relating to conveyancing and property matters together with reports of decisions on appeal, 1982-. Sydney, Butterworths, Australia, 1982- .

Published as part of: Charlebois, Francis and Young's Conveyancing service - New South Wales. Contains only decisions of the Supreme Court of New South Wales that are not reported in the authorized reports.

66. The Land and Valuation Court reports of New South Wales, 1922-70. Sydney, 1923-72. 49 v.

For the authorised reports of cases decided in the Court **see** The N.S.W. Local government reports.

67. [Land Court cases] Reports of cases determined in the Land Court of New South Wales, 1890/92-1921. Sydney, 1893-1922. 31 v.

68. New South Wales conveyancing reports, 1980- . North Ryde, CCH Australia, 1980- . 1 v.

Local Government

69. The Local Government Appeal Tribunal reports of New South Wales: the authorized reports of the Local Government Appeals Tribunal, 1972/73-1975/76. Sydney, 1973-79. 4 v.

70. The N.S.W. local government reports ... comprising selected decisions on local government law and practice of the various courts of New South Wales and the High Court of Australia, 1911/13 - 1955/56. Sydney, 1913-57. 20 v.

Continued by: Local government reports of Australia.

Mercantile Law

71. The New South Wales bankruptcy, company and probate cases, 1890/91-1899. Sydney, 1891-99. 9 v.

Incorporated in New South Wales weekly notes.

Revenue Notes

72. N.S.W. Court of Review decisions containing judgments of the N.S.W. Court of Review on appeals arising out of income tax assessments made under the Income Tax (Management) Act, 1912. As amended to 1st July, 1927, 1913-27. Sydney. 1 v.

NORTHERN TERRITORY

73. Northern Territory judgments: a selection of the judgments of the Supreme Court of the Northern Territory of Australia, 1951-76. Canberra, 1982. 1 v.

74. Northern Territory reports, being reports of cases decided in the Supreme Court of the Northern Territory, 1979- . Sydney, Butterworths, Australia, 1980- . 17 v.

The Northern Territory reports commenced as a separately paginated series in the Australian law reports, v. 27.

QUEENSLAND

75. Beor, H.R. The Queensland law reports. Cases in equity, common law, admiralty, insolvency and criminal law, 1876-78. Brisbane, 1878-80. 1 v.

Microfiche: Sydney, Law Book Company.

76. The Queensland justice of the peace reports, 1907-72. Brisbane, 1907-72. 66 v.

Superseded by: Queensland lawyer reports. Bound with: Queensland justice of the peace.

77. The Queensland law journal reports, 1879-1901. Brisbane, 1884-1902. 11 v.

Microfiche: Sydney, Law Book Company.

78. The Queensland lawyer reports, 1973- . Brisbane, Law Book Company, 1973- . 6 v.

Superseded: Queensland justice of the peace reports. Published as part of: Queensland lawyer.

79. Queensland reports: decisions of the Supreme Court of Queensland, 1958- . Brisbane, Incorporated Council of Law Reporting for the State of Queensland, 1960- . 22 v.

Microfiche: Sydney, Law Book Company.

Continuation of. Queensland state reports.

80. [Queensland state reports] State reports, Queensland. Decisions of the Supreme Court of Queensland, 1902/03-57. Brisbane, 1902-58. 32 v.

Microfiche: Sydney, Law Book Company.

Continued by: Queensland reports. Title varies: 1902-06 Queensland state reports.

81. [Queensland Supreme Court reports] Reports of cases argued and determined in the Supreme Court of Queensland, 1860-81. Brisbane, 1898-1902. 5 v.

Microfiche: Sydney, Law Book Company.

SUBJECT REPORTS

Criminal Law

82. The Queensland criminal reports being a reprint of all criminal cases reported in The Supreme Court reports, vols. 1 to 5. The Queensland law journal and notes of cases, vols. I to XI, and the Queensland state reports and weekly notes 1860-1907. Brisbane, 1913. 1 v.

Industrial Law

83. Workers compensation reports, 1916- . Brisbane, Government Printer, 1916- . 26 v.

Land Law

84. The Crown lands law reports, Queensland, 1859/1900-1973. Brisbane, 1911-73. 40 v.

Continued by: Queensland Land Court reports.

85. Queensland conveyancing reports, 1982- . North Ryde, CCH Australia, 1982- . 1 v.

86. Queensland Land Courts reports, 1974- . Brisbane, Government Printer, 1975- . 8 v.

Continuation of: The Crown lands law reports, Queensland.

87. Queensland unit & group titles law and practice: court reports and tribunal decisions, 1980- . North Ryde, CCH Australia, 1980- . 1 v.

SOUTH AUSTRALIA

88. Pelham, L.J. Reports of cases in the Supreme Court of South Australia and in the Vice-Admiralty Court from July 1865 to Dec. 1866. Adelaide, 1867.

Reprinted 1906.

Known as v.0 of the South Australian law reports.

89. South Australian law reports. Reports of cases argued and determined in the Supreme Court of South Australia, 1867-92; 1899-1920. Adelaide, 1868-95; [1899-20.] 48 v.

Reprinted: Alexander Bros. Microfiche: Sydney, Law Book Company.

Continued by: State reports South Australia. 1893-98 never published. Includes as v.0, Pelham's reports, no. 88.

90. The South Australian state reports, 1971- . Melbourne, Law Book Company, 1971- . 30 v.

Microfiche: Sydney, Law Book Company.

Continuation of: State reports South Australia.

91. The State reports, South Australia, 1921-70. Melbourne, 1922-71. 50 v.

Microfiche: Sydney, Law Book Company.

Continuation of: South Australian law reports. Continued by: South Australian State reports.

SUBJECT REPORTS

Industrial Law

92. South Australian industrial reports, 1916/18- . Adelaide, Government Printer, 1918- . 47 v.

Land Law

93. South Australian planning reports, 1967-81. Adelaide, 1968-81. 15 v.

Continued by: Australian planning appeal decisions.

Licensing

94. The South Australian Licensing Court reports including reports of decisions given by the Full Court of the Supreme Court of South Australia sitting on appeal from decisions of the Licensing Court, 1967/69- . Adelaide, Government Printer, 1970- . 5 v.

TASMANIA

95. Nicholls, H. and Stops, W.J.T. Reports of cases determined in the Supreme Court of Tasmania, 1897-1904. Melbourne, 1906-07. 2 v.

Microfiche: Sydney, Law Book Company.

96. The Tasmanian law reports, 1904-40. Hobart, 1908-40. 35 v.

Microfiche: Sydney, Law Book Company.

Continued by: The Tasmanian reports.

97. The Tasmanian reports, 1941/46- . Hobart, Law Book Company, 1941- . 38 v.

Microfiche: 1941-78 Sydney, Law Book Company.

Continuation of: The Tasmanian law reports. Title varies: 1941-53 State reports Tasmania; 1954-78 Tasmanian State reports.

VICTORIA

98. A'Beckett, W. Reserved judgments of the Supreme Court of New South Wales, for District of Port Phillip, 1846-51. Melbourne, 1947-53. 1 v.

Reprinted: Sydney, Butterworths, Australia.

Title varies: 1852-53 Judgments of ...

99. The Australian jurist reports, 1870-74. Melbourne, 1871-75. 5 v.

Reprinted: Butterworths, Australia.

100. The Australian law times, 1879-1928. Melbourne, 1880-1929. 49 v.

Early volumes also report a few cases from other Australian jurisdictions, and New Zealand. In 1929 incorporated in the Victorian law reports.

101. County Court reports, 1962-72. Sydney, 1965-73. 1 v.

102. Victoria law times and legal observer, 1856-57. Melbourne, 1856-57. 2 v.

Reprinted: Butterworths, Australia.

103. The Victorian law reports, 1875-1957. Melbourne, 1876-1957. 81 v.

Reprinted: Sydney, Butterworths, Australia.

Continued by: Victorian reports. Published in four series. I Cases in equity; II Cases at law; III Insolvency, ecclesiastical and matrimonial cases; IV Cases on appeal to Chief Judge of Court of Mines. Incorporating, in 1959, the Australian law times reports.

104. The Victorian reports, 1870-72. Melbourne, 1874-[78]. 3 v.

Reprinted: Sydney, Butterworths, Australia.

Also known as: Webb, A'Beckett & Williams. Published in four series. I Cases in equity; II Cases at law; III Insolvency, ecclesiastical and matrimonial cases; IV Cases on appeal to Chief Judge of Court of Mines.

105. Victorian reports: cases determined in the Supreme Court of Victoria, 1956/57- . Sydney, Butterworths, Australia, 1957- . 26 v.

Continuation of: Victorian law reports and Australian law times reports.

106. Wyatt, A. and Webb, G.H.F. and A'Beckett, T. Reports of cases argued and determined in the Supreme Court of Victoria, 1861-63. Melbourne, 1863-65. 2 v.

Reprinted: Sydney, Butterworths, Australia.

107. Wyatt, A., Webb, G.H.F. and A'Beckett, T. Reports of cases argued and determined in the Supreme Court of Victoria, 1863-69. Melbourne, 1866-71. 6 v.

Reprinted: Sydney, Butterworths, Australia.

SUBJECT REPORTS

Industrial Law

108. Decisions. Workers Compensation Board (Victoria), 1938- . Melbourne, Cambec Press, 1945- . 4 v.

109. Victorian industrial reports, being reports of decisions of the Industrial Relations Commission of Victoria, together with appeals therefrom and other decisions relating generally to industrial law (with notes of decisions not fully reported), 1982- . Sydney, Butterworths, Australia 1982- .

Published as part of: Alley's Industrial law Victora. 2nd ed.

110. Victorian workers compensation cases, 1976- . North Ryde, CCH Australia, 1980- . 1 v.

Includes a few early cases from other jurisdictions.

Land Law

111. Torrens title cases: being a collection of important cases decided by the courts of England, Australasia, and Canada upon statutes relating to the transfer of land by registration of title, with a full digest of the cases by W.H. Hunter, 1865-93. Toronto, 1895. 1 v.

Also known as: Hunter's Torrens Act cases. The majority of cases in this volume are decisions of the Supreme Court of Victoria, and are also reported in the Victorian law reports.

112. Victorian conveyancing reports, 1981- . North Ryde, CCH Australia, 1981- .

113. Victorian planning appeal decisions. The authorised reports of the Town Planning Appeals Tribunal, the Environment Protection Appeal Board, and the Arbitrators under the Local Government Act, 1969- . Melbourne, Law Book Company, 1970- . 26 v.

Licensing

114. Victorian licensing decisions, 1976- . Sydney, Butterworths, Australia 1982- . 1 v.

Published as part of: Bourke's Liquor law (Victoria). 5th ed.

Practice

115. Williams, E.E. Reports of practice cases argued and determined in the Supreme Court of New South Wales, for the District of Port Phillip, 1846. Melbourne, 1847. 1 v.

Reprinted: Sydney, Butterworths, Australia.

Tort

116. Victorian motor accidents cases, 1982- . North Ryde, CCH Australia, 1982- . 1 v.

WESTERN AUSTRALIA

117. The Western Australian law reports, 1898/99-1957/59. Perth, 1900-60. 60 v.

Reprinted: Sydney, Butterworths, Australia, in 17 v.

Incorporated in Western Australian reports.

118. Western Australian reports, 1960- . Sydney, Butterworths, Australia, 1960- . 18 v.

Incorporates Western Australian law reports.

SUBJECT REPORTS

Family Law

119. The State reports (Western Australia). Being the authorised reports of the Family Court of Western Australia in the exercise of state jurisdiction and of the District Court of Western Australia, 1979/83- . Sydney, Law Book Company, 1980- . 1 v.

The bound v. title page is dated 1984.

Industrial Law

120. [Western Australia arbitration reports] Reports of proceedings before the Court of Arbitration, 1901/03-1915/20. Perth, 1904-25, 14 v.

Continued by: Western Australia industrial gazette. V. 1-11 includes proceedings of the Boards of Conciliation.

121. The Western Australian industrial gazette, 1921- . Perth, Government Printer, 1921- . 62 v.

Continuation of: Western Australia arbitration reports.

122. Workers' compensation decisions, 1949-65. Perth, 1949-65. 1 v.

123. Workers' compensation reports Western Australia, 1982- . Perth, Workers' Compensation Board of Western Australia, 1983- .

B A H A M A S

See also no. 1862

124. Bahamas law reports, 1977, pt. 1. Nassau, n.d.

No further issues published.

125. Solomon, K. The Bahamas law reports. Supreme court and magisterial court cases, 1900-06. Nassau, 1907. 1 v.

V. 1 only issued.

BANGLADESH

From August 1947 to 1971 known as East Pakistan.

126. Bangladesh cases reporter, 1982- . Dhaka, 1983- . 3 v.

127. Bangladesh law reports, containing cases determined by the High Court Division and Appellate Division of the Supreme Court of Bangladesh, 1972- . Dhaka, 1972- .

V. 1 does not cover Supreme Court cases.

128. Bangladesh legal decisions, containing cases determined by the Supreme Court of Bangladesh, 1981- . Dhaka, Bangladesh Bar Council, 1981- . 4 v.

129. Bangladesh Supreme Court reports: reports of cases decided by the Appellate Division of the Supreme Court of Bangladesh, 1977 . Dhaka, Bangladesh Institute of Law and International Affairs, 1977- . 6 v.

130. Dhaka law reports: a journal of law reports, 1949- . Dhaka, Dhaka law reports, 1949- . 36 v.

Subtitle varies: - 1969 cases of the High Court of Dacca; 1970-71 cases of the Supreme Court of Pakistan; 1972- cases of the Supreme Court of Bangladesh.

131. The Pakistan law reports: Dacca series containing cases determined by the High Court of Dacca and by the Federal Court of Pakistan on appeal from that Court, 1951-68. Dacca, 1951-1969/71. c. 18 v.

Appeals were subsequently transferred to the Supreme Court of Pakistan.

SUBJECT REPORTS

Revenue Law

132. Bangladesh tax decisions, 1973- . Dhaka, Bangladesh Tax Decisions, 1973- . 10 v.

B A R B A D O S

See also nos. 1862, 1863

133. Barbados Law Reports, 1948/57- . Barbados, Ministry of the Attorney-General, 1981- . 4 v.

It is intended to publish current and retrospective reports for the period 1948 to date.

134. [Greaves' Barbados law reports] Reports of cases relating to Barbados to be found in the English law reports and of certain cases argued and determined in the local courts, edited by W.H. Greaves and C.P. Clarke, 1694/1893-1894/1903. Bridgetown, 1897-1904. 2 v.

Subtitle varies: v. 2 reports of cases in the Court of Error, edited by G.A. Field.

B E L I Z E

To 1964 called British Honduras
See also no. 1862

135. Belize gazette, 1863- . Bemopan, Government Printery, 1863- .

Title varies: 1863-1964 British Honduras gazette. Some individual judgments printed as supplements, 1933(?)- .

B E R M U D A

See also no. 1862

136. Beatty, K.J. Bermuda law reports: some decisions of the Supreme Court of Bermuda, 1904-26. Bermuda, 1925-27. 2 v.

B O T S W A N A

To 1966 called Bechuanaland

See also nos. 5, 6

137. [Botswana law reports] Republic of Botswana law reports, 1966 Gaborone, Government Printer, 1968- .

Continuation, in part, of: High Commission Territories law reports.

SUBJECT REPORTS

Mercantile Law

See also no. 1

B R U N E I

See no. 1463

B U R M A

See also the following series of no. 977: (Lower Burma) 1914-22; (Upper Burma) 1914-22.

Under British administration until 1948 when Burma left the Commonwealth.

138. Agabeg, A. Burma law reports, 1895-1909. Rangoon, n.d. 14 v.

139. Burma law journal reports, 1922-October 1927. Rangoon, 1922-27. 6 v.

Issued with the Burma law journal.

140. Burma law reports. Appeal cases before the Privy Council from British Burma, cases determined by the High Court of judicature at Fort William in Bengal, on appeal from the Recorder's courts, British Burma, cases determined by the Chief Court of British Burma; decisions of the Recorder's courts, 1865-70. Moulmain, 1870. 2 v.

141. Burma law reports, 1948- . Burma, 1948- .

Continuation of: Rangoon law reports. 1 vol. p.a. issued to 1967.

142. Burma law reports, 1907-20. Rangoon, 1907-20. 13 v.

Issued with the Burma law times.

143. Indian law reports: Rangoon series. Cases determined on appeal by the High Court at Rangoon and by the Privy Council on appeal from that court (including the late Chief Court of Lower Burma and the late Court of the Judicial Committee of Upper Burma) 1923-37. Rangoon, [1924-37]. 14 v.

Continued by: Rangoon law reports.

144. Rangoon law reports, 1937-Jan. 1942 and 1946-47. Rangoon, 1937-47. 6 v. & 1 pt.

Continuation of: Indian law reports, Rangoon series, continued by: Burma law reports. Burma under Japanese occupation, Feb. 1942-Aug. 1945.

LOWER BURMA

145. Lower Burma rulings, being the printed judgments of the Chief Court of Lower Burma, 1900-1919/22. n.d. 11 v.

Details of a collateral reprint given in no. 985.

146. Pegu Commissioner's cases, 1858. [Rangoon], c. 1858. 1 v.

147. Porter, W.A. Burmah law reports, 1865-70. Rangoon. 2 pts.

148. Printed judgments of the Court of the Judicial Commissioners, Lower Burma, and the special court for the period, 1893-1900. Rangoon, 1905. 1 v.

1st ed. 1903.

149. Ripley, E. Selected judgments and rulings of the Court of the Judicial Commissioner, and of the special court, 1872-92. Rangoon, 1907. 1 v.

1st ed. 1893.

150. Sparks, P. Rangoon Court select decisions, 1859-60. Rangoon, 1862. 1 v.

151. Warde Jones. Selected decisions and circulars, 1881-82. Rangoon, 1 v.

SUBJECT REPORTS

Buddhist Law

152. Judgments and rulings on Buddhist law, 1872-75. Rangoon, 1875. 1 v.

Criminal Law

153. Moyle, J.C. Criminal circulars, 1872-75. Rangoon, n.d. 3 v.

154. Rangoon criminal law journal, 1931. Rangoon, 1931. 1 v.

UPPER BURMA

155. Upper Burma rulings, civil and criminal. [Selected judgments of the Court of the Judicial Commissioner, Upper Burma.] 1892-1922. Rangoon, 190922. 14 v.

Reprints from official circulars and quarterlies, omitting obsolete cases.

C A N A D A

See also nos. 316, 747

156. Atlantic provinces reports, 1975- . Fredericton, Maritime Law Book Company, 1975- . 116 v.

Data base: QL.

Includes judgments of the courts of New Brunswick, Nova Scotia, Newfoundland and Prince Edward Island.

157. Cameron, E.R. Supreme Court cases. A collection of judgments of the Supreme Court of Canada in certain appeals in which the bare decisions only are reported in the appendixes to volumes XIV, XVI and XVIII of the official reports of the Court and with which have been included some judgments of the Supreme Court of Canada and of the Courts appealed from, not heretofore reported, 1880-1900. Toronto, 1905. 1 v. Some judgments in French.

158. [Canada Exchequer Court reports] Morse, C. Reports of the Exchequer Court of Canada, 1875-1922. Ottawa, 1891-1923. 21 v.

Data base: QL.

Continued by: Canada Law reports: Exchequer Court. Also known as: Exchequer Court reports, Canada; Morse's Exchequer reports, Canada.

159. Canada Federal Court reports. Recueil des arrets de la Cour federale du Canada, 1971- . Ottawa, Queen's Printer, 1972- . 22 v. Bi-lingual: English, French.

Data base: QL; Appeal decisions WLP 1982- .

Continuation of: Canada law reports: Exchequer Court.

160. Canada law reports: Exchequer Court of Canada. Rapports judiciaires du Canada: Cour de L'échiquier du Canada, 1923-70. Ottawa, 1923-70. 48 v. Bi-lingual: English, French.

Data base: QL.

Continuation of: Canada Exchequer Court reports. Continued by: Canada Federal Court reports.

161. Canada law reports: Supreme Court of Canada. Rapports judiciaires du Canada: Cour suprême du Canada, 1923-69. Ottawa, 1923-69. 47 v. Some judgments in French.

Continuation of: Supreme Court reports, Canada. Continued by: Canada Supreme Court reports.

162. Canada Supreme Court reports. Recueil des arrets de la Cour supreme du Canada, 1970- . Ottawa, Queen's Printer, 1971- . 15 v. Bi-lingual: English, French.

Data base: QL; WLP 1980- .

Continuation of: Canada law reports: Supreme Court of Canada.

163. Canadian reports. Appeal cases, 1807-1913. Toronto, 1910-20. 24 v.

Also known as: Appeal cases (Canada); Canadian appeal cases.

164. [Coutlee's Supreme Court cases] Coutlee, L.W. A collection of notes of unreported cases in the Supreme Court of Canada, 1875-1906. Toronto, 1907. 1 v. Some judgments in French.

165. Dominion law reports: a new annotated series of reports comprising every case reported in the courts of every province and also all the cases decided in the Supreme Court of Canada, Exchequer Court and the Railway Commission, together with Canadian cases appealed to the Privy Council, 1912- . Toronto, Canada Law Book Company, 1912- . 410 v.

Data base: QL 1955- .

1923-55 new series; 1956-68 2nd series; 1969-83 3rd series; 1984- 4th series. Subtitle varies.

166. Eastern law reporter, Canada, 1906-15. Toronto, 1906-15. 14 v.

Includes judgments of the courts of Nova Scotia, New Brunswick and Prince Edward Island and from v. 2 also Quebec.

167. Maritime provinces reports, 1929/30-1967/68. Toronto, 1931-68. 53 v.

Continuation of: New Brunswick reports **and** Nova Scotia reports; Continued by: New Brunswick reports 2nd series, Nova Scotia reports 2nd series, **and** Newfoundland & Prince Edward Island reports. Includes judgments of the courts of New Brunswick, Nova Scotia and Prince Edward Island and from v. 23 also Newfoundland.

168. National reporter: a series of law reports for the publishing of judgments of the Supreme Court of Canada and the Federal Court of Canada, 1974- . Fredericton, Maritime Law Book Company, 1974- . 44 v.

169. [Supreme Court reports, Canada] Reports of the Supreme Court of Canada, 1876-1922. Ottawa, 1878-1923. 64 v. Some judgments in French.

Reprinted with notes and annotations and index, London, Butterworths. 1925-34.

Continued by: Canada law reports. Supreme Court. Also known as: 1876-95 Duval's reports; 1896-1922 Masters' reports; 1898-1922 Cameron's reports, the latter being the publisher.

170. Western law reporter (Canada) and index - digest, 1905-16. Toronto, 1905-16. 34 v.

Incorporated in Western weekly reports.

171. Western weekly reports: all judgments of value ... in the courts of Alberta, British Columbia, Manitoba and Saskatchewan, 1911/12- . Calgary, Carswell Legal Publications (Western), 1912- . 254 v.

Data base: QL 1968- .

From 1951-70 called n.s. From 1951 includes decisions of the Supreme Court of Canada in Western Appeals; from 1970 includes decisions of the Supreme Court of Canada and the Federal Court of Canada. Incorporates Western law reporter.

SUBJECT REPORTS

Administrative Law

172. Administrative law reports, 1983- . Agincourt, Carswell, 1983- .

Building Law

173. Construction law reports, 1983- . Agincourt, Carswell, 1983 .

Constitutional Law

174. [Cameron's constitutional decisions of the Privy Council] Cameron, E.R. The Canadian constitution as interpreted by the Judicial Committee of the Privy Council in its judgments, together with a collection of all the decisions of the Judicial Committee which deal therewith, 1867-1929. Toronto, 1915-30. 2 v.

Continued by: Plaxton's constitutional decisions of the Privy Council.

175. [Cartwright's constitutional cases on the British North America Act, Canada] Cartwright, J.R. Cases decided on the British North America Act, 1867, in the Privy Council, the Supreme Court of Canada and the provincial courts, 1868-96. Toronto, 1882-97. 5 v.

176. Olmsted, R. Decisions of the Judicial Committee of the Privy Council relating to the British North America Act, 1867 and the Canadian constitution, 1867-1954. Ottawa, 1954. 3 v.

Also known as: Privy Council decisions (Olmsted), Decisions ... of the Privy Council (Olmsted).

177. Plaxton, C.P. Canadian constitutional decisions of the Judicial Committee of the Privy Council, 1930-39. Ottawa, 1939. 1 v.

Continuation of: Cameron's constitutional decisions of the Privy Council.

178. Wheeler, G.J. Confederation law of Canada: Privy Council cases on the British North-America Act, 1867, 1876-91. London, 1896. 1 v.

Also known as: Wheeler's Privy Council cases.

Criminal Law

179. Canadian criminal cases, a series of reports of important decisions in criminal and quasi-criminal cases, 1892- . Aurora, Canada Law Book Company, 1898- . 223 v.

1963-70 new series; 1970-82 2nd series; 1983- 3rd series.

180. Criminal reports (Canada). A series of reports with annotations and practice notes on criminal cases arising in the courts of the various provinces in Canada, 1946- . Toronto, Carswell, 1946- . 119 v. Some judgments in French.

Title varies: 1967- Criminal reports (annotated). 1967-78 new series; 1978 3rd series.

Customary Law

181. Canadian native law reporter, 1979- . Saskatoon, University of Saskatchewan Native Law Centre, 1979- . 16 v.

Environmental Law

182. Canadian environmental law reports, 1972-84, n.s. 1987- . Toronto, Carswell, 1972- . 11 v. Some judgments in French.

Title varies: nos. 1-6 Canadian environmental law news. Old series published by Canadian Environmental Law Research Foundation.

Family Law

183. Family Law Reform Act cases, 1978/83- . Toronto, Carswell, 1984- .

Originating in: Macdonald, J. and others. Law and practice under the Family Law Reform Act.

184. Reports of family law, 1971- . Toronto, Carswell, 1971- . 60 v.

1978- 2nd series.

185. Reports of family law. Reprint series, 1824-1970. Toronto, 1979-80. 5 v.

Contains cases of continuing authority with updated headnotes and annotations.

Human Rights

186. Canadian human rights reporter, 1980- . Saskatoon, Canadian Human Rights Reporter, 1980- . 3 v. Some judgments in French.

187. Canadian rights reporter: reports of cases decided under the Canadian Charter of Rights and Freedoms, 1982- . Scarborough, Butterworths, 1982- . 1 v.

Industrial Law

188. Canadian cases on employment law, 1983- . Toronto, Carswell, 1983- .

189. Canadian labour law cases: full text decisions of labour cases issued from Canadian Federal and provincial courts and from provincial labour boards, 1944/59-1960/64. Don Mills, 1964-66. 2 v.

Continued by: Canadian labour law reporter.

190. Canadian labour law reporter: 1964/66- . Don Mills, CCH Canadian, 1967- . 11 v.

Preceded by: Canadian labour law cases.

191. Labour arbitration cases, 1948- . Aurora, Canada Law Book Company, 1948- . 59 v.

1973-81 2nd series; 1982- 3rd series.

192. Western labour arbitration cases, 1966/67- . Vancouver, University of British Columbia, 1967- . [Looseleaf] 1 v.

Intellectual Property

193. Canadian intellectual property reports, 1984- . Agincourt, Carswell, 1984- .

194. Canadian patent reporter: containing the full report of all judgments of the Canadian courts relating to patents, copyrights, trademarks, trade names and industrial designs, together with general information in regard to the practice in this field and decisions, 1941- . Aurora, Canada Law Book Company, 1941- . 130 v.

1970- 2nd series.

195. Fox, H.G. Patent, trade mark, design and copyright cases, being reports of cases decided in the Canadian courts and on appeal therefrom to the Privy Council, 1941-71. Toronto, 1941-71. 44 v. Some judgments in French.

Land Law

See also no. 111

196. Real property reports [annotated], 1977- . Toronto, Carswell, 1977- . 24 v.

Local Government

197. Municipal and planning law reports [annotated], 1976- . Agincourt, Carswell, 1977- . 18 v.

Mercantile Law

198. Business law reports [annotated], 1977- . Toronto, Carswell, 1977 . 17 v.

199. Canadian bankruptcy reports, annotated, 1921- . Toronto, Burroughs & Company, 1921- . 81 v. Some judgments in French.

1961- new series.

200. Canadian cases on the law of insurance, 1982- . Toronto, Carswell, 1983- .

201. [Canadian commercial law reports] Commercial law reports (annotated) being reports of important decisions relating to companies, banks and banking, insurance, insolvency and similar subjects in the Federal and provincial courts, 1901-05. Toronto, 1903-05. 4 v.

Also known as: Commercial law reports of Canada; Commercial law reports annotated.

202. Canadian insurance law reporter, 1934- . Don Mills, CCH Canadian, 1934- . 14 v.

Also known as: Insurance law reporter.

Parliament

203. Decisions of the Speakers of the Legislative Assembly and House of Commons of Canada, 1841-72. Ottawa, 1972. 1 v.

204. Desjardins, L.G. Decisions of the Speakers of the House of Commons of Canada. Decisions des orateurs de la Chambre des Communes du Canada, 1867-1900. Quebec, 1901. 1 v.

Practice

205. Carswell's practice cases [annotated], 1976- . Agincourt, Carswell, 1977- . 29 v.

Property Law

206. Personal property security act cases, 1977/81- . Toronto, Carswell, 1982- . 1 v.

Originating in: Maclaren, R.H. Secured transactions in personal property.

Revenue Law

207. Canada Tax Appeal Board cases, 1949-71. Toronto, 1950-72. 51 v.

1967-71 n.s. Incorporated in Canada tax cases (n.s.). Also known as: Tax Appeal Board cases.

208. Canada tax cases, 1971/27- . Toronto, Richard De Boo, 1927- . 45 v.

1972- n.s. From 1972 incorporates Canada Tax Appeal Board cases.

209. Canadian customs and excise reports, 1980- . Toronto, Butterworths, 1980- . 3 v.

210. Dominion tax cases: the full text of all reported judgments on federal tax questions, 1920/40- . Ottawa, CCH Canadian, 1940- . 36 v. Some judgments in French.

Tort

211. Canadian cases on the law of torts [annotated], 1976/77- . Toronto, Carswell, 1977- . 21 v.

Transport

212. Canadian railway and transport cases affecting railways, aircraft and shipping and transportation in general ..., 1940-66. Toronto, 1940-66. 36 v.

Continuation of: Canadian railway cases. Continued by: Canadian transport cases.

213. Canadian railway cases containing a selection of cases affecting railways, 1902-39. Toronto, 1902-39. 49 v.

Continued by: Canadian railway and transport cases.

214. Canadian transport cases. Recueil d'arrets sur les transports, 1966/69- . Quebec, Canadian Government Publishing Centre, 1975- . 13 v. Bi-lingual: English, French.

Continuation of: Canadian railway and transport cases.

215. Motor vehicle reports [annotated], 1979- . Toronto, Carswell, 1979- . 17 v.

Trusts

216. Estates & trusts reports [annotated], 1977/78- . Toronto, Carswell, 1978- . 12 v.

ALBERTA

217. Alberta law reports: cases determined in the Supreme Court of Alberta, 1907- . Calgary, Carswell Legal Publications (Western), 1909- . 57 v.

1977- 2nd series.

218. Alberta reports: a series of law reports designated by the Law Society of Alberta for the publishing of judgments of the Alberta

courts, 1977- . Fredericton, Maritime Law Book Company, 1977- . 37 v.

Data base: QL from v. 35.

219. Alberta Supreme Court Appellate Division. Unreported decisions, 1954/64-1965/68. Edmonton, 1965-70. 2 v.

Also known as: Alberta unreported decisions; Unreported decisions of the ... Supreme Court of Alberta.

BRITISH COLUMBIA

220. British Columbia decisions. Civil cases, 1974- . Vancouver, Western Legal Publications, 1974- . [looseleaf] 1 v.?

Continuation of: British Columbia unreported decisions. Civil cases.

221. British Columbia law notes, 1894. Victoria, 1894. 1 v.

Reprinted 1968.

222. British Columbia law reports, 1867/89-1946/47; 1977- . Calgary, Carswell Legal Publications (Western), 1893- . 101 v.

Title varies: v. 2 - 63 British Columbia reports. 1977- also known as 2nd series.

223. British Columbia unreported decisions. Civil cases, 1972-73. Vancouver, 1972-73. [looseleaf] 3 v.

Continued by: British Columbia decisions. Civil cases.

SUBJECT REPORTS

Criminal Law

224. British Columbia decisions. Criminal conviction cases, 1974- . Vancouver, Western Legal Publications, 1974- . [looseleaf] 1 v.

Continuation of: British Columbia unreported decisions. Criminal conviction cases.

225. British Columbia decisions. Criminal sentence cases, 1974- . Vancouver, Western Legal Publications, 1974- . [looseleaf] 1 v.

Continuation of: British Columbia unreported decisions. Criminal sentence cases.

226. British Columbia unreported decisions. Criminal conviction cases, 1971-73. Vancouver, 1971-73. [looseleaf] 2 v.

Continued by: British Columbia decisions. Criminal conviction cases.

227. British Columbia unreported decisions. Criminal sentence cases, 1971-73. Vancouver, 1971-73. [looseleaf] 2 v.

Continued by: British Columbia decisions. Criminal sentence cases.

Mining Law

228. Martin, A. Reports of mining cases decided by the courts of British Columbia, 1867-1908. Toronto, 1903-08. 2 v.

Title varies: v. 2, pt. 1, Mining cases of British Columbia; v. 2 pt. 2, Mining and water cases. Both vols also contain statutes.

Parliament

229. [Fell and Langley] Decisions of the Speakers of the Legislative Assembly of British Columbia, 1877/1915-1931/43. Victoria, 1915-[44?]. 3 v.

Also known as: Speakers' decisions (Fell and Langley).

MANITOBA

230. Carey, D. Judgments in the Queen's Bench, Manitoba, 1875. Calgary, 1875. 1 v.

Reprinted: Calgary 1918.

Also known as: Carey's Manitoba reports; Carey's reports.

231. Manitoba reports, 1884-1963; 1979- . Fredericton, Maritime Law Book Company, 1884- . 84 v.

Data base: QL 1979- .

Continuation of: Manitoba reports temp. Wood. Title varies: v. 1-6 Reports of cases ... in the court of Queen's Bench, Manitoba. Also known as: Manitoba law reports. 1979- 2nd series.

232. [Manitoba reports temp. Wood] Reports of cases argued and determined in the court of Queen's Bench in Manitoba, 1875-83. Toronto, 1884. 1 v.

Continued by: Manitoba reports. Also known as: Armour's Queen Bench and County Court reports temp. Wood; Wood's Manitoba reports.

NEW BRUNSWICK

See also nos. 156, 166, 167

233. [New Brunswick equity reports] Trueman, W.H. Reports of cases determined by the Supreme Court in equity of New Brunswick, 1876-1911. Toronto, 1899-1912. 5 v.

Title varies: 1876-93 New Brunswick equity cases, being a selection of hitherto unreported cases. From v. 4 includes Chancery Division.

234. New Brunswick law news, 1966-68. Fredericton, 1966-68. 3 v.

Continued by: New Brunswick reports 2nd series.

235. New Brunswick reports. Recueil du Nouveau - Brunswick (second series), 1969- . Fredericton, Maritime Law Book Company, 1969- . 42 v. v. 1-44 some judgments in French. v. 45- bi-lingual: English, French.

Data base: QL.

Continuation, in part, of: Maritime provinces reports.

236. New Brunswick reports. Reports of cases ... in the Supreme Court of New Brunswick, 1825-1929. Toronto, 1925-29. 54 v.

Reprinted: v. 2 1882; v. 3-5 1894-95.

Continued by: Maritime Province reports. v. 1: W. Chapman; v. 2: G.F.S. Berton; v. 3-5: D.S. Kerr; v. 6-11: J.C. Allen; v. 12-13: J. Hannay; v. 14-16: W. Pugsley; v. 17-20: W. Pugsley and G.W. Burbridge, v. 1 20 numbered retrospectively. Also known as: Supreme Court of New Brunswick reports.

237. Stockton, A.A. Reports of cases decided in the Vice-Admiralty Court of New Brunswick, 1879-91. St. John, 1894. 1 v.

NEWFOUNDLAND

See also nos. 156, 167

238. Newfoundland & Prince Edward Island reports. A series of law reports designated by the Law Society of Newfoundland and the Law Society of Prince Edward Island for the publishing of judgments of the Newfoundland and Prince Edward Island courts, 1971- . Fredericton, Maritime Law Book Company, 1971- . 37 v.

Data base: QL from v. 36.

Continuation of: Maritime provinces reports.

239. [Newfoundland law reports] Decisions of the Supreme Court of Newfoundland, 1817/28-1941/46. St. Johns, 1901-56.

Also known as: Supreme Court reports; Decisions of the Supreme Court of Newfoundland.

240. Tucker, R.A. Select cases from the records of the Supreme Court of Newfoundland, 1817-28. St. Johns, 1829. 1 v.

Reprinted and annotated in Newfoundland law reports; Reprinted: Agincourt, Carswell, 1980.

Also known as: Newfoundland select cases, Tucker, Select cases, Newfoundland.

NORTHWEST TERRITORIES

241. [North-West Territories reports] The Territories law reports: reports of cases decided in the Supreme Court of the North-West Territories including revised reports of all cases hitherto reported in the NorthWest Territories reports, 1885-1907. Toronto, 1900-12. 7 v.

242. [North-West Territories. Supreme Court reports] Reports of the Supreme Court of the North-West Territories, 1887-98. Regina, 1889-[98]. 2 v.

Reprinted in North-West Territories reports.

Also known as: Supreme Court reports.

243. North-West Territories reports, 1983- . Toronto, Carswell, 1983- .

NOVA SCOTIA

See also nos. 156, 166, 167

244. Nova Scotia reports: cases argued and determined in the Supreme Court of Nova Scotia, 1834-1929. Toronto, 1855-1929. 55 v.

Continued by: Maritime Provinces reports. Also known by the name of the reporter as follows: v. 1, 3: J. Thomson; v. 2: A. James; v. 4: F. Cochran; v. 5-6: H. Oldright; v. 7-9: J.M. Geldert and J.M. Oxley; also known as Nova Scotia decisions: v. 10-12: B. Russell and S.A. Chesley; v. 13-27: B. Russell and J.M. Geldert; v. 28-39, 41-60: J.M. Geldert and F.W. Russell; v. 40: W.B. Wallace; v. 1-19 numbered retrospectively.

245. Nova Scotia reports 1965/69. 1965-69. Fredericton, 1973-75. 5 v.

246. Nova Scotia reports (second series), 1970- . Fredericton, Maritime Law Book Company, 1970- . 52 v.

Data base: QL.

Continuation, in part, of: Maritime provinces reports.

247. Ritchie, J.W. The equity decisions of the Hon. J.W. Ritchie, 1873-1882. Halifax, 1883. 1 v.

248. Stewart, J. Reports of cases argued and determined in the Court of Vice-Admiralty at Halifax, 1803-13. London, 1814. 1 v.

249. Young, W. The Admiralty decisions, 1865-80. Toronto, 1882. 1 v.

SUBJECT REPORTS

Parliament

250. Russell, B. Reports of cases determined in the Election Court for the Province of Nova Scotia, 1874. Halifax, 1874. 1 v.

ONTARIO

Until 1840, known as Upper Canada

251. Chancery Chambers reports, by A. Grant, 1857-72. Toronto, 1868-73. 4 v.

Microfiche: Upper Canada reports, Agincourt, Carswell.

2nd ed. 1877. Title varies: v. 2 Reports of cases adjudged in Chancery Chambers; v. 3, 4 Reports of cases decided in Chancery Chambers and in the master's office. Also known as: Upper Canada Chancery Chambers reports.

252. Draper, W.H. Reports of cases argued and determined in His Majesty's Court of King's Bench in and for the Provinces of Upper Canada, 1829-31. York, 1831. 1 v.

Microfiche: Upper Canada reports, Agincourt, Carswell.

2nd ed. Toronto, 1861. Continued by: Upper Canada Queen's Bench reports (o.s.). Entitled v. 1. No more published.

253. [Error and appeal reports (Grant)] Grant, A. Reports of cases adjudged in the Court of Error and Appeal, 1846-66. Toronto, 1865-66. 3 v.

Microfiche: Upper Canada reports, Agincourt, Carswell.

2nd ed. 1885. Also known as: Upper Canada error and appeal reports; Grant's error and appeal reports.

254. Fraser, A. Records of the early courts of justice of Upper Canada, 178994. Toronto, 1918. 1 v.

Also known as: Upper Canada court records. Published as the Fourteenth report of the Bureau of Archives.

255. Grant, A. Reports of cases adjudged in the Court of Chancery of Upper Canada, 1849/50-1881/82. Toronto, 1850-83. 29 v.

Microfiche: Upper Canada reports, Agincourt, Carswell.

Also known as: Grant's Chancery reports; Upper Canada Chancery (Grant's) reports. Title varies: of Upper Canada to v. 15 (1868), of Ontario from v. 16 (1869).

256. [Ontario appeal reports] Reports of cases decided in the Court of Appeal on appeal from the superior and county courts - appeals in insolvency and election cases, [v. 1-6] by J.S. Tupper, 1876-1900. Toronto, 1878-1901. 27 v.

Microfiche: Upper Canada reports, Agincourt, Carswell.

Continued by: Ontario law reports. Also known as: Tupper's appeal reports, Ontario.

257. Ontario law reports: cases determined in the Supreme Court of Ontario. (Appellate and High Court divisions), 1901-31. Toronto, 1901-31. 66 v.

Continuation of: Ontario reports; Ontario appeal reports; Ontario election cases; Ontario practice reports. Continued by: Ontario reports (n.s.). Title varies: v. 38, 39 Other law reports.

258. Ontario reports, containing reports of cases decided in the Queen's Bench and Chancery Divisions of the High Court of Justice for Ontario, 1882-1900. Toronto, 1882-1901. 32 v.

Microfiche: Upper Canada reports, Agincourt, Carswell.

Continued by: Ontario law reports.

258A. Ontario reports, incorporating Ontario weekly notes. Reports of cases determined in the courts of Ontario, 1863-73. Toronto, 1963-73. 26 v.

Continuation of: Ontario reports [n.s.]. Continued by: Ontario reports (second series).

258B. Ontario reports [n.s.]: cases determined in the Supreme Court of Ontario (Appellate and High Court divisions) 1931-62. Toronto, 1932-63. 32 v.

Continuation of: Ontario law reports. Continued by: Ontario reports incorporating Ontario weekly notes.

258C. Ontario reports (second series): Reports of cases determined in the courts of Ontario, 1974- . Scarborough, 1975- . 37 v.

Continuation of: Ontario reports incorporating Ontario weekly notes.

259. Ontario weekly notes, 1909-32. Toronto, 1909-32. 41 v.

Reprinted: Agincourt, Carswell.

1933-62 new series. 30 v.

Continued by: Ontario reports incorporating Ontario weekly notes.

260. Ontario weekly reporter and index - digest, 1902-16. Toronto, 1902-17. 27 v.

261. Taylor, T. Reports of cases argued and determined in the Court of King's Bench of Upper Canada, 1823-27. York, 1828. 1 v.

Microfiche: Upper Canada reports, Agincourt, Carswell.

2nd ed. 1862. Some cases for 1823-24 published under the same title 1824. Also known as: Upper Canada King's Bench reports.

262. [Upper Canada chamber reports] Reports of points of practice determined in chambers by 3 judges of the Courts of Queen's Bench and Common Pleas, 1846-52. Toronto, 1851-53. 2 v.

Microfiche: Upper Canada reports, Agincourt, Carswell.

2nd ed. 1877. Also known as: Upper Canada common law chamber reports; Chamber reports, Upper Canada.

263. [Upper Canada common pleas reports] Reports of cases decided in the Court of Common pleas of Upper Canada, 1850-82. Toronto, 1852-83. 32 v.

Microfiche: Upper Canada reports, Agincourt, Carswell.

v. 1, 2nd ed. 1869.

264. Upper Canada jurist: containing original and selected articles on legal studies; some important decisions in bankruptcy and chancery in Upper Canada and in the English common law, 1844-48. Toronto, 1845-48. 2 v.

Microfiche: Upper Canada reports, Agincourt, Carswell.

v. 1-2, 2nd ed. 1877. Also issued with parts forming v. 1-2 of Upper Queen's Bench reports (o.s.).

265. [Upper Canada Queen's Bench reports (n.s.)] Reports of cases in the Queen's Bench, 1844-81. Toronto, 1846-82. 46 v.

Microfiche: Upper Canada reports, Agincourt, Carswell.

v. 1, 2nd ed. 1858; 3rd ed. ?; 4th ed. 1890. Continuation of Upper Canada Queen's Bench reports (o.s.). Continued by: Ontario reports. Title varies: v. 1-6 Queen's Bench and Practice Court reports.

266. [Upper Canada Queen's Bench Reports (o.s.)] Queen's Bench and Practice Court reports, 1831-44. Toronto, 1845-58. 6 v.

Microfiche: Upper Canada reports, Agincourt, Carswell.

Continuation of: Draper. Reports of cases in K.B. Continued by: Upper Canada Queen's Bench reports (n.s.). 1844-81. v. 1-2 issued as part of Upper Canada Jurist and so titled; v. 2 subtitled King's Bench and Practice Court reports, v. 3-5 as above, v. 6 Queen's Bench reports.

SUBJECT REPORTS

Local Government

267. Clarke, A.H. and Scully, E.I. Reports of the decisions of the referees appointed for the purpose of the drainage laws and of the Court of Appeal for Ontario in cases where the Referees' decisions have been appealed from, relative to the drainage laws, 1898-1903. Toronto, 1898-1903. 2 v.

268. Harrison, R.A. and Hodgins, T. Municipal reports, containing reports of cases arising under the municipal and school laws of Upper Canada, 1845-51. Toronto, 1863. 1 v.

269. Ontario Municipal Board reports, 1972- . Aurora, Canada Law Book Company, 1973- . 12 v.

270. Smith, A.L. and Sager, L.M. Report of the decisions in cases arising out of the Municipal Drainage Act together with other cases analogous thereto; also the general rules relating to practice and procedure under the municipal procedure under the Municipal Drainage Act, 1904-16. Toronto, 1916. 1 v.

Parliament

271. Hodgins, T. Reports of the decisions of the judges for the trial of election petitions in Ontario, relating to elections to the Legislative Assembly of Ontario and to the House of Commons of Canada, 1871-79. Toronto, 1883. 1 v.

Microfiche: Upper Canada reports, Agincourt, Carswell.

272. [Ontario] Election cases. Reports of decisions under the Dominion and Ontario Controverted Election Acts relating to the election of members from the Province of Ontario to the House of Commons of Canada and to the Legislative Assembly, 1884-1900. Toronto, 1891-1901. 2 v.

Microfiche: Upper Canada reports, Agincourt, Carswell.

Continued by: Ontario law reports.

273. Patrick, A. Digest of "precedents or decisions" by selected committees appointed to try the merits of Upper Canada contested elections, 1824-49. Toronto, 1849. 1 v.

Microfiche: Upper Canada reports, Agincourt, Carswell.

2nd ed. 1851. Also known as: Patrick's election cases; Patrick, contested elections (Ontario).

Practice

274. Lefroy, A. and Cassel, R.S. Notes of practice cases, being notes of sessions and dicta (English and Canadian) illustrative of the Ontario Judicature Act and orders, subsequent to the annotated editions of the said Act, 1881-83. 1883. 1 v.

275. [Ontario practice reports] Reports of cases determined in the Practice Court and Chambers, with points of pleading and practice determined in the Courts of Queen's Bench and Common Pleas, 1848-1900. Toronto, 1856-1901. 19 v.

Microfiche: Upper Canada reports, Agincourt, Carswell.

Continued by: Ontario law reports. Also known as: Practice reports (Ontario). Title varies: Ontario practice reports from v. 16 (1869).

PRINCE EDWARD ISLAND

See also nos. 156, 166, 167, 238

276. Haszard, F.L. and Warburton, A.B. Reports of cases determined in the Supreme Court, Court of Chancery and Vice Admiralty Court of Prince Edward Island, 1850/74-1875/82. Charlottetown, 1885-86. 2 v.

Also known as: Prince Edward Island reports; Warburton and Haszard.

277. Peters, J.H. Reports of cases determined in the Supreme Court, Court of Chancery and Court of Vice Admiralty of Prince Edward Island, 1850-72. Charlottetown, 1872. 1 v.

Also known as: Prince Edward Island reports, Peters; Haviland's Prince Edward Island reports.

QUEBEC

Until 1840 known as Lower Canada

See also no. 166

278. Dorion, L.C.W. Decisions de la Cour d'Appel. Queen's Bench reports, Quebec, 1880-84. Montreal, 1881-84. 4 v. Some judgments in French.

Reprinted: Quebec revised reports.

Also known as: Queen's Bench reports, Quebec.

279. Jugements et deliberations du Conseil Superieur de Quebec, 1663-1710/16. Quebec, 1885-91. 6 v. In French.

Title varies: v. 1-4 Jugements et deliberations du Conseil Souverain de la Nouvelle France.

280. The Lower Canada jurist. Collection de decisions du Bas-Canada, 1848-91. Montreal, 1857-91. 35 v. Some judgments in French.

Reprinted: Quebec revised reports.

281. Lower Canada reports. Decisions des Tribunaux du Bas-Canada, 1850-67. Quebec, 1852-67. 17 v. Some judgments in French.

Reprinted: Quebec revised reports.

282. Montreal condensed reports. Precis de decisions du tribunaux du district de Montreal, 1853-54. Montreal, 1854. 1 v. Some judgments in French.

Reprinted: 2nd ed., 1884; Quebec revised reports.

A reprint of the reports published in the Law Reporter.

283. Montreal law reports, Court of Queen's Bench, 1885-91. Montreal, 1885-91. 7 v. Some judgments in French.

Reprinted: Quebec revised reports.

284. Montreal law reports, Superior Court, 1885-91. Montreal, 1885-91. 7 v. Some judgments in French.

Reprinted: Quebec revised reports.

285. [Perrault Conseil Superieur] Extraits ou precedents, des arrets tires des registres du Conseil Superieur de Quebec, 1727-59. Quebec, 1824. 1 v. In French.

286. [Perrault Prevoste de Quebec] Perrault, J.F. Extraits ou precedents, tires des Registres de la Prevoste de Quebec, 1726-59. Quebec, 1824. 1 v. In French.

287. Pyke, G. Reports of cases argued and determined in the court of King's Bench for the district of Quebec in the Province of Lower Canada, 1809-10. Quebec, 1811. 1 v.

Reprinted: Quebec revised reports.

Also known as: Pyke's reports, District of Quebec.

288. Quebec law reports. Rapports judiciaires de Quebec, 1874-91. Quebec, 1877-91. 17 v. Some judgments in French.

Reprinted: Quebec revised reports.

289. [Quebec official reports (Queen's Bench)] Les rapports judiciaires de Quebec. Cour du Banc de la Reine, 1892-1969. Montreal, 1892-1969. 99 v. Mainly in French.

Continued by: Les recueils de jurisprudence de Quebec. Cour d'Appel. Title varies: v. 1 Les rapports judiciaires officiel de Quebec; 1967-69 Les recueils de jurisprudence.

290. [Quebec revised reports] Rapports judiciaires revisés de la Province de Quebec, par M. Mathieu. Revision complète et annotee de toutes les causes rapportées dans les différences revues de droit de cette province. 1726-1892. Montreal, 1891-1903. 28 v. Some judgments in French.

Also known as: Revised reports, Province of Quebec; Mathieu.

291. [Questions seigneuriales] Lower-Canada reports: questions seigneuriales. Decisions des tribunaux de Bas-Canada, 1856. Montreal, 1856. 2 v. In French.

Also known as: Lower-Canada reports; Decisions des tribunaux du Bas-Canada.

292. Les recueils de jurisprudence du Quebec. Cour d'Appel, 1970- Montreal, La Societe quebecoise d'information juridique, 1970- . 13 v.

Continuation of: Quebec official reports. (Queen's Bench).

293. Recueils de jurisprudence du Quebec. Cour provinciale, Cour des Sessions de la Paix, Tribunal de la Jeunesse, 1975- . Montreal, Societe quebecoise d'information juridique, 1976- . 8 v. Mainly in French.

294. La revue legale, 1869-92; 1895- . Montreal, Wilson & Lafleur, 1869-92; 1895- . 108 v. Mainly in French.

1869-92 old series; 1895-42 new series.

295. Stuart, G. Reports of cases argued and determined in the Courts of King's Bench and in the Provincial Court of Appeals of Lower Canada, 1810-35. Quebec, 1834. 1 v. Some judgments in French.

Reprinted: Quebec revised reports.

SUBJECT REPORTS

Parliament

296. Desjardins, L.G. Decisions des orateur de L'Assemblee legislative de la Province de Quebec, 1867-1901. Quebec, 1902. 1 v. Bi-lingual; English, French.

Practice

297. Les rapports de Pratique de Quebec. Quebec practice reports, 1897-1982. Montreal, 1898-1982. 86 v. Mainly in French.

Continued, in part, by: Revue de droit judiciaire. Title varies: From v. 49 English title omitted.

Revenue Law

298. Periard, A. Causes celebres: rapports des jugements rendus en cour superieure a Montreal et dans la cour du Banc de la Reine (en appel) sur la constitutionalite de L'Acte imposant des taxes sur les Banques et les corporations commerciales, 1883-85. Montreal, 1985. 1 v. In French.

Also known as: Tax cases; causes celebres sur les taxes.

SASKATCHEWAN

299. Saskatchewan law reports: reports of cases decided in the Supreme Court of Saskatchewan, the Court of Appeal and in His Majesty's Court of King's Bench for the Province of Saskatchewan, 1907/08-1932/33. Toronto, 1909-1934. 25 v.

300. Saskatchewan reports: a series of law reports for the publishing of judgments of the Saskatchewan courts, 1980- . Fredericton, Maritime Law Book Company, 1980- . 20 v.

YUKON

301. Yukon reports: a series of law reports designated by the Law Society of Yukon for the publishing of judgments from the Yukon courts, 1987- . Fredericton, Maritime Law Book Company, 1987- .

C H A N N E L   I S L A N D S

GUERNSEY

302. Cases heard and determined at St. Peter's Port ... Guernsey before His Majesty's Commissioners, 16 October to 20 December, 1607. Guernsey, [1608]. 1 v.

303. Guernsey Court of Appeal (Civil Division) [reports], 1965- . Guernsey, Guernsey Herald, 1965- . 1 v.

SUBJECT REPORTS

Criminal Law

304. Guernsey Court of Appeal (Criminal Division) [reports], 1964- . Guernsey, Guernsey Herald, 1964- . 1 v.

JERSEY

305. Godfrey, H.M. and Messeroy, A. Ordres du conseil et pieces analogues enregistres a Jersey, 1536-1867. Jersey, 1897-1906. 6 v. In French

Includes decisions appeared to the Privy Council.

306. Judgments of the Royal Court of Jersey and of the Court of Appeal of Jersey, 1950-8. Jersey, Bigwoods, 1967-88. 13 v.

307. Table des decisions des Cour Royale de Jersey, 1885-1963. Jersey, Bigwoods, 1896-1964. 10 v. In French.

A classified summary of decisions.

C O M M O N W E A L T H

308. Law reports of the Commonwealth, 1985- . Abingdon, Professional Books, 1985- .

Published in 3 series. Commercial law, Constitutional and administrative law and Criminal law. Retrospective vols are planned.

C Y P R U S

309. Cacoyannis, G.P. Cyprus casebook: a selection of judicial

pronouncements on topics of general application, 1888-1977. Limassol. 1978-80. 3 v.

310. Cyprus law reports: cases decided by the High Court of Justice in its original jurisdiction and on appeal from the assize courts and district courts, 1883- . Nicosia, Printing office of the Republic, 1893- . 45 v.

Subtitle varies.

311. Judgments of the Supreme Court of Cyprus on appeal and in its original jurisdiction (not included in the Cyprus Law reports) and judgments of the District Courts in which there was no appeal, 1965- . Nicosia, Supreme Court, 1965- . 17 v.

Title varies: 1965-77 Monthly publication of judgments ... In mimeographed form.

SUBJECT REPORTS

Constitutional Law

312. Reports of cases decided by the Supreme Constitutional Court of Cyprus, 1960-63. Nicosia, 1961-63. 5 v.

Continued by: Cyprus law reports, pt. III.

E N G L A N D A N D W A L E S

313. The all England law reports annotated, 1936- . London, Butterworths, 1936- . 134 v.

Date base: LEXIS 1945- .

Incorporates: Law times reports from 1948; and Law journal reports from 1950.

314. The all England law reports reprint, 1558-1935. London, 1957-68. 36 v.

"A selection from early authorised reports", 1558-1842; "A selection from The law times reports 1843-1935."

315. Birkenhead, Lord. Judgments delivered by Lord Chancellor Birkenhead, 1911-22. London, 1923. 1 v.

316. British ruling cases from courts of Great Britain, Canada, Ireland, Australia and other divisions of the British Empire, 1905-31. Rochester, N.Y., 1911-31. 16 v.

317. Common law reports: reports of cases argued and determined in all the superior courts of common law, 1853-55. London, 1854-55. 3 v. in 5.

Microfilm: Dobbs Ferry, Oceana.

318. The English reports, 1220-1865. Edinburgh, London, 1900-32. 178 v.

Reprinted: Abingdon, Professional Books, 1974.

A collection of reprints in which series of reports are grouped together according to the court in which the cases were heard.

319. English reports annotated, 1866-1900. London, 1914. 10 v.

320. The equity reports, 1853-55. London, 1854-55. 3 v. in 4.

Microfilm: Dobbs Ferry, Oceana.

321. The jurist: containing reports of cases determined in law and equity, 1837-54. London, 1838-55. 18 v.

Microfilm: Dobbs Ferry, Oceana.

Continued by: The jurist, n.s. From v. 6 each volume published in two parts: part 1 contains reports of cases, part 2 contains articles, statutes, rules and orders, miscellaneous legal information.

322. The jurist, new series, 1855-66. London, 1856-67, 12 v.

Microfilm: Dobbs Ferry, Oceana.

Continuation of: The jurist. Each volume published in two parts: part 1 contains reports of cases, part 2 contains articles, statutes, rules and orders, miscellaneous legal information.

323. The law journal ... comprising reports of cases in the courts of Chancery, King's Bench, and Common Pleas, 1822-31. London, 1823-31. 9 v.

The reports were divided into several parts, each with its own pagination.

324. The law journal ... comprising reports of cases in the courts of Chancery, King's Bench, Common Pleas, Exchequer of Pleas, and Exchequer Chamber ... and cases connected with the duties and offices of magistrates. (The law journal reports ... from volume 4, 1835). [New series], 1831-1949. London, 1832-1949. 118 v.

Data base: LEXIS 1945- .

The reports were published in several parts, each with its own pagination and index, from 1832-1946. v 1-38 are also numbered old series, v. 10-47. Continued by: The all England law reports.

325. 'The law journal' notes of cases decided in all the superior courts of law and equity, 1866-92. London, 1866-92. 2 v.

326. The law reporter, consisting of early reports of cases heard in Banco and at Nisi Prius, 1821-22. London, 1821-22. 2 v.

327. The law reports. Courts of Probate and Divorce, 1865-75. London, 1869-75. 3 v.

Continued by: The law reports. Probate Division. Also known as: Probate and Divorce.

328. The law reports. High Court of Admiralty, and Ecclesiastical Courts, 1865-75. London, 1867-75. 4 v.

Continued by: The law reports. Probate Division. Also known as: Admiralty and ecclesiastical cases.

329. The law reports. Probate Division, 1875-90. London, 1876-90. 15 v.

Continuation of: The law reports. Courts of Probate and Divorce; The law reports. High Court of Admiralty and Ecclesiastical Courts. Continued by: The law reports. Probate Division. Courts of Probate, Divorce and Admiralty. Also known as: Probate reports.

330. The law reports. Probate Division. Courts of Probate, Divorce and Admiralty, and on appeal therefrom in the Court of Appeal; Ecclesiastical Courts and on appeal therefrom in the Privy Council, 1891-1971. London, 1891-1971. 80 v.

Data base: LEXIS 1945-71.

330 ENGLAND AND WALES

Continuation of: The law reports. Probate Division. Continued by: The law reports. Family Division. Also known as: Probate reports.

331. The law reports. Queen's Bench Division and on appeal therefrom in the Court of Appeal, decisions on Crown cases reserved and decisions of the Railway and Canal Commission, 1891- . London, Incorporated Council of Law Reporting, 1891- . 175 v.

Data base: LEXIS 1945- .

Continuation of: The law reports. Queen's Bench Division. Title varies: 1901-52 King's Bench Division. Also known as: Queen's Bench/ King's Bench reports.

332. The law times reports, 1843-59. London, 1843-59. 34 v.

Published in the Law times as part of the journal from 1843-51. Continued by: The law times reports, new series.

333. The law times reports [new series], 1859-1947. London, 1859-1947. 177 v.

Data base: LEXIS 1945-47.

1-4 are also numbered volumes 35-38 old series. Continued by: The all England law reports.

334. The new reports, containing cases decided in the courts of equity and common law, 1862-65. London, 1863-65. 6 v.

Microfilm: Dobbs Ferry, Oceana.

335. Newnam, W. The reports at large; or, Lawyer's complete assistant containing all the reports of cases of established reputation in the High Court of Chancery, Exchequer, King's Bench and Common Pleas. London, 1781. 5 v.

v. 1-2 reprinted Atkyns (Ch); v. 3-4 reprinted Strange (K.B.); a further v. 3 [sic] reprinted 3 Atkyns.

336. The reports ... decisions of the House of Lords, Privy Council, Probate, Divorce & Admiralty Division and Court of Appeal therefrom, 1893-95. London, 1894-96. 15 v.

337. Ruling cases, 1600?-1908. London, 1894-[1908]. 27 v.

The leading authorities of case law, arranged alphabetically by subject.

338. Searle, R. and Smith, J.C. Monthly reports of cases decided in the Court of Probate, and in the Court for Divorce and Matrimonial Causes, 1859-60. London, 1860. 1 v.

Microfilm: Dobbs Ferry, Oceana.

339. A second book of judgments ... [Compiled by] G. Huxley. [Edited by] G. Townsend, 1424-1622. London, 1675. 1 v.

Previous ed. 1674.

340. Select collection of cases, with the opinion of the principal counsel of the last two reigns ... also, Reports of some decisions in the House of Lords ..., 1722-70. London, 1825. 1 v.

341. Spinks, T. The Ecclesiastical and Admiralty reports; being reports of cases heard before the Arches' and Prerogative Courts of Canterbury and the Consistory Court of London ..., the High Court of Admiralty and the Admiralty Prize Court ... with ... Cases ... by appeal ... to the Privy Council, 1853-55. London, 1855. 2 v.

Reprinted: English reports; Microfilm: Dobbs Ferry, Oceana.

Originally issued with the Common law reports and Equity reports.

342. Swabey, M.C. and Tristram, T.H. Reports of cases decided in the Court of Probate and in the Court for Divorce and Matrimonial Causes, 1858-65. London, 1860-71. 4 v.

Reprinted: English reports; Microfilm: Dobbs Ferry, Oceana.

343. The Times law reports, 1884-1952. London, 1884-1952. 68 v.

Incorporates: Reports of commercial cases from 1941. Continued by Weekly law reports.

344. Weekly law reports, 1953- . London Incorporated Council of Law Reporting, 1953- . 90 v.

Data base: LEXIS.

Continuation of: Weekly notes, and the Times law reports.

345. The weekly notes, 1866-1952. London, 1866-1952. 87 v.

Data base: LEXIS 1945

Continued by: Weekly law reports.

346. The weekly reporter, 1852-1906. London, 1853-1906. 54 v.

PARTICULAR COURTS

Admiralty

347. Browning, W.E. and Lushingon, V. Reports of cases decided in the High Court of Admiralty of England, and an appeal to the Privy Council, 1863-66. London, 1868. 1 v.

Reprinted: English reports; Microfilm: Dobbs Ferry, Oceana.

348. Dodson, J. Reports of cases argued and determined in the High Court of Admiralty, 1811-22. London, 1815-28. 2 v.

Reprinted: English reports; Microfilm: Dobbs Ferry, Oceana.

349. Edward, T. Reports of cases argued and determined in the High Court of Admiralty, 1808-12. London, 1812. 1 v.

Reprinted: English reports; Microfilm: Dobbs Ferry, Oceana.

Entitled v. 1. No more published.

350. Haggard, J. Reports of cases argued and determined in the High Court of Admiralty, 1822-38. London, 1825-40. 3 v.

Reprinted: English reports; Microfilm: Dobbs Ferry, Oceana.

351. Hay, Sir G. and Marriott, Sir J. Decisions in the High Court of Admiralty [temp.] ... Hay and ... Marriott, 1776-79. London, 1801. 1 v.

Reprinted: English reports; Microfilm: Dobbs Ferry, Oceana.

Also known as: Marriott.

352. Lushington, V. Reports of cases decided in the High Court of Admiralty, 1859-62. London, 1864. 1 v.

Reprinted: English reports; Microfilm: Dobbs Ferry, Oceana.

353. Robinson, C. Reports of cases argued and determined in the High Court of Admiralty, 1798-1808. London, 1799-1808. 6 v.

Reprinted: v. 1 1801, 1806; v. 2 1808, 1812; v. 3 1810 [2nd ed.]; v. 4 1812; English reports; Microfilm: Dobbs Ferry, Oceana.

354. Robinson, W. Reports of cases argued and determined in the High Court of Admiralty, 1838-50. London, 1844-52. 3 v.

Reprinted: English reports; Microfilm: Dobbs Ferry, Oceana.

v. 3: pts. 1-2 only published.

355. Swabey, M.C.M. Reports of cases decided in the High Court of Admiralty of England, and on appeal to the Privy Council, 1855-59. London, 1860. 1 v.

Reprinted: English reports; Microfilm: Dobbs Ferry, Oceana.

Admiralty - Collaterale

356. Burrell, Sir W. Reports of cases determined by the High Court of Admiralty, 1758-74; together with extracts from the books and records of the High Court of Admiralty, and the Court of the Judges Delegates, 1584-1839, and a collection of cases and opinions on Admiralty matters, 1701-81, edited by R.G. Marsden [1584-1840]. London, 1885. 1 v.

Reprinted: English reports; Microfilm: Dobbs Ferry, Oceana.

Also known as: Burrell and Marsden. Admiralty cases.

357. Holt, W. Admiralty Court cases on the rule of the road ... at sea, 1863-67. London, 1867. 1 v.

Microfilm: Dobbs Ferry, Oceana.

358. Notes of cases in the Ecclesiastical and Maritime Courts, 1841-50. London, 1843-50. 7 v.

Microfilm: Dobbs Ferry, Oceana.

Bail Court

See also nos. 630, 636

359. Chitty, J. Reports of cases principally on practice and pleading determined in the Court of King's Bench, 1770-1822. London, 1820-23. 2 v.

Microfilm: Dobbs Ferry, Oceana.

v. 1 contains only cases in 1819.

360. Dowling, A.S. Reports of cases argued and determined in the King's Bench Practice Court; with the points of practice decided in

the Courts of Common Pleas and Exchequer, 1830-41. London, 1833-42. 9 v.

Microfilm: Dobbs Ferry, Oceana.

Continued by: Dowling and Dowling. Cases in King's Bench.

361. Dowling, A. [S.] and Dowling, V. Reports of cases argued and determined in the Queen's Bench Practice Court; with the points of pleading and practice decided in the Courts of Common Pleas and Exchequer, 1841-43. London, 1843-44. 2 v.

Microfilm: Dobbs Ferry, Oceana.

Continuation of: Dowling. Cases in King's Bench. Continued by: Dowling and Lowndes. Cases in Queen's Bench. Also known as: Dowling, new series.

362. Dowling, A. [S.] and Lowndes, J.J. Reports of cases argued and determined in the Queen's Bench Practice Court; with the points of pleading and practice decided in the Courts of Common Pleas and Exchequer, 1843-49. London, 1845-51. 7 v.

Microfilm: Dobbs Ferry, Oceana.

Continuation of: Dowling and Dowling. Cases in Queen's Bench.

363. Harrison, S.B. and Wollaston, F.L. Reports of cases argued and determined in the Court of King's Bench and in the Bail Court, 1835-36. London, 1836-37. 2 v.

Microfilm: Dobbs Ferry, Oceana.

Part of The new term reports.

364. Lowndes, J.J. and Maxwell, P.B. Bail Court cases, 1852-54. London, 1852-54. 1 v.

Microfilm: Dobbs Ferry, Oceana.

Continuation of: Lowndes, Maxwell and Pollock. Cases in Queen's Bench.

365. Lowndes, J.J., Maxwell, P.B. and Pollock, C.E. Reports of cases argued and determined in the Queen's Bench Practice Court: with points of practice and pleading decided in the Courts of Common Pleas and Exchequer, 1850-51. London, 1851-52. 2 v.

Microfilm: Dobbs Ferry, Oceana.

Continued by: Lowndes and Maxwell. Bail Court cases. Also known as: Bail Court reports.

366. Saunders, T.W. and Cole, H.T. Bail Court reports, 1846-48. London, 1847-49. 2 v.

Microfilm: Dobbs Ferry, Oceana.

367. Willmore, G., Wollaston, F.L. and Davison, H. Reports of cases argued and determined in the Court of King's Bench, and upon writs of error ... to the Exchequer Chamber, and in the Bail Court, 1837. London, 1839. 1 v.

Microfilm: Dobbs Ferry, Oceana.

Part of The new term reports.

368. Wollaston, F.L. Reports of cases argued and determined in the Bail Court, and the practice cases in all the courts of the common law, 1840-41. London, [1840-41]. 1 v.

Microfilm: Dobbs Ferry, Oceana.

Part of The new term reports.

Chancery

369. [Acta Cancellariae] Monro, C. Acta Cancellariae; or, Selections from the records of the Court of Chancery, 1545-1625. London, 1847. 1 v.

Microfilm: Dobbs Ferry, Oceana.

Also known as: Monro.

370. Ambler, C. Reports of cases argued and determined in the High Court of Chancery. 2nd ed. by J.E. Blunt, 1737-83. London, 1828. 2 v.

Reprinted: English reports; Microfilm: Dobbs Ferry, Oceana.

1st ed. 1790 [in 1 v.], also Dublin.

371. Atkyns, J.T. Reports of cases argued and determined in the High Court of Chancery in the time of Chancellor Hardwicke, 1736-54. 3rd ed. by F.W. Sanders. London, 1794. 3 v.

Reprinted: English reports; Microfilm: Dobbs Ferry, Oceana.

Previous eds: 1765-68, 1781-82.

372. Bacon, Sir F. Reports of cases decided by Francis Bacon in the High Court of Chancery, 1617-21. London, 1932. 1 v.

373. Barnardiston, T. Reports of cases determined in the High Court of Chancery, 1740-41. London, 1742. 1 v.

Reprinted: English reports; Microfilm: Dobbs Ferry, Oceana.

374. Belt, R. A supplement to the reports in Chancery of Francis Vesey, senior ... 1747-56, 2nd ed. London, 1825. 1 v.

Reprinted: English reports; Microfilm: Dobbs Ferry, Oceana.

1st ed. 1817. Sometimes known as: Vesey, sen., Belt's supp.; 3 Vesey, sen.

375. Brown, W. Reports of cases argued and determined in the High Court of Chancery ... 5th ed. by R. Belt, 1778-94. London, 1820. 4 v.

Reprinted: English reports; Microfilm: Dobbs Ferry, Oceana.

1st ed. 1785-94; 2nd ed. 1792-94; 3rd ed. 1801; 4th ed. 1819 (Eden).

376. Cary, Sir G. Reports of cases in Chancery, 1557-1604. London, 1872. 1 v.

Reprinted: English reports; Microfilm: Dobbs Ferry, Oceana.

Previous eds.: 1650, 1665, 1820.

377. [Cases in Chancery] Cases argued and decreed in the High Court of Chancery, 1660-97. 3rd ed. London, 1735. 3 v.

Reprinted: English reports; Microfilm: Dobbs Ferry, Oceana.

3 pts., separately paged but normally bound as one. Title varies: pt. 3 Select cases in the High Court of Chancery. Previous eds.: pt. 1 1697; 2nd ed. 1707; pt. 2 1701; pt. 3 1702: 2nd ed. 1715.

378. Cases in law and equity, 1720-73. London, 1776. 1 v.

Originally published as part of Lawyer's magazine. Not to be confused with Gilbert or Modern reports, v. 10.

379. [Cases temp. Talbot] Cases in equity during the time of the late Lord Chancellor Talbot, 1730-37. 3rd ed. by J.G. Williams. London, 1792. 1 v.

Reprinted: English reports; Microfilm: Dobbs Ferry, Oceana.

Previous eds.: 1741; 2nd ed. 1753.

380. Choyce cases in Chancery [**appended to** The practice of the High Court of Chancery unfolded], 1558-1605. London, 1870. 1 v.

Reprinted: English reports; Microfilm: Dobbs Ferry, Oceana.

Previous eds.: 1652, 1672.

381. Cooper, G. Cases argued and determined in the High Court of Chancery during the time of Lord Eldon, with a few cases of an earlier period, 1792-1815. London, 1815. 1 v.

Reprinted: English reports; Microfilm: Dobbs Ferry, Oceana.

Another impression of 1815 has imprint London and Dublin. Also known as: Cooper temp. Eldon.

382. Cox, S. Cases determined in the courts of equity, 1783-97. London, 1816. 2 v.

Reprinted: English reports; Microfilm: Dobbs Ferry, Oceana.

Contains a few cases of an earlier date (1745-60).

383. Craig, R.D. and Phillips, T.J. Reports of cases argued and determined in the High Court of Chancery during the time of Lord Chancellor Cottenham, 1840-41. London, 1842. 1 v.

Reprinted: English reports; Microfilm: Dobbs Ferry, Oceana.

384. De Gex, J.P. and Jones, H.C. Reports of cases heard and determined by the Lord Chancellor and the Court of Appeal in Chancery, 1857-59. London, 1858-81. 4 v.

Reprinted: English reports; Microfilm: Dobbs Ferry, Oceana.

Continuation of: De Gex, Macnaghten and Gordon. Chancery appeals. Continued by: De Gex, Fisher and Jones. Chancery appeals.

385. De Gex, J.P., Fisher, F. and Jones, H.C. Reports of cases heard and determined by the Lord Chancellor and the Court of Appeal in Chancery, 1859-62. London, 1861-70. 4 v.

Reprinted: English reports; Microfilm: Dobbs Ferry, Oceana.

Continuation of: De Gex and Jones. Chancery appeals. Continued by: De Gex, Jones and Smith. Chancery appeals.

386. De Gex, J.P., Jones, H.C. and Smith, R.H. Reports of cases heard and determined by the Lord Chancellor and the Court of Appeal in Chancery, 1862-65. London, 1865-73. 4 v.

Reprinted: English reports; Microfilm: Dobbs Ferry, Oceana.

Continuation of: De Gex, Fisher and Jones. Chancery appeals.

387. De Gex, J.P., Macnaghten, S. and Gordon, A. Reports of cases heard and determined by the Lord Chancellor and the Court of Appeal in Chancery, 1851-57. London, 1853-64. 8 v.

Reprinted: English reports; Microfilm: Dobbs Ferry, Oceana.

Continued by: De Gex and Jones. Chancery appeals.

388. Dickens, J. Reports of cases argued and determined in the High Court of Chancery, 1559-1797. London, 1803. 2 v.

Reprinted: English reports; Microfilm: Dobbs Ferry, Oceana.

Only a few cases before 1700.

389. Eden, R.H. Reports of cases in the High Court of Chancery ... from the original manuscripts of Lord Chancellor Northington. 2nd ed., 1757-66. London, 1827. 2 v.

Reprinted: English reports; Microfilm: Dobbs Ferry, Oceana.

1st ed. 1818. Also known as: Cases temp. Northington.

390. [Equity cases abridged] A general abridgment of cases in equity, argued and adjudged in the High Court of Chancery, by a Gentleman of the Middle Temple, 1677-1744. London, 1793-69. 2 v.

Reprinted: English reports; Microfilm: Dobbs Ferry, Oceana.

Previous eds.: v. 1: 1st ed. 1732; 2nd ed. 1734; 3rd ed. 1739; 4th ed. 1756. v. 2: 1st ed. 1756. Dublin, 1793. Sometimes called "3rd ed." but is a reprint of the last English edition.

391. Freeman, R. Reports of cases argued and determined in the High Court of Chancery, 1660-1706. 2nd ed. by J.E. Hovenden. London, 1823. 1 v.

Reprinted: English reports; Microfilm: Dobbs Ferry, Oceana.

1st ed. 1742. Also known as: 2 Freeman.

392. Gilbert, J. Reports of cases in equity argued and decreed in the Courts of Chancery and Exchequer. 2nd ed., 1705-26. London, 1742. 1 v.

Reprinted: English reports; Microfilm: Dobbs Ferry, Oceana.

1st ed. 1734. Includes some Irish cases.

393. Hovenden, J.E. A supplement of Vesey junior's Reports of cases in Chancery: containing notes ... from the mss. of Mr. Forrester, 1789-1817. London, 1827. 2 v.

Reprinted: English reports; Microfilm: Dobbs Ferry, Oceana.

Prepared without Vesey junior's sanction and in fact predates the 2nd ed. of his reports by a few months.

394. Jacob, E. Reports of cases argued and determined in the High Court of Chancery, 1821-22. Lonodn, 1828. 1 v.

Reprinted: English reports; Microfilm: Dobbs Ferry, Oceana.

395. Jacob, E. and Walker, J. Reports of cases argued and determined in the High Court of Chancery, 1819-21. London, 1821-23. 2 v.

Reprinted: English reports; Microfilm: Dobbs Ferry, Oceana.

396. Kelynge, W. A report of cases in Chancery, the King's Bench, 1730-34. London, 1873. 1 v.

Reprinted: English reports; Microfilm: Dobbs Ferry, Oceana.

Previous eds. 1740, 1764. 1873 ed. a reprint of 1764 ed. Sometimes known as: 2 Kelynge to distinguish it from Kelyng, J.

397. The law reports. Cases determined in the Chancery Division and in Lunacy and on appeal therefrom in the Court of Appeal, 1891- . London, Incorporated Council of Law Reporting, 1891- . 135 v.

Data base: LEXIS 1945- .

Continuation of: The law reports ... cases determined by the Chancery Division. Also known as: Chancery reports.

398. The law reports. Chancery appeal cases, including bankruptcy and lunacy cases before the Lord Chancellor and the Court of Appeal in Chancery, 1865-75. London, 1866-75. 10 v.

Continued by: The law reports ... cases determined by the Chancery Division.

399. The law reports. Division I - Chancery. Cases determined by the Chancery Division of the High Court of Justice and by the Chief Judge in Bankruptcy and by the Court of Appeal on appeal from the Chancery Division and the Chief Judge and in lunacy, 1875-90. London, 1876-90. 45 v.

Continuation of: The law reports. Chancery Appeal cases; The law reports. Equity cases. Continued by: The law reports. Cases determined in the Chancery Division. Also known as: Chancery Division.

400. The law reports. Equity cases before the Master of the Rolls and the Vice-Chancellors, 1865-75. London, 1866-75. 20 v.

Continued by: The law reports ... cases determined by the Chancery Division. Also known as: Equity cases.

401. MacNaghten, S. and Gordon, A. Reports of cases argued and determined in the High Court of Chancery [temp.] Cottenham, 1849-52. London, 1850-52. 3 v.

Reprinted by: English reports; Microfilm: Dobbs Ferry, Oceana.

402. Merivale, J.H. Reports of cases argued and determined in the High Court of Chancery, 1815-17. London, 1817-19. 3 v.

Reprinted: English reports; Microfilm: Dobbs Ferry, Oceana.

An appendix to v. 3 contains notes of cases 1805-15 not reported elsewhere.

403. Mosely, W. Reports of cases argued and determined in the High Court of Chancery [temp.] King. 1726-30. 2nd ed. London, 1803. 1 v.

Reprinted: English reports; Microfilm: Dobbs Ferry, Oceana.

Previous eds. Dublin, 1744, 1793.

404. Mylne, J. and Craig, R.D. Reports of cases argued and determined in the High Court of Chancery, 1835-41. London, 1837-48. 5 v.

Reprinted: English reports; Microfilm: Dobbs Ferry, Oceana.

Continuation of: Mylne and Keen. Chancery cases.

405. Mylne, J.W. and Keen, B. Reports of cases argued and determined in the High Court of Chancery, 1832-35. London, 1834-37. 3 v.

Reprinted: English reports; Microfilm: Dobbs Ferry, Oceana.

Continued by: Mylne and Craig. Chancery cases.

406. Nelson, W. Reports of special cases argued and decreed in the Court of Chancery, 1625-92. London, 1872. 1 v.

Reprinted: English reports; Microfilm: Dobbs Ferry, Oceana.

Previous ed. 1717.

407. Peere Williams, W. Reports of cases argued and determined in the High Court of Chancery, and of special cases adjudged in the Court of King's Bench. 6th ed., by J.B. Munro, W.L. Lowndes and J. Randall, 1695-1735. London, 1826. 3 v.

Reprinted: English reports; Microfilm: Dobbs Ferry, Oceana.

1st ed. 1740 (2 v.), 2nd ed. 1746-49; 3rd ed. 1768; 4th ed. 1787 (Cox); Dublin, 1790; 5th ed. 1793 (Cox). 6th ed. omits some cases inserted by Cox.

408. Phillips, T.J. Reports of cases argued and determined in the High Court of Chancery, 1841-49. London, 1847-49. 2 v.

Reprinted: English reports, Microfilm: Dobbs Ferry, Oceana.

409. Precedents in Chancery, being a collection of cases argued and adjudged in the High Court of Chancery. 2nd ed. by T. Finch, 1689-1722. London, 1786. 1 v.

Reprinted: Dublin, 1792, English reports; Microfilm: Dobbs Ferry, Oceana.

1st ed. 1733; 2nd ed. 1747, 1750. Sometimes known as: Finch's precedents.

410. Reports of cases taken and adjudged in the Court of Chancery. 3rd ed., 1625-1710. London, 1763. 3 v. [in 1].

Reprinted: English reports; Microfilm: Dobbs Ferry, Oceana.

Previous eds: 1st ed. 1693-4 (in 2 v.), 2nd ed. 1715-6. Black letter.

411. Reports [temp. Finch] of cases decreed in the High Court of Chancery during the time Sir Heneage Finch, afterwards Earl of Nottingham, was Lord Chancellor, collected by [W.N.], 1673-80. London, 1725. 1 v.

Reprinted: English reports; Microfilm: Dobbs Ferry, Oceana.

W.N. is William Nelson. Also known as: Nelson temp. Finch.

412. Ridgeway, W. Reports of cases argued and determined in the King's Bench and Chancery [temp.] Lord Hardwicke, 1733-45. London, 1794. 1 v.

Reprinted: Dublin, 1794, English reports; Microfilm: Dobbs Ferry, Oceana.

The volume consists of two parts paged consecutively: pp. 1-162 contains King's Bench cases, 1733-36, pp. 163-345 contains Chancery cases 1744-45.

413. Russell, J. Reports of cases argued and determined in the High Court of Chancery, 1823-29. London, 1827-29. 5 v.

Reprinted: English reports; Microfilm: Dobbs Ferry, Oceana.

v. 5: pts 1-2 only published. A title page and index was issued in 1872.

414. Russell, J. and Mylne, J.W. Reports of cases argued and determined in the High Court of Chancery, 1829-33. London, 1832-37. 2 v.

Reprinted: English reports; Microfilm: Dobbs Ferry, Oceana.

415. [Select cases temp. King] Select cases argued and adjudged in the High Court of Chancery [temp.] King. 2nd ed., by S. Macnaghten, 1724-33. London, 1850. 1 v.

Reprinted: English reports; Microfilm: Dobbs Ferry, Oceana.

Previous ed. 1740. 2nd ed. sometimes known as: Macnaghten's select cases; Select cases in Chancery.

416. Swanston, C.T. Reports of cases argued and determined in the High Court of Chancery, 1818-19. London, 1821-27. 3 v.

Reprinted: English reports; Microfilm: Dobbs Ferry, Oceana.

Contains a few cases 1816-21 and in the Appendix 1673-1792.

417. Tothill, W. Transactions of the High Court of Chancery ... Reviewed by Sir R.O. Holborne, 1559-1646. London, 1872. 1 v.

Reprinted: English reports; Microfilm: Dobbs Ferry, Oceana.

Previous eds. 1649, 1671, 1820. 1872 ed. reprinted from 1820.

418. Turner, G. and Russell, J. Reports of cases argued and determined in the High Court of Chancery [temp.] Lord Chancellor Eldon, 1822-24. London, 1832. 1 v.

Reprinted: English reports; Microfilm: Dobbs Ferry, Oceana.

Entitled v. 1. No more published.

419. Vernon, T. Cases argued and adjudged in the High Court of Chancery, 1680-1719. 3rd ed., by J. Raithby. London, 1828. 2 v.

Reprinted: English reports; Microfilm: Dobbs Ferry, Oceana.

1st ed. 1726-28; 2nd ed. 1806 (Raithby), Dublin, 1726-29; 3rd ed. Dublin, 1793.

420. Vesey, F., sen. Reports of cases argued and determined in the High Court of Chancery [temp.] Lord Chancellor Hardwicke, 1747-56. 4th ed., by R. Belt. London, 1818. 2 v.

Reprinted: English reports; Microfilm: Dobbs Ferry, Oceana.

1st ed., 1771; 2nd ed. 1773; 3rd ed. 1788. For supplement see No. 374.

421. Vesey, F., jun. Reports of cases argued and determined in the High Court of Chancery, 1789-1817. London, 1827. 19 v.

Reprinted: English reports; Microfilm: Dobbs Ferry, Oceana.

The publishing history of Vesey jun. is complicated. v. 1-6 were published in folio, 1793-1802, v. 1 being reprinted in 1795. v. 7-19 were published in octavo 1804-22. v. 1-6 were reprinted in octavo as a '2nd ed.' in 1801-02 and as a '3rd ed.' in 1814. v. 7-8 were published as a '2nd ed.' in 1814. Variant title-pages may be found in v. 9-18. The true 2nd ed. was published in 1827. Indexes: to v. 1-14, by R. Belt, 1810, to v. 1-19, anon., 1822; to v. 1-19, by F. Vesey jun., 1833 (entitled Vol. 20). There is a supplement by J.E. Hovenden, 2 v., 1827, published without Vesey's sanction. Vesey jun. is sometimes simply cited as Vesey from v. 4 onwards, when ther is no need to avoid confusion with Vesey sen. A gap in reporting from Trinity, 1812 to Hilary 1815 is filled by Vesey and Beames.

422. Vesey, F. jun. and Beames, J. Reports of cases argued and determined in the High Court of Chancery [temp.] Lord Chancellor Eldon. 1812-14. 2nd ed. London, 1818. 3 v.

Reprinted: English reports; Microfilm: Dobbs Ferry, Oceana.

1st ed. 1813-15. In America sometimes known as: 21-22 Vesey jun.

423. West, M.J. Reports of cases argued and determined in the High Court of Chancery ... from the original manuscripts of Lord Chancellor Hardwicke, 1736-39. London, 1827. 1 v.

Reprinted: English reports; Microfilm: Dobbs Ferry, Oceana.

Entitled v. 1. No more published.

Chancery - Collaterale

424. Cooper, C.P. Reports of cases in Chancery decided by Lord Cottenham, 1846-48. London, 1846-48. 2 v.

Reprinted: English reports; Microfilm: Dobbs Ferry, Oceana.

v. 2: pts. 1-2 only published.

425. Cooper, C.P. Reports of some cases adjudged in the courts of the Lord Chancellor, Master of the Rolls and Vice-Chancellor, 1837-38. London, 1838-41. 1 v.

Reprinted: English reports; Microfilm: Dobbs Ferry, Oceana.

Also known as: Cooper's practice cases.

426. Cooper, C.P. Select cases decided by Lord Brougham in the Court of Chancery, 1833-34. London, 1835. 1 v.

Reprinted: English reports; Microfilm: Dobbs Ferry, Oceana.

427. Donnelly, R. Minutes of cases argued and determined in the High Court of Chancery, 1836-37. London, 1837. 1 v.

Reprinted: English reports; Microfilm: Dobbs Ferry, Oceana.

Pt. 1 only of a new series was published in 1838. This part is not reprinted in English reports.

428. Hall, F.J. and Twells, P. Reports of cases argued and determined in the High Court of Chancery [temp.] Lord Chancellor Cottenham, 1848-50. London, 1850-51. 2 v.

Reprinted: English reports; Microfilm: Dobbs Ferry, Oceana.

429. Romilly, Sir S. Notes of cases extracted from the manuscripts of Sir Samuel Romilly. With notes of Edward Romilly, 1767-87. London, 1872. 1 v.

Microfilm: Dobbs Ferry, Oceana.

Pt. 1 only published.

430. Wilson, J. Reports of cases argued and determined in the High Court of Chancery, 1818-19. London, [1819]. 2 v.

Reprinted: English reports; Microfilm: Dobbs Ferry, Oceana.

v. 2: pt. 1 only published.

431. Wyatt, J. The practical register in Chancery, with the addition of the modern cases. London, 1800. 1 v.

Microfilm: Dobbs Ferry, Oceana.

Previous ed. 1714 (anonymous). Also known as: Practical register, Chancery.

Common Pleas

See also No. 623

432. Anderson, E. Les reports ... del Common-Bank, 1535-1603. London, 1664-65. 2 v. In Anglo-French.

Reprinted: English reports; Microfilm: Dobbs Ferry, Oceana.

Pt. 2 contains cases in the Court of Wards.

433. Barnes, H. Notes of cases in points of practice, taken in the Court of Common Pleas, 1732-69. 3rd ed. London, 1790. 1 v.

Reprinted: English reports; Microfilm: Dobbs Ferry, Oceana.

Previous eds.: 1741 (1732-40); 1754 (2 v 1732-54 with supp. 1756), 2nd ed. 1772 (1732-60), also Dublin, 1788.

434. Benloe, W. Les reports ... de divers pleadings et cases, 1358-1579. [and] Dalison, W. Les reports de divers special cases, 1546-74. London, 1689. 1 v. In Latin, Anglo-French or English.

Reprinted: English reports; Microfilm: Dobbs Ferry, Oceana.

Also known as: Old Benloe. Benloe sometimes spelt Bendloe, Bendoes, Benlowes and Bendloes.

435. Bingham, P. New cases in the Court of Common Pleas and other courts, 1834-40. London, 1835-41. 6 v.

Reprinted: English reports; Microfilm: Dobbs Ferry, Oceana.

Continuation of: Bingham. Reports in Common Pleas.

436. Bingham, P. Reports of cases argued and determined in the Court of Common Pleas and other courts, 1822-34. London; 1824-34. 10 v.

Reprinted: English reports; Microfilm: Dobbs Ferry, Oceana.

Continued by: Bingham. New cases in Common Pleas.

437. Blackstone, H. Reports of cases argued and determined in the Courts of Common Pleas and Exchequer Chamber, 1788-96. 4th ed. London, 1827. 2 v.

Reprinted: English reports; Microfilm: Dobbs Ferry, Oceana.

Previous eds: 1791-96, (2 v.); 1792-96, (Dublin, 2 v.); 3rd ed. 1801 (2 v.); 5th ed. 1837 by F.W. Meymott. 5th ed. in small type and not preferred to 4th ed.

438. Bosanquet, J.B. and Puller, C. New reports of cases argued and determined in the Courts of Common Pleas and other courts, 1804-07. 2nd ed. London, 1826. 2 v.

Reprinted: English reports; Microfilm: Dobbs Ferry, Oceana.

Previous ed: 1806-08.

439. Bosanquet, J.B. and Puller, C. Reports of cases argued and determined in the Courts of Common Pleas and Exchequer Chamber, 1796-1804. 3rd ed. London, 1826. 3 v.

Reprinted: English reports; Microfilm: Dobbs Ferry, Oceana.

Previous eds: Dublin, 1804 (1800-04); 2nd ed. 1814. No. 455 generally bound with this item.

440. Bridgman, Sir J. Reports of that grave and learned judge, 1613-21. London, 1659. 1 v.

Reprinted: English reports; Microfilm: Dobbs Ferry, Oceana.

Contains 2 cases of a later date.

441. Bridgman, Sir O. Reports of judgments delivered by Sir Orlando Bridgman when Chief Justice of the Common Pleas, edited by S. Bannister, 1660-67. London, 1823. 1 v.

Reprinted: English reports; Microfilm: Dobbs Ferry, Oceana.

442. Broderip, W.J. and Bingham, P. Reports of cases argued and determined in the Court of Common Pleas and other courts, 1819-22. London, 1820-22. 3 v.

Reprinted: English reports; Microfilm: Dobbs Ferry, Oceana.

443. Brownlow, R. and Goldesborough, J. Reports of divers choice cases in law, 1569-1624. [Pt. 1, 3rd ed. Pt. 2, 2nd ed.]. London, 1675. 2 v.

Reprinted: English reports; Microfilm: Dobbs Ferry, Oceana.

Previous eds: Pt. 1 1651, 1654; Pt. 2 1652. Pt. 2 is by Brownlow alone.

444. Carter, S. Reports of several special cases argued and resolved in the Court of Common Pleas, 1664-75. London, 1688. 1 v.

Reprinted: English reports; Microfilm: Dobbs Ferry, Oceana.

445. Common Bench reports. Cases argued and determined in the Court of Common Pleas, 1845-56. London, 1846-56. 18 v.

Reprinted: English reports; Microfilm: Dobbs Ferry, Oceana.

v. 1-8 by Manning, Granger & Scott; v. 9 by Granger and Scott; v. 10-18 by Scott. Continuation of Manning and Granger. Cases in Common Pleas. Continued by: Common Bench reports, new series.

446. Common Bench reports, new series. Reports of cases argued and determined in the Court of Common Pleas and in the Exchequer Chamber, by J. Scott, 1856-65. London, 1857-66. 20 v.

Reprinted: English reports; Microfilm: Dobbs Ferry, Oceana.

Continuation of: Common Bench reports.

447. Cooke, Sir G. Reports and cases of practice in the Court of Common Pleas, 1706-47. 3rd ed. by T.T. Bucknill. London, 1872. 1 v.

Reprinted: English reports; Microfilm: Dobbs Ferry, Oceana.

Previous eds.: 1742, 1747.

448. Hetley, Sir T. Reports and cases taken ... , 1627-31. London, 1657. 1 v.

Reprinted: English reports; Microfilm: Dobbs Ferry, Oceana.

449. Hutton, Sir R. The reports of ... Sir Richard Hutton. 2nd ed., 1612-38: London, 1682. 1 v.

Reprinted: English reports; Microfilm: Dobbs Ferry, Oceana.

1st ed. 1658.

450. The law reports. Common Pleas Division, 1875-80. London, 1876-80. 5 v.

Continuation of: The law reports. Court of Common Pleas. Continued by: The law reports. Queen's Bench Division.

451. The law reports. Court of Common Pleas, 1865-75. London, 1866-75. 10 v.

Continued by: The law reports. Common Pleas Division. Also known as: Common Pleas.

452. Littleton, E., Baron. Les reports ... en le Courts del Common Bank & Exchequer, 1627-31. London, 1683. 1 v. In French.

Reprinted: English reports; Microfilm: Dobbs Ferry, Oceana.

453. Lutwyche, Sir E. The reports of the resolutions of the court on divers exceptions taken to pleadings ... arising ... in the Court of Common Pleas, 1683-1704. London, 1718. 2 v.

Reprinted: English reports; Microfilm: Dobbs Ferry, Oceana.

1st ed. 1704 (in French and Latin); another trans. 1718 (1 v. by W. Nelson, omitting the entries). The English reports reprints the 1704 ed. which is entitled 'Un livre des entries; contenant auxi un reports des resolutions del court.' The Nelson trans. is held a poor ed.

454. Manning, J. and Granger, T.C. Cases argued and determined in the Court of Common Pleas, 1840-45. London, 1841-46. 7 v.

Reprinted: English reports; Microfilm: Dobbs Ferry, Oceana.

Continued by: Common Bench reports.

455. Moore, A. Reports of cases in the Courts of Common Pleas and Exchequer Chamber and in the House of Lords, 1795-97. London, 1800. 1 v.

Reprinted: English reports.

Generally bound as: Bosanquet & Puller, v. 1, pp. 471 ff. Occasionally is found bound separately.

456. Savile, Sir J. Les reports ... de divers special cases cybien en le Court de Common Bank, Come l'Exchequer, 1580-94. London, 1688. 1 v. In Anglo-French.

Reprinted: English reports; Microfilm: Dobbs Ferry, Oceana.

Previous ed. 1675. Black letter.

457. Taunton, W.P. Reports of cases argued and determined in the Court of Common Pleas and other courts, 1807-19. London, 1811-23. 8 v.

Reprinted: English reports; Microfilm: Dobbs Ferry, Oceana.

458. Vaughan, Sir J. The reports and arguments of ... 2nd ed., 1666-73. London, 1706. v. 1.

Reprinted: English reports; Microfilm: Dobbs Ferry, Oceana.

1st ed. 1677. Black letter. A tract is appended entitled 'Concerning process out of the courts at Westminster into Wales.'

459. Willes, Sir J. Reports of adjudged cases in the Court of Common Pleas [temp.] Lord Chief Justice Willes. [Ed.] by C. Durnford, 1737-58. Dublin, 1800. 1 v.

Reprinted: English reports; Microfilm: Dobbs Ferry, Oceana.

Previous ed. London, 1799.

460. Winch, Sir H. Reports of ... , 1621-25. London, 1657. 1 v.

Reprinted: English reports; Microfilm: Dobbs Ferry, Oceana.

Common Pleas - Collaterals

461. Arnold, T.J. Reports of cases argued and determined in the Court of Common Pleas, 1838-39. London, 1840. 2 v.

Microfilm: Dobbs Ferry, Oceana

Part of The new term reports.

462. Drinkwater, W.L. Reports of cases argued and determined in the Court of Common Pleas, 1840-41. London, 1840-41. 1 v.

Microfilm: Dobbs Ferry, Oceana.

Part of The new term reports.

463. Harrison, O.B.C. and Rutherford, H. Reports of cases argued and determined in the Court of Common Pleas, and the Court of Exchequer Chamber on appeal from the Court of Common Pleas, with tables of the names of the cases reported and cited, and an index of the contents. 1865-66. London, 1868. 1 v.

Microfilm: Dobbs Ferry, Oceana.

Continuation of: Common Bench reports (new series).

464. Hodges, W. Reports of cases argued and determined in the Court of Common Pleas, 1835-37. London, 1836-39. 3 v.

Microfilm: Dobbs Ferry, Oceana.

Part of The new term reports.

465. Marshall, C. Reports of cases argued and determined in the Courts of Common Pleas and Exchequer Chamber, 1813-16. London, 1815-17. 2 v.

Microfilm: Dobbs Ferry, Oceana.

466. Moore, J.B. Reports of cases argued and determined in the Court of Common Pleas and Exchequer Chamber, 1817-27. London, 1818-31. 12 v.

Microfilm: Dobbs Ferry, Oceana.

Continued by: Moore and Payne.

467. Moore, J.B. and Payne, J. Reports of cases argued and determined in the Courts of Common Pleas and Exchequer Chamber, 1827-31. London, 1828-32. 5 v.

Microfilm: Dobbs Ferry, Oceana.

Continuation of: Moore.

468. Moore, J.B. and Scott, J. Cases argued and determined in the Courts of Common Pleas and Exchequer Chamber, and in the House of Lords, 1831-34. London, 1833-34. 4 v.

Microfilm: Dobbs Ferry, Oceana.

469. Scott, J. Cases in the Court of Common Pleas and Exchequer Chamber, 1834-40. London, 1835-41. 8 v.

Microfilm: Dobbs Ferry, Oceana.

Continued by: Manning and Granger. Cases in Common Pleas and Exchequer.

470. Scott, J. Scott's new reports in the Court of Common Pleas and Exchequer Chamber, 1840-45. London, 1841-45. 8 v.

Microfilm: Dobbs Ferry, Oceana.

County Courts

471. Austin, R.C. Reports of cases (principally under the County Court Equitable Jurisdiction Act, 1865, and the County Courts Amendment Act, 1867) in the county courts included in Circuit No. 45, heard and determined by Henry James Stonor, Esq., Judge of the said courts. With a preface, notes and appendix, 1867-69. London, 1869. 1 v.

472. [County court cases] Reports of county court cases and appeals argued and determined in the superior courts, 1847-58. London, 1852-58. 3 v.

Microfilm: Dobbs Ferry, Oceana.

Title varies: v. 2 adds 'also reports of cases relating to insolvency' after 'superior courts' and deletes 'Reports of' from start of title. v.1. (Cox, Macrae and Hertslet) 2-3 (Saunders and Macrae). Also known as Cox, Macrae and Hertslet's county court cases; Cox, Macrae and Hertlet's county court reports. Insolvency reports issued with v. 1-2, paged separately and usually bound separately.

473. [County court reports] Reports of county court cases and appeals decided by all the superior courts, and of decisions in the county courts, together with cases in bankruptcy, new series, 1860-1920. London, 1861-1920. 34 v.

Title varies: v. 34 Reports of county court and bankruptcy cases argued and determined in the superior courts. Published in the County courts chronicle and gazette of bankruptcy, v. 14-47 (1860-1920) in continuation of earlier reports in the text of the chronicle; these being paged separately in v. 5, 7, 12 and 13. Also issued separately in quarterly parts as Cox's county courts equity and bankruptcy cases. Also known as Cox's county court reports after the publisher's name.

474. De Colyar, H.A. Reports of cases in the county courts included in Circuits Nos. 45 & 46. Heard and determined by Henry James Stoner, Esq., judge of the said courts, including recent cases under the Employers' Liability Act, with a preface, notes, and full index, 1867-82. London, 1883. 1 v.

Microfilm: Dobbs Ferry, Oceana.

475. Francillon, J. Judgments in cases reserved for consideration in the County Courts of Gloucestershire and Wiltshire, 1847-52. Cheltenham, 1850-52. 1 v.

476. [Hampshire County Courts reports] Reports of cases in the Hampshire County Courts during the years 1917-1920, being judgments delivered by Judge Bernard Lailey; Edited by F.E.B. Duff, 1917-20. Portsmouth, 1920 1 v.

477. The law journal county courts reporter: a monthly record of county court decisions and appeals with notes, 1912-33. London, 1912-33. 30 v.

Continued by: The law journal county courts reports. Published in The law journal, with separate annual title pages. Also known as: Law journal county courts reports. Not published 1925.

478. The law journal county court reports, 1934-47. London, 1934-48. 14 v.

Continuation of: The law journal county court reporter. Published as a supplement to The law journal

479. 'The law journal' newspaper county court appeals, 1935. London, 1935. 1 v.

Supplement to The law journal, Dec. 28, 1935.

480. Roberts, W.H., Leeming, H. and Wallis, J.E. Reports of cases in the superior courts on the law and practice of the new county courts, 1849-51. London, 1850-51. 1 v.

Microfilm: Dobbs Ferry, Oceana.

Ecclesiastical Courts

See also subject sequence under Ecclesiastical law.

481. Addams, J. Reports of cases argued and determined in the ecclesiastical courts, 1822-26. London, 1823-26, 3 v.

Reprinted: English reports; Microfilm: Dobbs Ferry, Oceana.

v. 3: pt. 1 only published.

482. Curteis, W.C. Reports of cases argued and determined in the Ecclesiastical Courts at Doctors' Commons, 1834-44. London, 1840-44. 3 v.

Reprinted: English reports; Microfilm: Dobbs Ferry, Oceana.

483. Deane, J.P. and Swabey, M.C.M. Reports of cases decided in the Ecclesiastical Courts at Doctors' Commons, 1855-57. London, 1858. 1 v.

Reprinted: English reports; Microfilm: Dobbs Ferry, Oceana.

484. Haggard, J. Reports of cases argued and determined in the Consistory Court of London [temp.] Scott, 1789-1821. London, 1822. 2 v.

Reprinted: English reports; Microfilm: Dobbs Ferry, Oceana.

485. Haggard, J. Reports of cases argued and determined in the Ecclesiastical Courts of Doctors' Commons and in the High Court of Delegates, 182733. London, 1829-34. 4 v.

Microfilm: Dobbs Ferry, Oceana.

Appendices to v. 1-2 contain cases 1700-1827. v. 4: pts. 1-2 only published.

486. Lee, Sir G. Reports of cases argued and determined in the Arches and Prerogative Courts of Canterbury, and in the High Court of Delegates: containing the judgments of ... Sir George Lee, 1752-58. London, 1833-32. 2 v.

Reprinted: English reports; Microfilm: Dobbs Ferry, Oceana.

An appendix to v. II contains some cases, 1726-32.

487. Phillimore, J. Reports of cases argued and determined in the Ecclesiastical Courts at Doctors' Commons; and in the High Court of Delegates, 1809-21. London, 1818-27. 3 v.

Reprinted: English reports; Microfilm: Dobbs Ferry, Oceana.

Includes notes of a few earlier cases.

488. Phillimore, Sir R. The principal ecclesiastical judgments delivered in the Court of Arches, 1867-75. London, 1876. 1 v.

Microfilm: Dobbs Ferry, Oceana.

Also known as: Phillimore's ecclesiastical reports.

489. Robertson, J.E.P. Reports of cases argued and determined in the Ecclesiastical Courts at Doctors' Commons, 1844-53. London, 1850-53. 2 v.

Reprinted: English reports; Microfilm: Dobbs Ferry, Oceana,

v. 2: pts. 1-3 only published. The text breaks off in the middle of a case.

490. Tristram, T.H. The principal judgments delivered in the Consistory Courts of London, Hereford, Ripon and Wakefield, and in the Commissary Court of Canterbury, 1872-90. London, 1893, 1 v.

Microfilm: Dobbs Ferry, Oceana.

Exchequer

491. Anstruther, A. Reports of cases argued and determined in the Court of Exchequer, 1792-97. London, Dublin, 1817. 3 v.

Reprinted: English reports; Microfilm: Dobbs Ferry, Oceana.

1st ed. 1796-97.

492. Bunbury, W. Reports of cases in the Court of Exchequer, 1713-41. 2nd ed. Dublin, 1793. 1 v.

Reprinted: English reports; Microfilm: Dobbs Ferry, Oceana.

Previous eds.: London, 1755; Dublin, 1756; 2nd ed. London, 1802 identical to Dublin 1793 ed.

493. Crompton, C. and Jarvis, J. Reports of cases argued and determined in the Courts of Exchequer and Exchequer Chamber, 1830-32. London, 1832-33. 2 v.

Reprinted: English reports; Microfilm: Dobbs Ferry, Oceana.

Continued by: Crompton and Meeson. Cases in Exchequer.

494. Crompton, C. and Meeson, R. Reports of cases argued and determined in the Courts of Exchequer and Exchequer Chamber, 1832-34. London, 1834-35. 2 v.

Reprinted: English reports; Microfilm: Dobbs Ferry, Oceana.

Continuation of: Crompton and Jarvis. Continued by: Crompton, Meeson and Roscoe. Cases in Exchequer.

495. Crompton, C., Meeson, R. and Roscoe, H. Reports of cases argued and determined in the Courts of Exchequer and Exchequer Chamber, 1834-55. London, 1835-36. 2 v.

Reprinted: English reports; Microfilm: Dobbs Ferry, Oceana.

Continuation of: Crompton and Meeson. Cases in Exchequer.

496. Daniell, E.R. Reports of cases argued and determined on the equity side of the Court of Exchequer, 1817-20. London; 1824. 1 v.

Reprinted: English reports; Microfilm: Dobbs Ferry, Oceana.

497. Exchequer reports [Welsby, Hurlstone and Gordon]. Reports of cases argued and determined in the Courts of Exchequer and Exchequer Chamber, by W.N. Welsby, E.T. Hurlstone and G. Gordon, 1847-56. London, 1849-56. 11 v.

Reprinted: English reports; Microfilm: Dobbs Ferry, Oceana.

v. 10-11 are by Hurlstone and Gordon alone.

498. Forrest, R. Reports of cases argued and determined in the Court of Exchequer, 1800-01. London, 1884. 1 v.

Reprinted: English reports; Microfilm: Dobbs Ferry, Oceana.

Previous ed. 1802.

499. Hardres, Sir T. Reports of cases adjudged in the Court of Exchequer, 1655-69. Dublin, 1792. 1 v.

Reprinted: English reports; Microfilm: Dobbs Ferry, Oceana.

Previous ed. (black letter) London, 1693.

500. Hurlstone, E.T. and Coltman, F.J. The Exchequer reports. Reports of cases argued and determined in the Courts of Exchequer and Exchequer Chamber, 1862-66. London, 1863-68. 4 v.

Reprinted: English reports; Microfilm: Dobbs Ferry, Oceana.

Continuation of: Hurlstone and Norman. Exchequer reports.

501. Hurlstone, E.T. and Norman, J.P. The Exchequer reports. Reports of cases argued and determined in the Courts of Exchequer and Exchequer Chamber, 1856-62. London, 1857-62. 7 v.

Reprinted: English reports; Microfilm: Dobbs Ferry, Oceana.

Continued by: Hurlstone and Coltman. Exchequer reports.

502. Jenkins, D. Eight centuries of reports; or; eight hundred cases solemnly adjudged in the Exchequer Chamber. 1220-1623. 4th ed. by C.F. Morrell. London, 1885. 1 v.

Reprinted: English reports; Microfilm: Dobbs Ferry, Oceana.

1st ed. (in French) 1661; 2nd ed. 1734, 3rd ed. 1771, 1777.

503. Lane, R. Reports in the Court of Exchequer. With notes and a life of the reporter, by C.F. Morrell, 1605-11. London, 1884. 1 v.

Reprinted: English reports; Microfilm: Dobbs Ferry, Oceana.

Reprinted from the original 1657 ed.

504. The law reports. Court of Exchequer, 1865-75. London, 1866-75. 10 v.

Continued by: The law reports. Exchequer Division. Also known as: Exchequer cases.

505. The law reports. Exchequer Division, 1875-80. London, 1876-80. 5 v.

Continuation of: The law reports. Court of Exchequer. Continued by: The law reports. Queen's Bench Division. Also known as: Exchequer cases.

506. M'Cleland, T. Reports of cases argued and determined in the Courts of Exchequer and Exchequer Chamber, 1824. London, 1825. 1 v.

Reprinted: English reports; Microfilm: Dobbs Ferry, Oceana.

507. M'Cleland, T. and Younge, E. Reports of cases argued and determined in the Courts of Exchequer and Exchequer Chamber, 1824-25. London, 1827. 1 v.

Reprinted: English reports; Microfilm: Dobbs Ferry, Oceana.

Entitled v. 1. No more published.

508. Meeson, R. and Welsby, W.N. Reports of cases argued and determined in the Court of Exchequer and Exchequer Chamber, 1836-47. London, 1837-49. 17 v.

Reprinted: English reports; Microfilm: Dobbs Ferry, Oceana.

v. 15 is reported in part by R.P. Tyrwhitt. v. 16 is by R.P. Tyrwhitt and E.T. Hurlstone.

509. Parker, Sir T. Reports of cases concerning the revenue, argued and determined in the Court of Exchequer, ... 1743-67. London, 1800. 1 v.

Reprinted: English reports; Microfilm: Dobbs Ferry, Oceana.

Previous eds. 1776, 1791, Dublin 1791. Usually catalogued as 1791. 1800 ed. merely a change of date on the title page.

510. Price, G. Notes of points in practice rules in the Exchequer of Pleas, and the cases at law and in revenue argued and determined in the Court of Exchequer and the Courts of Error and Appeal, 1830-31. London, 1831. 1 v.

Microfilm: Dobbs Ferry, Oceana.

Pt. 1 only published.

511. Price, G. Reports of cases argued and determined in the Court of Exchequer, 1814-24. London, 1816-28. 13 v.

Reprinted: English reports; Microfilm: Dobbs Ferry, Oceana.

512. Wightwick, J. Reports of cases argued and determined in the Court of Exchequer, 1810-11. London, 1819. 1 v.

Reprinted: English reports; Microfilm: Dobbs Ferry, Oceana.

Contains one case from 1754.

513. Wilson, J. Reports of cases argued and determined in the Court of Exchequer, 1805-17. London, [1817]. 1 v.

Reprinted: English reports; Microfilm: Dobbs Ferry, Oceana.

v. 1, pt. 1 only published.

514. Younge, E. Reports of cases argued and determined in the Court of Exchequer in equity, 1830-32. London, 1833. 1 v.

Reprinted: English reports; Microfilm: Dobbs Ferry, Oceana.

Entitled v. 1. No more published.

515. Younge, E. and Collyer, J. Reports of cases argued and determined in the Court of Exchequer in equity, 1834-42. London, 1836-46. 4 v.

Reprinted: English reports; Microfilm: Dobbs Ferry, Oceana.

516. Younge, E. and Jervis, J. Reports of cases argued and determined in the Courts of Exchequer and Exchequer Chamber, at law, in equity, and in error, 1826-30. London, 1828-30. 3 v.

Reprinted: English reports; Microfilm: Dobbs Ferry, Oceana.

Exchequer - Collateral

517. Gale, C.J. Reports of cases argued and determined in the Court of Exchequer, 1835-36. London, 1836-38. 2 v.

Microfilm: Dobbs Ferry, Oceana.

Part of The new term reports.

518. Horn, H. and Hurlstone, E.T. Reports of cases argued and determined in the Court of Exchequer and upon writs of error from that court to the Exchequer Chamber, 1838-39. London, 1840. 2 v.

Microfilm: Dobbs Ferry, Oceana.

Part of The new term reports.

519. Hurlstone, E.T. and Walmsley, T. Reports of cases argued and determined in the Court of Exchequer, 1840-41. London, 1841. 1 v.

Microfilm: Dobbs Ferry, Oceana.

Part of The new term reports.

520. Murphy, F.S. and Hurlstone, E.T. Reports of cases argued and determined in the Court of Exchequer, 1837. London, 1838. 1 v.

Microfilm: Dobbs Ferry, Oceana.

Part of The new term reports.

521. Tyrwhitt, R.P. Reports of cases argued and determined in the Courts of Exchequer and Exchequer Chamber, 1830-35. London, 1832-37. 5 v.

Microfilm: Dobbs Ferry, Oceana.

Continued by: Tyrwhitt and Granger. Reports in Exchequer.

522. Tyrwhitt, R.P. and Granger, T.C. Reports of cases argued and determined in the Courts of Exchequer and Exchequer Chamber, 1835-36. London, 1837. 1 v.

Microfilm: Dobbs Ferry, Oceana.

Continuation of: Tyrwhitt. Reports in Exchequer.

House of Lords

See also no. 1654

523. Bligh, R. New reports of cases heard in the House of Lords, 1827-37. London, 1829-38. 11 v.

Reprinted: English reports; Microfilm: Dobbs Ferry, Oceana.

v. 11: pts. 1-3 only published.

524. Bligh, R. Reports of cases heard in the House of Lords, 1819-21. London, 1823-27. 4 v.

Reprinted: English reports; Microfilm: Dobbs Ferry, Oceana.

v. 4: pt. 1 only published.

525. [Brown's Parliament cases] Brown, J. Reports of cases upon appeals and writs of error determined in the High Court of Parliament, 1702-1800. 2nd ed., [continued] by T.E. Tomlins. London, 1803. 8 v.

Reprinted: English reports; Microfilm: Dobbs Ferry, Oceana.

1st ed. 1779-83 (7 v., 1702-79); Dublin, 1779 (v. 1-2) 1784-89 (7 v., with supp. by Colles). 2nd ed. does not include Colles.

526. Clark, C. and Finnelly, W. Reports of cases heard and decided in the House of Lords on appeals and writs of error, 1831-46. London, 1835-47. 12 v.

Reprinted: English reports; Microfilm: Dobbs Ferry, Oceana.

527. Colles, R. Reports of cases upon appeals and writs of error in the High Court of Parliament; being a supplementary volume to Brown's Cases of Parliament, 1697-1713. Dublin, 1789. 1 v.

Reprinted: English reports; Microfilm: Dobbs Ferry, Oceana.

528. Dow, P. Reports of cases upon appeals and writs of error in the House of Lords, 1813-18. London, 1814-19. 6 v.

Reprinted: English reports; Microfilm: Dobbs Ferry, Oceana.

529. Dow, P. and Clark, C. Reports of cases upon appeals and writs of error in the House of Lords, 1827-32. London, 1830-32. 2 v.

Reprinted: English reports; Microfilm: Dobbs Ferry, Oceana.

Also known as: Dow, new series.

530. House of Lords cases on appeal and writs of error, by C. Clark and W. Finnelly, 1847-66. London, 1849-66. 11 v.

Reprinted: English reports; Microfilm: Dobbs Ferry, Oceana.

v. 1-2 (Clark and Finnelly); v. 3-11 (Clark). v 1-2 sometimes known as: Clark and Finnelly, new series.

531. The law reports. Appeal cases before the House of Lords (English- Irish- and Scotch) and the Judicial Committee of Her Majesty's Most Honourable Privy Council, 1875-90. London, 1876-90. 15 v.

Continuation of: Law reports. Scotch and Divorce Appeal Cases; Law reports. Privy Council appeals; Law reports. English and Irish appeal cases. Continued by: Law reports. House of Lords, Judicial Committee of the Privy Council. Also known as: Appeal cases.

532. The law reports. English and Irish appeal cases and claims of peerage before the House of Lords, 1866-75. London, 1866-75. 7 v.

Continued by: The law reports. Appeal cases. Also known as: House of Lords cases.

533. The law reports. House of Lords, Judicial Committee of the Privy Council, and peerage cases, 1891- . London, Incorporated Council of Law Reporting, 1891- . 97 v.

Data base: LEXIS 1945- .

Continuation of: The law reports. Appeal cases before the House of Lords. Also known as: Appeal cases.

534. The law reports. Scotch and divorce appeal cases before the House of Lords, 1866-75. London, 1869-75. 2 v.

Continued by: The law reports. Appeal cases before the House of Lords. Also known as: House of Lords Scotch and divorce appeals.

535. Maclean, C.H. and Robinson, G. House of Lords cases on appeals and writs of error, 1839. London, 1840. 1 v.

536. Shower, Sir B. ... Cases in Parliament resolved and adjudged upon petitions and writs of error. 4th ed., by R.L. Loveland, 1694-99. London, 1876. 1 v.

Reprinted: English reports; Microfilm: Dobbs Ferry, Oceana.

1st ed. 1698 (anonymous); 3rd ed. 1740. No 2nd ed. known.

537. West, M.J. Cases heard and determined by the House of Lords, on appeals from the courts of equity, and on writs of error in England and Ireland; and questions of peerage, 1839-41. London, 1842. 1 v.

Reprinted: English reports; Microfilm: Dobbs Ferry, Oceana.

Entitled: v. 1. No more published.

King's Bench / Queen's Bench

538. Adolphus, J.L. and Ellis, T.F. Reports of cases argued and determined in the Court of King's Bench, 1834-40. London, 1835-42. 12 v.

Reprinted: English reports; Microfilm: Dobbs Ferry, Oceana.

Continued by: Queen's Bench reports.

539. Aleyn, J. Select cases in the King's Bench, 1646-48. London, 1688. 1 v.

Reprinted: English reports; Microfilm: Dobbs Ferry, Oceana.

Previous ed. 1681.

540. Andrews, G. Reports of cases argued and adjudged in the Court of King's Bench, 1737-38. 2nd ed. by G.W. Vernon. London, Dublin, 1791. 1 v.

Reprinted: English reports; Microfilm: Dobbs Ferry, Oceana.

1st ed. 1754. London ed. sometimes dated 1792.

541. Barnardiston, T. Reports of cases determined in the Court of King's Bench, 1726-34. London, 1744. 2 v.

Reprinted: English reports; Microfilm: Dobbs Ferry, Oceana.

542. Barnewall, R.V. and Adolphus, J.L. Reports of cases argued and determined in the Court of King's Bench, 1830-34. London, 1831-35. 5 v.

Reprinted: English reports; Microfilm: Dobbs Ferry, Oceana.

Continuation of: Barnewall and Cresswell. Reports in King's Bench.

543. Barnewall, R.V. and Alderson, E.H. Reports of cases argued and determined in the Court of King's Bench, 1817-22. London, 1818-22. 5 v.

Reprinted: English reports; Microfilm: Dobbs Ferry, Oceana.

Continued by: Barnewall and Cresswell. Reports in King's Bench.

544. Barnewall, R.V. and Cresswell, C. Reports of cases argued and determined in the Court of King's Bench, 1822-30. London, 1823-32. 10 v.

Reprinted: English reports; Microfilm: Dobbs Ferry, Oceana.

Continuation of: Barnewall and Alderson. Reports in King's Bench.
Continued by: Barnewall and Adolphus. Reports in King's Bench.

545. Bellewe, R. Les ans du Roy Richard le second collect' ensembl' hors de les Abridgments de Statham, Fitzherbert et Brooke, 1378-1400. London, 1869. 1 v. In Anglo-French.

Reprinted: English reports; Microfilm: Dobbs Ferry, Oceana.

Reprint of 1585 ed.

546. Benloe, W. Les reports, 1514-1627. London, 1661. 1 v. In French.

Reprinted: English reports; Microfilm: Dobbs Ferry, Oceana.

Also known as: New Benloe.

547. Best, W.M. and Smith, G.J.P. Reports of cases argued and determined in the Court of Queen's Bench, 1861-69. London, 1862-71. 10 v.

Reprinted: English reports; Microfilm: Dobbs Ferry, Oceana.

548. Blackstone, W. Reports of cases determined in the several courts of Westminster Hall, 1746-79. 2nd ed. by C.H. Elsley. London, 1828. 2 v.

Reprinted: English reports; Microfilm: Dobbs Ferry, Oceana.

Previous ed.: 1781, reprinted Dublin, 1781-1789.

549. Brook, Sir R. Some new cases of the years and time of King Hen. VIII, Edw. VI, and Qu, Mary; written out of the Great Abridgement ... Trans. by J. March, 1514-58. London, 1873. 1 v.

Reprinted: English reports; Microfilm: Dobbs Ferry, Oceana.

Previous eds: 1578, 1587, 1597, 1604, 1625 in Anglo-French. These eds. also known as Petit Brook or Petty Brook from their small size. Collected anonymously by Bellewe from Brooke's Abridgment and sometimes cited as: Bellewe's Cases temp. Henry VIII.

550. Bulstrode, E. The reports ... of divers resolutions and judgments ... given in the Court of King's Bench, 1610-26. 2nd ed. London, 1688. 3 v.

Reprinted: English reports; Microfilm: Dobbs Ferry, Oceana.

1st ed. 1657-59.

551. Burrow, Sir J. Reports of cases argued and adjudged in the Court of King's Bench, 1756-72. 5th ed. London, 1812. 5 v.

Reprinted: English reports; Microfilm: Dobbs Ferry, Oceana.

Previous eds.: v. 1-2 1766, 1771, 1777, 1790; v. 3 1771, 1779, 1790; v. 4 1777, 1790; v. 5 1780, 1790. Dublin eds.: v.1-2 1781; v. 1-5 1784-85.

552. Cababe, M. and Ellis, C.G. Reports of actions tried in the Queen's Bench Division of the High Court of Justice, 1882-85. London, 1885. 1 v.

Microfilm: Dobbs Ferry, Oceana.

553. Carthew, T. Reports of cases adjudged in the Court of King's Bench, 1687-1700. 2nd ed. London, 1741. 1 v.

Reprinted: 1743, English reports; Microfilm: Dobbs Ferry, Oceana

1st ed.: 1728.

554. [Cases temp. Hardwicke] Cases argued and adjudged in the Court of King's Bench ... during [the time of] Lord Chief Justice Hardwicke, 1733-38. 2nd ed. by T. Lee. London, 1815. 1 v.

Reprinted: English reports; Microfilm: Dobbs Ferry, Oceana.

Previous eds.: 1770; 2nd ed. 1811. Dublin, 1769. Also known as: Lee temp. Hardwicke.

555. Coke, Sir E. The reports ... in thirteen parts. New ed. by J.H. Thomas and J.F. Fraser, 1572-1616. London, 1826. 13 pts. in 6.

Reprinted: English reports; Microfilm: Dobbs Ferry, Oceana

Each part printed separately in several editions. In Anglo-French, pts. 1-10 1600-36, with collected eds. of pts. 1-11 1672-80; In English, pts. 12-13 1656-97, with collected eds. of pts. 1-11 1658-80 and collected eds. of pts. 1-13 1727-97. For further details see Sweet and Maxwell's Bibliography.

556. Comberbach, R. The reports of several cases argued and adjudged in the Court of King's Bench, 1685-98. London, 1724. 1 v.

Reprinted: English reports; Microfilm: Dobbs Ferry, Oceana.

557. Comyns, Sir J. Reports of cases argued and determined in the Court of King's Bench, Common Pleas and Exchequer, 1696-1740. 2nd ed. by S. Rose. London, 1792. 2 v.

Reprinted: English reports; Microfilm: Dobbs Ferry, Oceana.

Previous eds.: 1744 (in 1 v.); 2nd ed. 1791 (1 v. Dublin, by L. McNally).

558. Cowper, H. Reports of cases adjudged in the Court of King's Bench, 1774-78. 2nd ed. London, 1800. 2 v.

Reprinted: English reports; Microfilm: Dobbs Ferry, Oceana.

Previous eds. (all 1 v.): 1783; Dublin, 1788, 1794.

559. Croke, Sir G. Reports of ... select cases. Rev. ... by Sir H. Grimstone, 1582-1641. London, 1790-92. 4 v.

Reprinted: English reports; Microfilm: Dobbs Ferry, Oceana.

Previous eds.: 1st. 1657-61 (3 v.): 2nd. 1669 (3 v.): 3rd. 1683 (3 v.) In 3 parts, cited Cro. Eliz., Cro. Jac. & Cro. Car. (or 1, 2, 3 Croke, except in 1st ed., where the numerical order is reversed, i.e. Cro. Eliz. = 3 Croke). In Leach's ed. v. 1-2 contains Cro. Eliz., v. 3 Cro. Jac., & v. 4 Cro. Car.

560. Cunningham, T. Reports of cases argued and adjudged in the Court of King's Bench, 1734-35. 3rd ed. by T.T. Bucknill. London, 1871. 1 v.

Reprinted: English reports; Microfilm: Dobbs Ferry, Oceana.

1st ed. 1766; 2nd ed. 1770. Title page states 'Cases in 7, 8, 9, and 10 Geo. II' but only Part 1, containing cases in 7 and 8 Geo. II was published.

561. Douglas, S., Baron Glenbervie. Reports of cases argued and determined in the Court of King's Bench, 1778-85. 4th ed. [of v. 1-2] by W. Frere and H. Roscoe. London, 1813-31. 4 v.

Reprinted: English reports; Microfilm: Dobbs Ferry, Oceana.

1st ed. 1783; 2nd ed. 1786. 3rd ed. 1790. Dublin, 1783. v. 3 (Roscoe) and v. 4 (Frere and Roscoe) not in previous eds.

562. Dyer, Sir J. Reports of cases ... 1513-81 translated by J. Vaillant. London, Dublin, 1794. 3 v.

Reprinted: English reports; Microfilm: Dobbs Ferry, Oceana.

Previous eds. (In French) 1585; 1592; 1601; 1621; 1672; 1688.

563. East, E.H. Reports of cases argued and determined in the Court of King's Bench, 1800-12. London, 1801-14. 16 v.

Reprinted: English reports; Microfilm: Dobbs Ferry, Oceana.

Some vols. were reprinted from 1805 onwards. Intended as a new series of the Term reports but not generally regarded as such.

564. Ellis, T.F. and Blackburn, C. Reports of cases argued and determined in the Court of Queen's Bench, 1852-58. London, 1853-59. 8 v.

Reprinted: English reports; Microfilm: Dobbs Ferry, Oceana.

Continued by: Ellis, Blackburn and Ellis. Cases in Queen's Bench.

565. Ellis, T.F., Blackburn, C. and Ellis, F. Reports of cases argued and determined in the Court of Queen's Bench, 1858. London, 1860. 1 v.

Reprinted: English reports; Microfilm: Dobbs Ferry, Oceana.

Continuation of: Ellis and Blackburn. Cases in Queen's Bench.
Continued by: Ellis and Ellis. Cases in Queen's Bench.

566. Ellis, T.F. and Ellis, F. Reports of cases argued and determined in the Court of Queen's Bench, 1858-61. London, 1863-67. 3 v.

Reprinted: English reports; Microfilm: Dobbs Ferry, Oceana.

Continuation of: Ellis, Blackburn and Ellis. Cases in Queen's Bench.

567. Fitzgibbons, J. Reports of several cases argued and adjudged in the Court of King's Bench, 1727-32. London, 1732. 1 v.

Reprinted: English reports; Microfilm: Dobbs Ferry, Oceana.

568. Fortescue, J., 1st Baron. Reports of select cases in all the Courts of Westminster-Hall, 1692-1736. London, 1748. 1 v.

Reprinted: English reports; Microfilm: Dobbs Ferry, Oceana.

569. Freeman, R. Reports of cases argued and determined in the Court of King's Bench and Common Pleas, 1670-1704. 2nd ed. by E. Smirke. London, 1826. 1 v.

Reprinted: English reports; Microfilm: Dobbs Ferry, Oceana.

1st ed. 1742. Also known as: 1 Freeman.

570. Gilbert, J. Cases in law and equity: argued, debated and adjudged in the King's Bench and Chancery, 1713-14, London, 1760. 1 v.

Reprinted: English reports; Microfilm: Dobbs Ferry, Oceana.

Previous ed. 1740. 2nd ed. Dublin, 1792. Despite title, contains no equity cases.

571. Godbolt, J. Reports of certain cases arising in the several courts of record at Westminster, 1575-1637. London, 1652. 1 v.

Reprinted: English reports; Microfilm: Dobbs Ferry, Oceana.

Some copies are dated 1653.

572. Gouldsborough, J. Reports ... in all the Courts at Westminster. 2nd ed. 1586-1602. London, 1682. 1 v.

Reprinted: English reports; Microfilm: Dobbs Ferry, Oceana.

1st ed. 1653. The author's name is also spelt Goldesborough.

573. Hobart, Sir H. The reports. 5th ed. by E. Chilton, 1603-25. London, 1724. 1 v.

Reprinted: English reports; Microfilm: Dobbs Ferry, Oceana.

1st ed. 1641; 2nd ed. 1650, 1658; 3rd ed. 1671; 4th ed. 1678, 1683.

574. Holt, Sir J. A report of all the cases determined by Sir John Holt ... during which time he was Lord Chief Justice of England ... also several cases in Chancery and the Exchequer-Chamber, 1688-1710. London, 1738. 1 v.

Reprinted: English reports; Microfilm: Dobbs Ferry, Oceana.

575. Jones, Sir T. The reports of several special cases adjudged in the Courts of King's Bench and Common Pleas, 1667-84. 2nd ed. London, 1729. 1 v. In French and English.

Reprinted: English reports; Microfilm: Dobbs Ferry, Oceana.

Previous ed.: 1692 (in French).

576. Jones, Sir W. Les reports ... , 1620-40. London, 1675. 1 v. In Anglo-French.

Reprinted: English reports; Microfilm: Dobbs Ferry, Oceana.

Black letter.

577. Keble, J. Reports in the Court of King's Bench at Westminster, 1661-78. London, 1685. 3 v.

Reprinted: English reports; Microfilm: Dobbs Ferry, Oceana.

578. Keilwey, R. Reports d' ascuns cases ... seliges hors des papiers de ... Par-J. Croke. 3ème éd., 1469 1529. London, 1688. 1 v. In Anglo-French.

Reprinted: English reports; Microfilm: Dobbs Ferry, Oceana.

1st ed. 1602; 2nd ed. 1633. To the third edition are appended a few cases reported by Dalison and by Bendloes.

579. Kelynge, W. A report of cases in Chancery, the King's Bench, etc., 1730-34. London, 1873. 1 v.

Reprinted: English reports; Microfilm: Dobbs Ferry, Oceana.

580. Kenyon, L., Lord. Notes of cases argued and adjudged in the Court of King's Bench [etc.], 1753-59. London, 1819-25. 2 v.

Reprinted: English reports; Microfilm: Dobbs Ferry, Oceana.

v. 2 is in 2 parts, the second part containing notes of Chancery cases. This part is sometimes cited as 3 Kenyon.

581. Latch, J. Plusiers tres-bon cases ... en la Court de Bank le Roy. Avec duex tables ... per Edward Walpoole, 1623-27. London, 1662. 1 v. In French.

Reprinted: English reports; Microfilm: Dobbs Ferry, Oceana.

An English translation by F.X. Martin, omitting "cases relating to spiritual matters", was published Newbern, N.C., in 1793.

582. The law reports. Court of Queen's Bench, 1865-75. London, 1866-75. 10 v.

Continued by: The law reports. Queen's Bench Division. Also known as: Queen's Bench.

583. The law reports. Queen's Bench Division, 1875-90. London, 1876-90. 25 v.

Continuation of: The law reports. Cases determined by the Court for Crown Cases Reserved; The law reports. Court of Queen's Bench; The law reports. Common Pleas Division (from 1880); The law reports. Exchequer Division (from 1880). Continued by: The law reports. Queen's Bench Division and on appeal therefrom in the Court of Appeal. Also known as: Queen's Bench reports.

584. Leonard, W. Reports and cases of law: argued and determined in the Courts at Westminster, 1553-1614. 2nd imp. London, 1687, 4 v.

Reprinted: English reports; Microfilm: Dobbs Ferry, Oceana.

Originally published 1658-75. Some copies dated 1686. 4 v. Black letter.

585. Leving, Sir C. Reports ... containing cases heard and determined in the Court of King's Bench ... Trans. by Mr. Serjeant Salkeld. 1660-96. 3rd ed. by T. Vickers, London, 1802. 3 v.

Reprinted: English reports; Microfilm: Dobbs Ferry, Oceana.

1st ed. (in French) 1702; 2nd ed. (French and English) 1722; 3rd ed. Dublin, 1793-97.

586. Ley, Sir J. Reports of divers resolutions in law, arising upon cases in the Court of Wards, and other courts at Westminster, 1609-28. London, 1659. 1 v.

Reprinted: English reports; Microfilm: Dobbs Ferry, Oceana.

587. Lofft, C. Reports of cases adjudged in the Court of King's Bench, 1772-74. Dublin, 1790. 1 v.

Reprinted: English reports; Microfilm: Dobbs Ferry, Oceana.

Previous ed. London, 1776.

588. March, J. Reports: or, New cases, 1639-42. London, 1675. 1 v.

Reprinted: English reports; Microfilm: Dobbs Ferry, Oceana.

1st ed. 1648.

589. Maule, G. and Selwyn, W. Reports of cases argued and determined in the Court of King's Bench, 1813-17. London, 1814-29. 6 v.

Reprinted: English reports; Microfilm: Dobbs Ferry, Oceana.

Modern Reports: In 1793-96 a new edition (called 5th ed.), edited by T. Leach, brought together a number of previously published parts. For details of individual parts see nos. 590-600 below.

590. [1 Modern reports] Modern reports, or, Select cases adjudged in the Courts of King's Bench, Chancery, Common Pleas and Exchequer, 1669-77. 5th ed. London, 1796. 1 v.

Reprinted: English reports; Microfilm: Dobbs Ferry, Oceana.

Previous eds.: 1682; 2nd ed. 1700; 3rd ed. 1720; 4th ed. 1757; 5th ed. also 1793 and Dublin, 1794. Also known as Colquitt.

591. [2 Modern reports] The second part of Modern reports, being a collection of several special cases, most of them adjudged in the Court of Common Pleas ... , 1674-82. 5th ed. London, 1793. 1 v.

Reprinted: English reports; Microfilm: Dobbs Ferry, Oceana.

Previous eds.: 1698; 2nd ed. 1709; 3rd ed. 1725; 4th ed. 1757; 5th ed. also Dublin, 1794.

592. [3 Modern reports] The third part of Modern reports, being a collection of several cases adjudged in the Court of King's Bench, 1682-90. 5th ed. London, 1793. 1 v.

Reprinted: English reports; Microfilm: Dobbs Ferry, Oceana.

Previous eds.: 1700; 2nd ed. 1712; 3rd ed. 1725; 4th ed. 1757; 5th ed. also Dublin, 1794.

593. [4 Modern reports] The fourthe part of Modern reports, being a collection of several special cases argued and adjudged in the Court of King and Queen's Bench, 1690-95. 5th ed. London, 1793. 1 v.

Reprinted: English reports; Microfilm: Dobbs Ferry, Oceana.

Previous eds.: 1703; 2nd ed. 1722; 4th ed. 1737; 5th ed. also Dublin, 1794.

594. [5 Modern reports] The fifth part of Modern reports, being a continuation of several special cases in the Court of King's Bench, 1690-99. 5th ed. London, 1794. 1 v.

Reprinted: English reports; Microfilm: Dobbs Ferry, Oceana.

Previous eds.: 1711; 2nd ed. 1720; 3rd ed. 1729; 4th ed. 1757; 5th ed. also Dublin, 1794.

595. [6 Modern reports] Modern cases argued and adjudged in the Court of Queen's Bench [temp.] Holt, 1703-04. 5th ed. London, 1796. 1 v.

Reprinted: English reports; Microfilm: Dobbs Ferry, Oceana.

Previous eds.: 1713; 2nd ed. 1719; 1733 [3rd ed.?]; 4th ed. 1757; 5th ed. also Dublin, 1794. Also known as: 1 Modern cases.

596. [7 Modern reports] Farresley, T. Modern cases argued and adjudged in the Court of King's Bench at Westminster [temp.] Holt, 1702-44. 5th ed. London, 1796. 1 v.

Reprinted: English reports; Microfilm: Dobbs Ferry, Oceana.

Previous eds.: 1716; 2nd ed. 1725; 4th ed. 1737; 5th ed. also Dublin, 1794. Also known as: Farresley, Modern cases; Modern cases per Farresley; Modern cases temp. Holt.; Benne.

597. [8-9 Modern reports] Modern cases in law and equity. Part 1, Cases in the King's Bench, 1721-26; Part, 2 Cases in Chancery 1712-25. 5th ed. London, 1795. 2 v.

Reprinted: English reports; Microfilm: Dobbs Ferry, Oceana.

Previous eds.: 1730; 2nd ed. 1769; 5th ed. also Dublin 1794. Part II not included in previous eds. Also known as: 2 Modern cases; New cases in equity: Equity cases. Part II as Cases in Chancery.

598. [10 Modern reports] Lucas, R. Cases in law and equity, chiefly [temp.] Macclesfield, 1709-25. 5th ed. London, 1795. 1 v.

Reprinted: English reports; Microfilm: Dobbs Ferry, Oceana.

Previous eds.: 1736, 1741; 2nd ed. 1769; 5th ed. also Dublin 1794. Also known as: Cases temp. Macclesfield; Cases in law and equity; Lucas.

599. [11 Modern reports] A report of cases argued, debated and adjudged in B.R. [temp.] Queen Anne, 1702-10. 5th ed. London, 1796. 1 v.

Reprinted: English reports; Microfilm: Dobbs Ferry, Oceana.

Previous eds.: 1737, 1969; 2nd ed. 1781; 5th ed. also Dublin 1794. Also known as Cases [or] Reports temp. Queen Anne.

600. [12 Modern reports] Cases adjudged in the Court of King's Bench [temp.] King William III, 1690-1702. 5th ed. London, 1796. 1 v.

Reprinted: English reports; Microfilm: Dobbs Ferry, Oceana.

Previous eds.: 1738; 2nd ed. 1741. 1769; 5th ed. also Dublin, 1794. Also known as: Cases temp. William III.

601. Moore, Sir F. Cases collect et report ... imprime et publie per l'original jadis remainent en les mains de Sir Gefrey Palmer, 1485-1620, 2nd ed. London, 1688. 1 v. In Anglo-French.

Reprinted: English reports; Microfilm: Dobbs Ferry, Oceana.

1st ed. 1663; 2nd ed. [sic] 1675. Also known as: Moore's King's Bench cases. Includes K.B., C.P., Ex., Ch. cases.

602. Noy, W. Reports and cases ... collected ... by ... , 1559-1649. 2nd ed. London, 1669. 1 v.

Reprinted: English reports; Microfilm: Dobbs Ferry, Oceana.

1st ed. 1656. Black letter.

603. Owen, T. Reports in the King's Bench and Common Pleas, 1557-1614. London, 1656. 1 v.

Reprinted: English reports; Microfilm: Dobbs Ferry, Oceana.

Black letter. Pages 76-81 not printed.

604. Palmer, Sir J. The reports ... 2nd ed., 1619-28. London, 1721. 1 v. In French.

Reprinted: English reports; Microfilm: Dobbs Ferry, Oceana.

Previous eds. 1678, 1688.

605. Plowden, E. The commentaries, or reports ... containing divers cases upon matters of law ... [with his] quaeries, 1550-79. London, 1816. 2 v.

Reprinted: English reports; Microfilm: Dobbs Ferry, Oceana.

Previous eds. in French, pt. 1, 1571, 1578, 1571-88, 1588, 1599, 1613; pt. 2 1579, 1584, 1610. 2 pts. in 1 v. 1659, 1681-84, 1684. In English, 1761, 1779. Dublin, 1782, 1792.

606. Pollexfen, Sir H. The arguments and reports ... in some special cases ... together with divers decrees in the High Court of Chancery ... , 1670-84. London, 1702. 1 v.

Reprinted: English reports; Microfilm: Dobbs Ferry, Oceana.

There are several mistakes in paging, v. 2, pp. 173-176, 181-184, 649-652 are mispaged, p. 189 is repeated.

607. Popham Sir J. Reports and cases ... [with] some remarkable cases reported by other learned pens ... , 1592-1627. 2nd ed. London, 1682. 1 v.

Reprinted: English reports; Microfilm: Dobbs Ferry, Oceana.

Previous ed.: 1656. Popham's cases cover 1592-97 in only 123 pp. The cases "by other learned pens" cover 1618-27 and are occasionally found cited as 2 Popham. Black letter.

608. Queen's Bench reports, by J.L. Adolphus and T.F. Ellis. New series, 1841-52. London, 1843-56. 18 v.

Reprinted: English reports; Microfilm: Dobbs Ferry, Oceana.

Continuation of: Adolphus and Ellis. Queen's Bench reports.

609. Raymond, R., 1st Baron. Reports of cases argued and adjudged by the Courts of King's Bench and Common Pleas, 1694-1732. 4th ed., by J. Bayley. London, 1790. 3 v.

Reprinted: English reports; Microfilm: Dobbs Ferry, Oceana.

1st ed. 1743 (2 v.); 2nd ed. 1765 (Wilson); 3rd ed. 1775 (Wilson); 4th ed. Dublin, 1792; 5th ed. 1832 (Gale). The latter is not preferred to 4th ed.

610. Raymond, Sir T. Reports of divers special cases, adjudged in

1st ed. 1969; 2nd ed. 1743; 3rd ed. Dublin, 1793. Includes one case from 1653.

611. Rolle, Sir H. Les reports ... de divers cases en le Court del' Banke le Roy, 1614-25. London, 1675-76. 2 v. In French.

Reprinted: English reports; Microfilm: Dobbs Ferry, Oceana.

Black letter.

612. Salkeld, W. Reports of cases adjudged in the Court of King's Bench: with some special cases in the Courts of Chancery, Common Pleas, and Exchequer, 1689-1712. 6th ed. by W.D. Evans. London, 1795. 3 v.

Reprinted: English reports; Microfilm: Dobbs Ferry, Oceana.

v. 1-2 1st ed. 1717-18; 2nd ed. 1721-22; 3rd ed. 1731-32. v. 3 1724; 4th ed. 1742-43; 5th ed. 1773 (Wilson); 6th ed. Dublin, 1791. v. 1-2 paged consecutively.

613. Saunders, Sir E. The reports ... of several pleadings and cases in the Court of King's Bench. 6th ed., by E.V. Williams, 1666-72. London, 1845. 2 v [in 3].

Reprinted: English reports; Microfilm: Dobbs Ferry, Oceana.

1st ed. 1686 (in French and Latin); 2nd ed. 1722, Dublin, 1791 (in French and English); 3rd ed. 1799-1802 (Williams); 4th ed. 1899 (Williams); 5th ed. 1824 (Patterson and Williams); v 2 usually divided into 2 parts. Later eds. sometimes known as: Williams' Saunders.

614. Sayer, J. Reports of cases adjudged in the Court of King's Bench, 175156. Dublin, 1790. 1 v.

Reprinted: English reports; Microfilm: Dobbs Ferry, Oceana.

Previous ed. London, 1775. These cases are more accurately reported in Dunning.

615. Shower, Sir B. Reports of cases adjudged in the Court of King's Bench. 2nd ed., by T. Leach, 1678-95. London, 1794. 2 v.

Reprinted: English reports; Microfilm: Dobbs Ferry, Oceana.

1st ed. 1708-20. 3rd ed. (in 1 v.) 1836, by G. Butts, is in small type and not preferred.

616. Siderfin, T. Les reports des divers special cases argue & adjudge en le Court del Bank le Roy, et auxy en le Co. Ba. & l'Exchequer. 2nd ed., 165770. London, 1714. 2 v. In Anglo-French.

Reprinted: English reports; Microfilm: Dobbs Ferry, Oceana.

Previous eds.: Pt. 1 1683; Pt. 2 1684, 2nd ed. 1689. Black letter.

617. Skinner, R. Reports of cases adjudged in the Court of King's Bench, 1681-97. London, 1728. 1 v.

Reprinted: English reports; Microfilm: Dobbs Ferry, Oceana.

618. Strange, Sir J. Reports of adjudged cases in the Courts of Chancery, King's Bench, Common Pleas, and Exchequer. 3rd ed., by M. Nolan, 1716-48. London, 1795. 2 v.

Reprinted: English reports; Microfilm: Dobbs Ferry, Oceana.

Previous eds.: 1st ed. 1755, 2nd ed. 1782. Dublin, 1792. There is also an inaccurate 8 vol. edition of 1781-82. (v. 3-4 of Newman's Reports as large). For the the volume sometimes cited as Octavo Strange **see** Select cases relating to evidence.

619. Style, W. Narrations moderne, or Modern reports begun in the now Upper Bench Court at Westminster, 1646-55. London, 1658. 1 v.

Reprinted: English reports; Microfilm: Dobbs Ferry, Oceana.

620. Term reports in the Court of King's Bench, by C. Durnford and E.H. East. New ed., 1785-1800. London, 1817. 8 v.

Reprinted: English reports; Microfilm: Dobbs Ferry, Oceana.

Previous eds. 1787-1800; 2nd ed. 1794-1802; Dublin, 1788-1800. There were 6 editions. Also known as: Durnford and East's Term reports.

621. Ventris, Sir P. The reports of ... , 1668-91, 4th imp. London, 1726. 2 v [in 1].

Reprinted: English reports; Microfilm: Dobbs Ferry, Oceana.

1st imp. 1696; 2nd imp. 1701; 3rd imp. 1716 (Richardson). Black letter.

622. Wilmot, Sir J.E. Notes of opinions and judgements delivered in different courts, 1757-70. London, 1802. 1 v.

Reprinted: English reports; Microfilm: Dobbs Ferry, Oceana.

623. Wilson, G. Reports of cases argued and adjudged in the King's Courts at Westminster, 1742-74, 3rd ed. London, 1799. 3 v.

Reprinted: English reports; Microfilm: Dobbs Ferry, Oceana.

1st ed. 1770-75 (in 2 v.); 2nd ed. 1779-84; 4th ed. [sic] Dublin, 1792.

624. Yelverton, Sir H. The reports ... of divers special cases in the Court of King's Bench, 1602-13, 4th ed. London, 1803. 1 v.

Reprinted: English reports; Microfilm: Dobbs Ferry, Oceana.

1st ed. 1661 (in French); 2nd ed. 1674 (in French); 3rd ed. 1735; 4th ed. Dublin, 1792.

King's Bench - Collateral

625. Arnold, T. and Hodges, Sir W. Reports of cases argued and determined in the Court of Queen's Bench, 1840-41. London, 1841. 1 v.

Microfilm: Dobbs Ferry, Oceana

Part of The new term reports.

626. Davison, H. and Merivale, H. Reports of cases argued and determined in the Court of Queen's Bench, 1843-44. London, 1844. 1 v.

Microfilm: Dobbs Ferry, Oceana

627. Dowling, J. and Ryland, A. Reports of cases aruged and determined in the Court of King's Bench, 1822-27. London, 1822-31. 9 v.

Microfilm: Dobbs Ferry, Oceana

628. Dunning, J., Baron Ashburton. Reports of cases argued and adjudged in the Court of King's Bench, 1753-54. Boston, 1885. 1 v.

Microfilm: Dobbs Ferry, Oceana

The cases appear in Sayer, but are imperfectly reported there.

629. Gale, C.J. and Davison, H. Reports of cases aruged and determined in the Court of Queen's Bench, 1841-43. London, 1842-43. 3 v.

Microfilm: Dobbs Ferry, Oceana

630. Harrison, S.B. and Wollaston, F.L. Reports of cases argued and determined in the Court of King's Bench and in the Bail Court, 1835-36. London, 1836-37. 2 v.

Microfilm: Dobbs Ferry, Oceana

Part of The new term reports.

631. Manning, J. and Ryland, A. Reports of cases argued and determined in the Court of King's Bench, 1827-30. London, 1828-37. 5 v.

Microfilm: Dobbs Ferry, Oceana

632. Nevile, S. and Manning, W.M. Reports of cases argued and determined in the Court of King's Bench, 1832-36. London, 1834-39. 6 v.

Microfilm: Dobbs Ferry, Oceana

Continued by: Nevile and Perry. Reports in King's Bench.

633. Nevile, S. and Perry, T.E. Reports of cases argued and determined in the Court of King's Bench, and upon writs of error ... to the Exchequer Chamber, 1836-38. London, 1837-38. 3 v.

Microfilm: Dobbs Ferry, Oceana

Continuation of: Nevile and Manning. Reports in King's Bench.

634. Perry, T.E. and Davison, H. Reports of cases argued and determined in the Court of Queens's Bench, and upon writs of error ... to the Exchequer Chamber, 1838-41. London, 1839-42. 4 v.

Microfilm: Dobbs Ferry, Oceana

635. Smith, J.P. Reports of cases argued and determined in the Court of King's Bench, with some cases in the High Court of Chancery, 1803-06. London, 1806-07. 3 v.

Microfilm: Dobbs Ferry, Oceana

1st ed. of v. 1, 1804 reprinted from Law journal.

636. Willmore, G., Wollaston, F.L. and Hodges, W. Reports of cases argued and determined in the Court of Queen's Bench, and upon writs of error ... to the Exchequer Chamber, and in the Bail Court, 1838-39. London, 1839-41. 2 v.

Microfilm: Dobbs Ferry, Oceana

Part of The new term reports.

Magistrates Courts

637. Blackerby, S. Cases in law, 1327-1734. London, 1734. 1 v.

Microfilm: Dobbs Ferry, Oceana

Previous eds. 1717, 1729. The 1734 edition forms the second part of The Justice of the Peace, his companion.

638. The handbook for magistrates and quarter sessions, 1853-55. London, 1953-55. 1 v.

Continuation of: The magistrate. Includes 'New magistrates and sessions cases'.

639. The law reports. Sessions cases, 1869-72. London, 1872. 1 v.

640. The magistrate, 1848-53. London, 1848-53. 5 v.

Continued by: Handbook for magistrates. v. 3-5 originally appeared as supplements to The magistrate.

641. Reports of new magistrates' cases argued and determined in the Courts of Common Law at Westminster, 1844-51. London, 1846-[51]. 5 v.

Microfilm: Dobbs Ferry, Oceana

Title varies: v. 3-4 Reports of new magistrates' and municipal corporations cases; v. 5 lacks title page, has running title Magistrates' courts and parish law cases. v. 3-5 originally appeared as supplements to The magistrate with which it was then incorporated. v. 1-2 (Bittleston and Wise); v. 3-4 (Bittleston and Parnell).

Nisi Prius

642. Campbell, J. [1st Baron]. Reports of cases determined at Nisi Prius in the Courts of King's Bench and Common Pleas, 1807-16. London, 1816-18. 4 v.

Reprinted: v. 1; 1833, English reports; Microfilm: Dobbs Ferry, Oceana.

Previous ed.: 1809-16.

643. Carrington, F.A. and Kirwan, A.V. Reports of cases argued and ruled at Nisi Prius in the Courts of Queen's Bench, Common Pleas and Exchequer, 1843-53. London, 1845-53. 3 v.

Reprinted: English reports; Microfilm: Dobbs Ferry, Oceana.

v. 3 pts. 1-2 only published.

644. Carrington, F.A. and Marshman, J.R. Reports of cases argued and ruled at Nisi Prius in the Courts of Queen's Bench, Common Pleas and Exchequer; together with cases tried on the circuits and in the Central Criminal Court, 1840-42. London, 1843. 1 v.

Reprinted: English reports; Microfilm: Dobbs Ferry, Oceana.

Continuation of: Carrington and Payne. Reports at Nisi Prius.

645. Carrington, F.A. and Payne, J. Reports of cases argued and ruled at Nisi Prius in the Courts of King's Bench, Common Pleas and on the circuit, 1823-41. London, 1825-41. 9 v.

Reprinted: English reports; Microfilm: Dobbs Ferry, Oceana.

Continued by: Carrington and Marsham. Reports at Nisi Prius.

646. [Clayton, J.] Reports and pleas of Assises at Yorke, 1631-50. London, 1651. 1 v.

Microfilm: Dobbs Ferry, Oceana.

Dublin edition, 1741. Also known as: Clayton's York Assizes.

647. Dowling, J. and Ryland, A. Cases argued and ruled at Nisi Prius in the Court of King's Bench, and on the Home Circuit, 1822-23. London, 1923. 1 v.

Reprinted: English reports; Microfilm: Dobbs Ferry, Oceana.

Pt. 1 only published.

648. Espinasse, I. Reports of cases argued and ruled at Nisi Prius in the Courts of King's Bench and Common Pleas, 1793-1810. London, 1802-11. 6 v.

Reprinted: 1819, English reports; Microfilm: Dobbs Ferry, Oceana.

Previous eds.: v 1: 1st ed. 1796, Dublin, 1797; 2nd ed. 1801. v. 2: 1st ed. 1798, Dublin, 1800; v. 1-2 paged continuously. 2nd ed. (in 1 v.), 1803.

649. Foster, T.C. and Finlason, W.F. Reports of cases decided at Nisi Prius and at the Crown side on circuit; with select decisions at chambers, 1856-57. London, 1860-67. 4 v.

Reprinted: English reports; Microfilm: Dobbs Ferry, Oceana.

650. Lilly, J. Reports and pleadings of cases in assize, 1688-93. London, 1719. 1 v.

Reprinted: English reports; Microfilm: Dobbs Ferry, Oceana.

A treatise, with forms, but containing a few cases.

651. Peake, T. Additional cases; being a continuation of cases at Nisi Prius ... , 1795-1812. London, 1829. 1 v.

Reprinted: English reports; Microfilm: Dobbs Ferry, Oceana.

Continuation of: Peake, T. Cases at Nisi Prius.

652. Peake, T. Cases determined at Nisi Prius, in the Court of King's Bench. 3rd ed., 1790-94. London, 1820. 1 v.

Reprinted: English reports; Microfilm: Dobbs Ferry, Oceana.

1st ed. 1795; 2nd ed. 1810; Dublin, 1795. Continued by: Peake. Additional cases at Nisi Prius.

653. Starkie, T. Reports of cases determined at Nisi Prius, in the Courts of King's Bench and Common Pleas, and on the circuit, 1814-23. London, 181723. 3 v.

Reprinted: English reports; Microfilm: Dobbs Ferry, Oceana.

v. 3: pt. 1 only published.

Nisi Prius - Collaterals

654. Bartholoman, A. Complete law reports of all the trials and cases ... at the Yorkshire Lent Assize ... 1811. York, 1811. 1 v.

Microfilm: Dobbs Ferry, Oceana

655. Gow, N. Reports of cases argued and ruled at Nisi Prius in the Court of Common Pleas ... and on the Oxford Circuit, 1818-20. London, 1828. 1 v.

Reprinted: English reports; Microfilm: Dobbs Ferry, Oceana.

656. Holt, F.L. Reports of cases ruled and determined at Nisi Prius, in the Court of Common Pleas, and on the Northern Circuit, 1815-17. London, 1818. 1 v.

Reprinted: English reports; Microfilm: Dobbs Ferry, Oceana.

Entitled v. 1. No more published.

657. Moody, W. and Malkin, B.H. Reports of cases determined at Nisi Prius, in the Courts of King's Bench and Common Pleas, and on the Western and Oxford Circuits, 1826-30. London, 1831. 1 v.

Reprinted: English reports; Microfilm: Dobbs Ferry, Oceana.

Entitled v. 1. No more published. Continued by: Moody and Robinson. Reports at Nisi Prius.

658. Moody, W. and Robinson, F. Reports of cases, determined at Nisi Prius, in the Courts of King's Bench, Common Pleas and Exchequer, and on the Northern and Western Circuits, 1830-44. London, 1837-44. 2 v.

Reprinted: English reports; Microfilm: Dobbs Ferry, Oceana.

Continuation of: Moody and Malkin. Reports at Nisi Prius.

659. Ryan, E. and Moody, W. Reports of cases determined at Nisi Prius, in the Courts of King's Bench and Common Pleas, and on the Oxford and Western Circuits, 1823-26. London, 1827. 1 v.

Reprinted: English reports; Microfilm: Dobbs Ferry, Oceana.

Privy Council

See also 1, 3, 4, 8, 10, 12, 57, 140, 143, 165, 174-8, 305, 330, 336, 341, 347, 355, 531, 533, 735-6, 738, 977-8, 980, 983-5, 988, 992-3, 995-9, 1004, 1008, 1013, 1021, 1025-8, 1080, 1107, 1109, 1127, 1187-8, 1193, 1213, 1215, 1232, 1246, 1274-5, 1308, 1440-1, 1443, 1490, 1521, 1563-4, 1568, 1580, 1699, 1779, 1782, 1791, 1795-6, 1804, 1809, 1818, 1833, 1841, 1853-5.

660. Knapp, J.W. Reports of cases argued and determined before the Committee of ... Privy Council, 1829-36. London, 1831-36. 3 v.

Reprinted: English reports; Microfilm: Dobbs Ferry, Oceana.

661. The law reports. Privy Council appeals, 1865-75. London, 1867-75. 6 v.

Continued by: The law reports. Appeal cases before the House of Lords. Also known as: Privy Council appeals.

662. Moore, E.F. Reports of cases heard and determined by the Judicial Committee and the Lords of ... Privy Council, 1836-62. London, [1840-67]. 15 v.

Reprinted: English reports; Microfilm: Dobbs Ferry, Oceana.

Continued by: Moore. Reports of Privy Council, n.s.

663. Moore, E.F. Reports of cases heard and determined by the Judicial Committee and the Lords of ... Privy Council, [new series], 1862-73. London, [1862-73]. 9 v.

Reprinted: English reports; Microfilm: Dobbs Ferry, Oceana.

From v. 3, p. 347, ff. the reports are identical with 1-4 L.R.P.C. Continuation of: Moore. Reports of Privy Council.

Rolls Court

664. Beavan, C. Reports of cases in Chancery, argued and determined in the Rolls Court, 1838-66. London, 1840-69. 36 v.

Reprinted: English reports; Microfilm: Dobbs Ferry, Oceana.

665. Keen, B. Reports of cases in Chancery, argued and determined in the Rolls Court [temp.] Langdale, 1836-38. London, 1837-39. 2 v.

Reprinted: English reports; Microfilm: Dobbs Ferry, Oceana.

666. Tamlyn, J. Reports of cases decided in the High Court of Chancery [temp.] Leach, 1829-30. London, 1831. 1 v.

Reprinted: English reports; Microfilm: Dobbs Ferry, Oceana.

Entitled v.1. No more published.

Vice-Chancellors' Courts

667. Collyer, J. Reports of cases decided in the High Court of Chancery [temp.] Knight Bruce, 1844-46. London, 1845-47. 2 v.

Reprinted: English reports; Microfilm: Dobbs Ferry, Oceana.

668. De Gex, J.P. and Smale, J. Reports of cases decided in the High Court of Chancery [temp.] Knight Bruce [and Parker], 1846-52. London, 1849-53. 5 v.

Reprinted: English reports; Microfilm: Dobbs Ferry, Oceana.

Vols. 1-4 report Knight Bruce, v. 5 reports Parker.

669. Drewry, C.S. Reports of cases decided in the High Court of Chancery [temp.] Kindersley, 1852-59. London, 1853-60. 4 v.

Reprinted: English reports; Microfilm: Dobbs Ferry, Oceana.

Continued by: Drewry and Smale. Cases in Chancery.

670. Drewry, C.S. and Smale, J.J. Reports of cases decided in the High Court of Chancery [temp.] Kindersley, 1859-65. London, 1862-67. 2 v.

Reprinted: English reports; Microfilm: Dobbs Ferry, Oceana.

Continuation of: Drewry. Cases in Chancery.

671. Giffard, J.W. de L. Reports of cases adjudged in the High Court of Chancery [temp.] Stuart, 1856-65. London, 1860-71. 5 v.

Reprinted: English reports; Microfilm: Dobbs Ferry, Oceana.

672. Hare, T. Reports of cases adjudged in the High Court of Chancery [temp.] Wigram, Turner and Wood, 1841-53. London, 1843-58. 11 v.

Reprinted: English reports; Microfilm: Dobbs Ferry, Oceana.

673. Hemming, G.W. and Miller, A.E. Reports of cases adjudged in the High Court of Chancery [temp.] Wood, 1862-65. London, 1864-66. 2 v.

Reprinted: English reports; Microfilm: Dobbs Ferry, Oceana.

674. Johnson, H.R.V. and Hemming, G.W. Reports of cases adjudged in the High Court of Chancery [temp.] Wood, 1858-60. London, 1860. 1 v.

Reprinted: English reports; Microfilm: Dobbs Ferry, Oceana.

675. Johnson, H.R.V. and Hemming, G.W. Reports of cases adjudged in the High Court of Chancery [temp.] Wood, 1859-62. London, 1861-63. 2 v.

Reprinted: English reports; Microfilm: Dobbs Ferry, Oceana.

676. Kay, E.E. Reports of cases adjudged in the High Court of Chancery [temp.] Wood, 1853-54. London, 1854. 1 v.

Reprinted: English reports; Microfilm: Dobbs Ferry, Oceana.

Continued by: Kay and Johnson. Reports in Chancery.

677. Kay, E.E. and Johnson, H.R.V. Reports of cases adjudged in the High Court of Chancery, 1854-58. London, 1855-59. 4 v.

Reprinted: English reports; Microfilm: Dobbs Ferry, Oceana.

Continuation of: Kay. Reports in Chancery.

678. Maddock, H. Reports of cases argued and determined in the Court of the Vice Chancellor of England [temp. Plumer, Leach], 1815-22. London, 181729. 6 v.

Reprinted: English reports; Microfilm: Dobbs Ferry, Oceana.

v. 6 is by Maddock and T.C. Geldart, but is usually cited as 6 Maddock.

679. Simons, N. Reports of cases decided in the High Court of Chancery [temp.] Leach, Hart, (Shadwell and Kindersley), 1826-52. London, 1829-54. 17 v.

Reprinted: English reports; Microfilm: Dobbs Ferry, Oceana.

Contains cases 1849-50 by Simons and ten additional cases reported by Drewry, 1849-52.

Reprinted: English reports; Microfilm: Dobbs Ferry, Oceana.

680. Simons, N. Reports of cases decided in the High Court of Chancery [new series], [temp.] Cranworth and Kindersley, 1850-52. London, 1851-52. 2 v.

Reprinted: English reports; Microfilm: Dobbs Ferry, Oceana.

681. Simons, N. and Stuart, J. Reports of cases decided in the High Court of Chancery [temp.] Leach, 1822-26. London, 1824-27. 2 v.

Reprinted: English reports; Microfilm: Dobbs Ferry, Oceana.

682. Smale, J. and Giffard, J.W. de L. Reports of cases adjudged in the High Court of Chancery [temp.] Stuart, 1852-57. London, 1855-58. 3 v.

Reprinted: English reports; Microfilm: Dobbs Ferry, Oceana.

683. Younge, E. and Collyer, J. Reports of cases decided in the High Court of Chancery [temp.] Knight Bruce, 1841-43. London, 1843-44. 2 v.

Reprinted: English reports; Microfilm: Dobbs Ferry, Oceana.

Vice-Chancellors' Court - Collaterals

684. Holt, W. Equity reports: [temp.] Knight Bruce and Wigram, 1845. London, 1845. 2 v.

Reprinted: English reports; Microfilm: Dobbs Ferry, Oceana.

SUBJECT REPORTS

Annuities

685. Hunt, W. A collection of cases on the Annuity Act. 2nd ed., 1777-96. Birmingham, 1796. 1 v.

1st ed. London, 1794.

Armed Forces

686. Ministry of Labour and National Service. National Service (Armed Forces) Act, 1939 [to National Service Acts, 1948-55]. Selected decisions given by the Umpire in respect of applications for postponement of liability to be called up for service in the armed forces of the Crown, 1940-59. [London], 1940-59. 16 v.

At head of title: N.S. Code 2. Pamphlet No. 1/40 [- Pamphlet No. 2/59]. Not published 1947, 1950, 1954, 1955.

687. Rowe, R.R. Reports of interesting cases argued and determined in the King's law courts of England and Ireland, the Houses of Parliament and military courts ... , 1798-1823. Dublin, 1824. 1 v.

Reprinted: English reports; Microfilm: Dobbs Ferry, Oceana.

Bankruptcy

688. [Bankruptcy and company reports] Reports of bankruptcy and companies winding-up cases decided in the High Court of Justice, the Court of Appeal and House of Lords, ed. by A. Roper, 1918-42. London, 1919-43. 17 v.

Continuation of: Hansell's Bankruptcy reports from v. 4-20. v. 20, parts 1-2 only published.

689. Bankruptcy and insolvency reports, 1853-55. London, 1855.

Microfilm: Dobbs Ferry, Oceana.

v. 2 edited by J.B. Dasent.

690. Buck, J.W. Cases in bankruptcy, 1816-20. London, 1820. 1 v.

Microfilm: Dobbs Ferry, Oceana.

Entitled v. 1. No more published.

691. Cresswell, R.N. Reports of cases heard and decided in the Court for Relief of Insolvent Debtors, 1827-29. London, 1830. 1 v.

Microfilm: Dobbs Ferry, Oceana.

692. De Gex, J.P. Reports of cases in bankruptcy, 1844-50. London, 1952. 2 v.

Microfilm: Dobbs Ferry, Oceana.

v. 2: pt. 1 only published. Continued by: De Gex, Macnaghten and Gordon. Bankruptcy appeals.

693. De Gex, J.P., Fisher, E. and Jones, H.C. Reports of bankruptcy appeals heard and determined by the Lord Chancellor and the Court of Appeal in Chancery, 1859-60. London, 1862. 1 v.

Pt. 1. only published. Reprinted from the same reporters' Chancery reports, with new pagination. Continuation of: De Gex and Jones. Reports of bankruptcy appeals. Continued by: De Gex, Jones and Smith. Reports of bankruptcy appeals.

694. De Gex, J.P. and Jones, H.C. Reports of bankruptcy appeals heard and determined by the Lord Chancellor and the Court of Appeal in Chancery, 185759. London, 1861. 1 v.

Reprinted from the same reporters' Chancery reports, with new pagination.

Continuation of: De Gex, Macnaghten and Gordon. Bankruptcy appeals. Continued by: De Gex, Fisher and Jones. Reports of bankruptcy appeals.

695. De Gex, J.P., Jones, H.C. and Smith, R.H. Reports of bankruptcy appeals heard and determined by the Lord Chancellor and the Court of Appeal in Chancery, 1862-65. London, 1874. 1 v.

Reprinted from the same reporters' Chancery reports, with new pagination. Continuation of: De Gex, Fisher and Jones. Reports of bankruptcy appeals.

696. De Gex, J.P., Macnaghten, S. and Gordon, A. Bankruptcy appeals. Reports of cases heard and determined by the Lord Chancellor and the Court of Appeal in Chancery, 1851-55. London, 1851-57. 1 v.

Reprinted from the same reporters' Chancery reports, with new pagination.

Continuation of: De Gex, Reports of cases. Continued by: De Gex and Jones. Reports of bankruptcy appeals.

697. Deacon, E.E. Reports of cases in bankruptcy, 1835-40. London, 1837-41. 4 v.

Microfilm: Dobbs Ferry, Oceana.

Continuation of: Deacon and Chitty. Reports of cases in bankruptcy.

698. Deacon, E.E. and Chitty, E. Reports of cases in bankruptcy, 1832-35. London, 1833-37. 4 v.

Microfilm: Dobbs Ferry, Oceana.

Continued by: Deacon. Reports of cases in bankruptcy.

699. Fonblanque, T.W.M. Reports of cases adjudicated in the several courts of the Commissioners in Bankruptcy, 1849-52. London, 1851-52. 1 v.

Microfilm: Dobbs Ferry, Oceana.

v. 1: pts. 1-3 only published.

700. The gazette of bankruptcy, 1862-63. London, 1862-63. 4 v.
v. 4: nos. 177-185 only published.

701. Glyn, T.C. and Jameson, R.S. Cases in bankruptcy, 1821-28. London, 1824-28. 2 v.

Microfilm: Dobbs Ferry, Oceana.

702. Hansell, M.E. Reports of bankruptcy and companies winding-up cases decided in the High Court of Justice, the Court of Appeal, and the House of Lords, 1915-17. London, 1916-18. 3 v.

Continuation of: Manson. Reports of cases. Continued by: Bankruptcy and company reports.

703. Macrae, D.C. and Hertslet, C.J.B. Reports of cases relating to insolvency, 1847-54. London, 1852-54. 2 v.

Microfilm: Dobbs Ferry, Oceana.

v. 2: pt. 1 only published.

704. Manson, E. Reports of cases in bankruptcy and companies, winding-up, decided in the High Court of Justice, the Court of Appeal, and the House of Lords, 1894-1914. London, 1894-1915. 21 v.

Continuation of: Morrell's bankruptcy reports. Continued by: Hansell's bankruptcy reports. Title varies: v. 6-21 Reports of bankruptcy and company cases. From v. 13 includes Privy Council decisions. Also known as Manson's bankruptcy reports. v. 3 edited by E. Manson and J.S. Henderson; v. 4-12 edited by E. Manson and W.I. Cook; v. 13-21 edited by E. Manson and A.J. Spencer.

705. Montagu, B. Reports of cases in bankruptcy decided by the Lord Chancellors Lyndhurst and Brougham, the Vice-Chancellor ... Shadwell, and the Court of Review, 1829-32. London, 1832. 1 v.

Microfilm: Dobbs Ferry, Oceana.

Continuation of: Montagu and MacArthur. Cases in bankruptcy. Continued by: Montagu and Bligh. Cases in bankruptcy.

706. Montagu, B. and Ayrton, S. Reports of cases in bankruptcy, decided by the Lord Chancellor Brougham, the Court of Review and Subdivision Courts, 1833-38. London, 1834-38. 3 v.

Microfilm: Dobbs Ferry, Oceana.

Continuation of: Montagu and Bligh: Cases in bankruptcy. Continued by: Montagu and Chitty: Cases in bankruptcy.

707. Montagu, B. and Bligh, R. Reports of cases in bankruptcy, decided by the Lord Chancellor Brougham, the Vice-Chancellor ... Shadwell, and the Court of Review, 1832-33. London, 1835. 1 v.

Microfilm: Dobbs Ferry, Oceana.

Continuation of: Montagu. Cases in bankruptcy. Continued by: Montagu and Ayrton. Cases in bankruptcy.

708. Montagu, B. and Chitty, E. Reports of cases in bankruptcy, decided by the Lord Chancellor Cottenham and the Court of Review, 1838-40. London, 1840. 1 v.

Microfilm: Dobbs Ferry, Oceana.

Continuation of: Montagu and Ayrton. Cases in bankruptcy. Continued by: Montagu, Deacon and De Gex. Cases in bankruptcy.

709. Montagu, B., Deacon, E.E. and De Gex, J. Reports of cases in bankruptcy, argued and determined in the Court of Review, and on appeal before the Lord Chancellor, 1840-44. London, 1842-45. 3 v.

Microfilm: Dobbs Ferry, Oceana.

Continuation of: Montagu and Chitty. Cases in bankruptcy.

710. Montagu, B. and MacArthur, J. Reports of cases [in bankruptcy] decided by the Lord Chancellor and Vice-Chancellor, 1826-30. London, 1830. 1 v.

Microfilm: Dobbs Ferry, Oceana.

Entitled v. 1. No more published. Continued by: Montagu. Cases in bankruptcy.

711. Morrell, C.F. Reports of cases under the Bankruptcy Act, 1883, decided in the High Court of Justice & the Court of Appeal, 1884-93. London, 188594. 10 v.

Continued by: Manson's bankruptcy reports. Also known as: Morrell's bankruptcy reports.

712. Perry, T. Reports of insolvents; Cases heard by the Commissioners in the Court for the Relief of Insolvent Debtors, 1831. London, 1831. 1 v.

713. Rose, G. Cases in bankruptcy, 1810-16. 2nd ed. London, 1821. 2 v.

Microfilm: Dobbs Ferry, Oceana.

1st ed. 1813-16.

Building Law

714. The architects' law reports (illustrated): a series of revised reports of cases decided in the superior courts, of importance to architects, surveyors and others interested in the construction and maintenance of buildings in London and the provinces, 1904-09. London, 1904-09. 4 v.

Title varies: v. 2-4 The architects' law reports and review.

715. Building law reports, 1841- . London, Longman, 1976- . 20 v.

Data base: LEXIS

City of London

716. Calthorp, Sir H. Reports of special cases touching several customs and liberties of the City of Londons, 1609-17. London, 1872. 1 v.

Reprinted: English reports; Microfilm: Dobbs Ferry, Oceana.

Previous eds.: 1655, 1670.

Criminal Law

717. Bell, T. Crown cases reserved for consideration, and decided by the judges of England, 1858-60. London, 1861. 1 v.

Reprinted: English reports; Microfilm: Dobbs Ferry, Oceana.

718. Central Criminal Court sessions papers ... Minutes of evidence, 1834-1913. London, 1834-1913. 158 v.

Continuation of: Old Bailey Sessions papers. Also known as: Sessions Papers [Central Criminal Court]

719. The criminal appeal reports, 1908- . London, Stevens, 1909- . 75 v.

Data base: LEXIS 1945- .

720. The criminal appeal reports (sentencing), 1979- . London, Sweet & Maxwell, 1980- . 4 v.

Data base: LEXIS.

721. Dearsley, H.R. Crown cases reserved for consideration ... argued and determined in the Court of Queen's Bench and the Courts of Error, 1852-56. London, 1856. 1 v.

Reprinted: English reports; Microfilm: Dobbs Ferry, Oceana.

Continued by: Dearsley and Bell. Crown cases reserved.

722. Dearsley, H.R. and Bell, T. Crown cases reserved for consideration ... argued and determined in the Court of Queen's Bench and the Courts of Error, 1856-58. London, 1858. 1 v.

Reprinted: English reports; Microfilm: Dobbs Ferry, Oceana.

Continuation of: Dearsley. Crown cases reserved.

723. Denison, S.C. Crown cases reserved for consideration, 1844-52. London, 1850-52. 2 v.

Reprinted: English reports; Microfilm: Dobbs Ferry, Oceana.

v. 2 completed by R.R. Pearce. Also known as: Denison and Pearce.

724. Foster, Sir M. Reports of some proceedings on the Commission for the trial of rebels in the year 1746 in the County of Surrey, and of other Crown cases, 1743-60. 3rd ed. by M. Dodson. London, 1809. 1 v.

Reprinted: English reports; Microfilm: Dobbs Ferry, Oceana.

1st ed. Oxford, 1762; 2nd ed. 1776 (Dodson); 3rd ed. 1792 (Dodson). Dublin, 1763, 1767; 2nd ed. 1791.

725. Hale, W.H. A series of precedents and proceedings in criminal causes ... extracted from act-books of ecclesiastical courts in the diocese of London, illustrative of the discipline of the Church of England, 1475-1640. London, 1847. 1 v.

Also known as: Hale's criminal precedents.

726. Kelyng, Sir J. Reports of Crown cases, 1662-69. 3rd ed., edited by R.L. Loveland. London, 1873. 1 v.

Reprinted: English reports; Microfilm: Dobbs Ferry, Oceana.

1st ed. 1708; 2nd ed. 1739; Dublin, 1789. Sometimes known as: 1 Kelyng to distinguish it from Kelynge, W.

727. The law reports. Cases determined by the Court for Crown Cases Reserved, 1865-75. London, 1872-75. 2 v.

Continued by: The law reports. Queen's Bench Division. Also known as: Crown cases reserved.

728. Leach, T. Cases in Crown law, 1730-1814. 4th ed. London, 1815. 2 v.

Reprinted: English reports; Microfilm: Dobbs Ferry, Oceana.

1st ed. 1789; 2nd ed. 1792; 3rd ed. 1800.

729. Leigh, E. and Cave, L.W. Crown cases reserved for consideration, 1861-65. London, 1866. 1 v.

Reprinted: English reports; Microfilm: Dobbs Ferry, Oceana.

730. Lewin, Sir G.A. A report of cases determined on the Crown side of the Northern Circuit, 1822-34. London, 1834-39. 2 v.

Reprinted: English reports; Microfilm: Dobbs Ferry, Oceana.

731. Moody, W. Crown cases reserved for consideration, 1824-44. London, 1837-44. 2 v.

Reprinted: English reports; Microfilm: Dobbs Ferry, Oceana.

732. [Old Bailey Sessions Papers] ... Proceedings on the King's Commission of the peace and oyer and terminer, and gaol delivery of Newgate ... for the City of London and ... county of Middlesex ... at Justice Hall in the Old Bayly, Dec. 1714-1833. London, 1714-1833. c. 100 v.

Continued by: Central Criminal Court Sessions Papers. Also known as: Sessions Papers [Old Bailey]. Issued in pts. since early sessions were held irregularly. Believed no 'complete' set held in U.K. but near 'complete' set held at Harvard. (Inner Temple records show the series was issued as early as 1678). Total vols. in sets held is variable.

733. Russell, W.O. and Ryan, E. Crown cases reserved for consideration, 1800-23. London, 1825. 1 v.

Reprinted: English reports; Microfilm: Dobbs Ferry, Oceana.

734. Temple, L. and Mew, G. Reports of cases, argued and determined in the Court of Criminal Appeal, 1848-51. London, 1852. 1 v.

Reprinted: English reports; Microfilm: Dobbs Ferry, Oceana.

Entitled v. 1. No more published.

Ecclesiastical Law

See also Tithes; nos. 328, 341

735. Brodrick, G.C. and Fremantle, W.H. A collection of the judgments of the Judicial Committee of the Privy Council in ecclesiastical cases relating to doctrine and discipline, 1695-1864. London, 1865. 1 v.

Microfilm: Dobbs Ferry, Oceana.

736. Brooke, W.G. Six judgments of the Judicial Committee of the Privy Council in ecclesiastical cases, 1850-72. London, 1872. 1 v.

737. Cripps, H.W. Reports of new cases decided in the Chancery, common law and ecclesiastical courts ... relating to the church and clergy, 1847-50. London, 1849-50. 1 v.

Microfilm: Dobbs Ferry, Oceana.

v. 1: pts. 1-2 only published.

738. [Dale's ecclesiastical reports] Dales, J.M. Legal ritual. The judgments delivered by the Privy Council and Dean of Arches in the recent cases of Martin v. Mackonochie and Elphinstone v. Purchas and Hebbert v. Purchas, with notes and suggestions for the guidance of incumbents, churchwardens, and parishioners, 1868-71. London, 1871. 1 v.

Microfilm: Dobbs Ferry, Oceana.

739. Hale, W.H. Precedents in causes of office against churchwardens and others, 1583-1736. London, 1841. 1 v.

Also known as: Hale's ecclesiastical precedents.

740. **No entry**

741. Stillingfleet, E., Bishop. Ecclesiastical cases relating to the duties and rights of the parochial clergy. London, 1702-04. 2 v.

Microfilm: Dobbs Ferry, Oceana.

1st ed. of pt. 1, 1698.

Family Law

742. Family law reports, 1980- . Bristol, Family Law, 1980- . 3 v.

Data base: LEXIS

Earliest case reported: 1973.

743. The law reports. Family Division and on appeal therefrom in the Court of Appeal and decisions in the Ecclesiastical Courts, 1972- . London, Incorporated Council of Law Reporting, 1972- . 11 v.

Continuation of: The law reports. Probate Division. Courts of Probate, Divorce and Admiralty. Also known as: Family reports.

Friendly Societies

744. Diprose, J. [and] Gammon, J. Reports of law cases affecting friendly societies, 1801-97. Manchester, 1897. 1 v.

Housing Law

745. Housing law reports, 1949- . London, Sweet & Maxwell, 1982- . 4 v.

Data base: LEXIS

Immigration Law

746. Immigration appeals: selected determinations of the Immigration Appeal Tribunal and of Immigration Appeal Adjudicators ... , 1970- London, H.M.S.O., 1972- . 11 v.

Data base: LEXIS

Also known as: Immigration appeal reports.

Industrial Law

747. Butterworths' workmen's compensation cases, 1907-49. London, 1909-50. 41 v.

Data base: LEXIS 1945- .

Continuation of: Workmen's compensation cases. From v. 24, 1931 separate supplement containing Scottish and Irish cases. Edited by Ruegg, A.H., Coltman, F.I. [and others].

748. Central Arbitration Committee [awards], v. 57, 1976- . London, H.M.S.O., [1976]- 7 v. in 20.

748 ENGLAND AND WALES

Continuation of: The Industrial Arbitration Board [awards].

749. The Industrial Arbitration Board [awards], v.54 1972-76. London, 1972-76. 5 v.

Continuation of: The Industrial Court awards. Continued by: Central Arbitration Committee awards. Title varies: Industrial Court decisions to 1973.

750. Industrial assurance. Reports of selected disputes referred to the Industrial Assurance Commissioner under the Industrial Assurance Act, 1923 ... , 1938-49. London, 1950. 1 v.

751. The Industrial Court (The Industrial Courts Act, 1919). Decisions, 1919-71. London, 1920-72. 53 v.

Continued by: Industrial Arbitration Board awards.

752. Industrial Court reports, 1972- . London, Incorporated Council of Law Reporting, 1972- . 11 v.

Data base: LEXIS.

Continuation of: The law reports. Reports of restrictive practices cases. Title varies: Industrial cases reports, 1975- .

753. Industrial Disputes Tribunal awards, 1951-59. London, 1951-59. 1,270 pts.

Leaflet form.

754. Industrial relations law reports, 1972- . London, Industrial Relations Law Reports, 1972- . 11 v.

Data base: LEXIS.

755. Industrial tribunals: reports of decisions of the Industrial Tribunals ... , 1965-78. London, 1967-79. 13 v.

Data base: LEXIS.

Title varies: v. 6-13 Industrial tribunal reports: reports of decisions of the Industrial tribunals, including reports of decisions on appeal therefrom.

756. Knight's industrial and commercial reports, 1966-74. London, 1967-75. 17 v.

Data base: LEXIS.

Continued by: Knight's industrial law reports. Title varies: v. 10-17 Knight's industrial reports.

757. Knight's industrial law reports, 1973-74. London, 1975. 1 v.

Data base: LEXIS.

Continuation of Knight's industrial reports. Continued by: Managerial law (summaries of cases only).

758. The law reports. Reports of restrictive practices cases heard in the Restrictive Practices Court and on appeal therefrom and other cases arising under the Restrictive Trade Practices Act, 1956, in England, Scotland and Northern Ireland, 1957-72. London, 1958-73. 7 v.

Data base: LEXIS.

Continued by: Industrial Court reports. Also known as: Restrictive practice cases.

759. Reinstatement in Civil Employment Act, 1944. Selected decisions given by the Umpire in respect of applications for reinstatement in civil employment under the above-mentioned act, 1944-52. London, 1944-53. 89 pts.

At head of title: Office of the Umpire. R.E. Code 1/Pamphlet No. 1 [-89]. Nos. 87-89 headed: National Service Act, 1948.

760. Reports of cases under the Workmen's Compensation Acts including all cases relating thereto decided in the Court of Appeal (England), Court of Session (Scotland), Court of Appeal (Ireland) and on appeal therefrom to the House of Lords, 1912-33. London, [1912-33]. 22 v.

Title varies: v. 3-22 Workmen's compensation and insurance reports. From v. 2 includes cases on insurance law, including those under the National Insurance Act (exclusive of marine insurance).

761. Workmen's compensation cases: being reports of cases decided under the Workmen's Compensation Act, 1897, principally taken from The law times reports and The Times law reports, 1898-1907. London, 1902-08. 9 v.

Continued by: Butterworths' workmen's compensation cases.

Intellectual Property

762. Austen-Cartmell, J. Abstract of reported cases relating to trade marks, 1876-92. London, 1893. 1 v.

Microfilm: Dobbs Ferry, Oceana.

Also known as: Cartmell's trade mark cases.

763. Carpmael, W. Law reports of patent cases, 1602-1842. London, 1843-51. 3 v.

Microfilm: Dobbs Ferry, Oceana.

v. 3: pt. 1 only published.

764. Davies, J. A collection of the most important cases respecting patents of invention and the rights of patentees, 1785-1816. London, 1816. 1 v.

Microfilm: Dobbs Ferry, Oceana.

765. Fleet Street reports of industrial property cases from the Commonwealth and Europe, 1963- . London, European Law Centre, 1963- . 19 v.

Title varies: 1963-78 Fleet Street patent law reports.

766. Goodeve, T.M. Abstract of reported cases relating to letters patent for inventions (bringing the cases down to the end of the year 1883), 1776-1883. London, 1884. 1 v.

Microfilm: Dobbs Ferry, Oceana.

767. Griffin, R. Abstract of reported cases relating to letters patent for inventions ... together with some unreported cases, and cases decided by the Law Officers and the Comptroller General, 1884-86. London, 1887. 1 v.

Microfilm: Dobbs Ferry, Oceana.

768. Griffin, R. Patent cases decided by the Comptroller-General and Law Officers of the Crown ... together with some unreported cases in the courts of law, 1885-87. London, 1888. 1 v.

Microfilm: Dobbs Ferry, Oceana.

769. Intellectual property decisions, 1977- . London, Centre for Legal and Business Administration, 1978- . 5 v.

770. MacGillivray, E.J. Copyright cases, 1901-49. London, 1905-51. 8 v.

771. Macrory, E. Reports of cases relating to letters patent for inventions, 1852-60. London, [1860?]. 1 v.

Microfilm: Dobbs Ferry, Oceana.

The title page and index were issued undated in 1901.

772. Reports of patent cases decided by courts of law in the United Kingdom, 1884- . London, Patent Office, 1884- . 99 v.

Data base: LEXIS 1945- .

Title varies: v. 3 - Reports of patent, design and trademark cases decided by courts of law in the United Kingdom. A supplement to the official journal of the Patent Office.

773. Webster, T. Reports and notes of cases on letters patent for inventions, 1601-1855. London, 1844-55. 2 v.

Microfilm: Dobbs Ferry, Oceana.

v. 2: pt. 1 only published.

Land Law

See also no. 111

774. Burrow, Sir J. A series of the decisions of the Court of King's Bench upon settlement cases, 1733-76. 2nd ed. London, 1786. 1 v.

Reprinted: Dublin, 1790; English reports; Microfilm: Dobbs Ferry, Oceana.

Previous eds.: 1768 (in 2 v.) with continuation v. 1772, 1776. Continued by: Caldecott. Magistrates cases.

775. [Cases of settlement] Cases and resolutions of cases adjudged in the Court of King's Bench concerning settlements and removals, 1695-1732. 4th ed. London, 1742. 1 v.

Microfilm: Dobbs Ferry, Oceana.

Previous eds.: 2nd ed. 1729; 3rd ed. 1732. 1st ed. not recorded.

776. Daniels, G. St. L. A compendium of commission cases: being a collection of cases on the law relating to auctioneers' and estate agents' commission, 1878-1900. London, 1900. 1 v.

Previous eds.: 1893, 1898. Reprinted from Estates Gazette.

777. Daniels, G. St. L. A compendium of compensation cases. Containing a summary of all cases reported in the Estates gazette, 1892-1902. London, 1903. 1 v.

778. [Estates gazette digest of cases] A digest of law and arbitration cases including commission, compensation, landlord and tenant, distress and rating cases, disputes arising under the Agricultural Holdings Acts and the London Building Act, etc., 1902-84. London, 1903-85. 81 v.

Data base: LEXIS 1945- .

Continued by: Estates gazette law reports. Title varies: 1933-38 The estates gazette digest of cases; 1939-45 The estates gazette digest of cases (and arbitration); 1946-84 The estates gazette digest of land and property.

779. Estates gazette law reports, 1985- . London, Estates Gazette, 1986- .

Data base: LEXIS

Continuation of: Estates gazette digest of cases.

780. Lands Tribunal cases, 1972-78. Chichester, 1974-79. 6 v.

Originally published in Local government review.

781. Reports of cases in the law of real property and conveyancing argued and determined in all the courts of law and equity, 1843-48. London, 1846-48. 2 v.

Reprinted from The law times.

782. Sessions cases adjudged in the Court of King's Bench, chiefly touching settlements, 1710-47. 2nd ed. London, 1760. 1 v.

Reprinted: 1873; English reports; Microfilm: Dobbs Ferry, Oceana.

Previous eds. (in 2 v.) 1750, 1754. 1873 reprint now usually cited has no indication of original pagination.

Licensing Law

783. Brewing trade licensing law reports. A complete yearly record of all judicial decisions affecting the brewing and licensing trades, with notes, 1913-76. London, 1914-76. 31 v. to 1958.

Title varies: 1936-53 Brewing trade review law reports; 1954-57 the law reports; 1959-c.73 incorporated in Brewing trade review, retitled The brewing review, c.1974-76.

Local Government

784. Conder, J.B.R. A hand-book of highway cases noted in The surveyor and municipal and county engineer, 1894-98. London, 1899. 1 v.

785. Conder, J.B.R. A handbook of sewer and drain cases noted in The surveyor and municipal and county engineer, 1894-1903. London, 1904. 1 v.

786. Cox, E.W. Reports of all the cases decided by all the superior courts relating to magistrates, municipal and parochial law, 1859-1919. London, 1862-1919. 27 v.

Title varies: v. 5-6 Reports of all the cases ... relating to magistrates, municipal and parochial, ecclesiastical and election law. Also known as: Cox's magistrates cases.

787. Decision of the Local Government Board. Collected from all sources, and reprinted from the Local government chronicle ... with introduction, explaining the practice of the Local Government Board in dealing with questions submitted for its decision, 1902-16. London, 1904-17. 14 v.

788. The Justice of the Peace, county, borough, Poor Law Union and Parish law recorder, 1837- . London, Justice of the Peace, 1837-. 146 v.

Data base: LEXIS 1945- .

Title varies: v. 67-90 The Justice of the Peace reports; v. 91 The Justice of the Peace and Local Government review reports. v. 1-66 published as part of the Justice of the Peace.

789. [Local government reports] Knight's local government reports, 1903- . London, Charles Knight, 1903- . 80 v.

Data base: LEXIS 1945- .

Locus Standi

790. [Bidder's locus standi reports] Bidder, H.F. Court of Referees on Private Bills in Parliament. Cases decided during the sessions, 1920-1936. London, 1937. 1 v.

Continuation of: Saunders and Bidder locus standi reports.
Continued by: Locus standi reports.

791. [Clifford and Rickard's locus standi reports] Clifford, F. and Rickards, A.G. Cases decided by the Court of Referees on Private Bills in Parliament, 1873-84. London, 1877-85. 3 v.

Continuation of: Clifford and Stephen's locus standi reports.
Continued by: Rickards and Michael's locus standi reports.

792. [Clifford and Stephen's locus standi reports] Clifford, F. and Stephens, P.S. Practice of the Court of Referees on Private Bills in Parliament; with reports of cases as to the locus standi of petitioners, 1867-72. London, 1870-73. 2 v.

Continued by: Clifford and Rickard's locus standi reports. Title varies: v. 2 Court of Referees on Private Bills in Parliament. Cases as to the 'locus standi' of petitioners.

793. [Fawcett, Court of Referees] Fawcett, J.H. A treatise on the Court of Referees in Parliament containing chapters on the practice and jurisdiction of the court, on the locus standi of petitioners in the House of Commons, and reports of the cases decided in that court, 1865. London, 1866. 1 v.

Reprinted (with additions) from The law times.

794. Locus standi reports. Court of Referees on Private Bills in Parliament. Cases decided during the sessions, 1936/37- . London, Butterworths, 1960- . 2 v.

Continuation of: Bidder's locus standi reports.

795. Newbon, H. The 'Private Bills' reports. A record of proceedings in Parlimentary Committees, including cases of 'locus standi' in the House of Lords, 1895-96. London, 1895-96. 2 v.

796. [Rickards and Michael's locus standi reports] Rickards, A.G. and Michael, M.J. Cases decided during the sessions, by the Court of Referees on Private Bills in Parliament, 1885-89. London, 1891. 1 v.

Continuation of: Clifford and Rickard's locus standi reports.

Continued by: Rickards and Saunders' locus standi reports.

797. [Rickards and Saunders' locus standi reports] Rickards, A.G. and Saunders, R.C. Cases decided during the sessions, by the Court of Referees on Private Bills in Parliament, 1890-94. London, 1895. 1 v.

Continuation of: Rickards and Michael's locus standi reports. Continued by: Saunders and Austin's locus standi reports.

798. [Saunders and Austin's locus standi reports] Saunders, R.C. and Austin, E. Court of Referees on Private Bills in Parliament. Cases decided ... , 1895-1904. London, 1900-05. 2 v.

Continuation of: Rickards and Saunders' locus standi reports. Continued by: Saunders and Bidder's locus standi reports.

799. [Saunders and Bidder's locus standi reports] Saunders, R.C. and Bidder, H.F. Court of Referees on Private Bills in Parliament. Cases decided ... , 1905-19. London, 1910-22. 2 v.

Continuation of: Saunders and Austin's locus standi reports. Continued by: Bidder's locus standi reports.

800. Stone, A.P. and Graham, W. Courts of Referees. Reports of the decisions on private bills, 1865. London, 1866. 1 v.

Pt. 1 only published.

Magistrates

801. Caldecott, T. Reports of cases relative to the duty and office of a Justice of the Peace, 1777-87. London, 1800. 1 v.

Microfilm: Dobbs Ferry, Oceana.

Previous eds.: 1786, 1797. Dublin 1790. Continuation of: Burrow. Settlement cases.

802. Dowling, J. and Ryland, A. Reports of cases relating to the duty and office of magistrates determined in the Court of King's Bench, 1822-27. London, 1823-31. 4 v.

Microfilm: Dobbs Ferry, Oceana.

v. 1, 2nd ed., 1835.

803. Magisterial cases, reprinted from ... The Justice of the Peace, 1896-1946. London, 1897-[1946]. 51 v.

804. Manning, J. and Ryland, A. Reports of cases relating to the duty and office of magistrates, determined in the Court of King's Bench, 1827-30. London, 1829-32. 3 v.

Microfilm: Dobbs Ferry, Oceana.

v. 3: pt. 1 only published. Continued by: Nevile and Manning. Magistrates' cases.

805. Nevile, S. and Manning, W.M. Reports of cases relating to the duty and office of magistrates determined in the Court of King's Bench and other courts, 1831-36. London, 1834-38. 3 v.

Continuation of: Manning and Ryland. Magistrates' cases. Continued by: Nevile and Perry. Magistrates' cases.

806. Nevile, S. and Perry, T.E. Reports of cases relating to the office of magistrates, determined in the Court of King's Bench, 1836-37. London, 1837. 1 v.

Microfilm: Dobbs Ferry, Oceana.

Continuation of: Nevile and Manning. Magistrates' cases.

807. New sessions cases, containing reports of cases relating to the duties and liabilities of magistrates, 1844-51. London, 1845-51. 4 v.

Microfilm: Dobbs Ferry, Oceana.

v. 1-2 (Carrow, Hamerton and Allen); v. 3 (Hamerton, Allen and Otter); v. 4 (Prideaux and Cole).

808. Nolan, M. Reports of cases relating to the duty and office of a Justice of Peace, 1791-92. London, 1793. 1 v.

Maritime Law

809. Acton, T.H. Reports of cases argued and determined before the Lords Commissioners of Appeals in prize causes, 1809-11. London, 1811-12. 2 v.

Reprinted: English reports; Microfilm: Dobbs Ferry, Oceana.

v. 2: pt. 1 only published.

810. Aspinall, J.P. Reports of cases relating to maritime law, containing all the decisions of the courts of law and equity in the United Kingdom, and selections from the more important decisions in the colonies and the United States, 1870-1940. London, 1873-1961. 20 v.

Also known as: Aspinall's maritime cases.

811. [British and colonial prize cases] Prize cases heard and decided in the Prize Court during the Great War by The Right Hon. Sir Samuel Evans, ... and in the courts of the overseas dominions and on appeal to the Judicial Committee of the Privy Council, 1914-22. London, 1916-22. 3 v.

812. [Crockford's maritime law reports] Reports of the cases relating to maritime law, decided by the Court of Admiralty, and by all the superior courts of law and equity; salvage awards; and a selection of cases decided in the courts of the United States, the consular courts, &c. &c., 1860-71. London, 1864-71. 3 v.

Microfilm: Dobbs Ferry, Oceana.

813. Lloyd's reports of prize cases heard before and decided by the Right Honourable Sir Samuel Evans, ... during the European War which began in August, 1914, 1914-22. London, 1915-24. 10 v.

Also known as: Lloyd's list prize cases.

814. Lloyd's reports of prize cases (second series), 1939-53. London, 1957. 1 v.

815. Pratt, F.T. Law of contraband of war: with a selection of cases from the papers of the Right Hon. Sir Geo. Lee ... , 1740-50. London, 1861. 1 v.

Microfilm: Dobbs Ferry, Oceana.

Previous imp. 1856. Most of the volume consists of cases.

816. Roscoe, E.S. Reports of prize cases determined in the High Court of Admiralty, before the Lords Commissioners of Appeals in Prize Causes, and before the Judicial Committee of the Privy Council, 1745-1858. London, 1905. 2 v.

Microfilm: Dobbs Ferry, Oceana.

817. Rothery, H.C. A digest of the judgments in Board of Trade inquiries into shipping casualties, delivered by H.C. Rothery, Esq. (The Wreck Commissioner), 1876-80. London, 1882. 1 v.

Microfilm: Dobbs Ferry, Oceana.

Also known as: Rothery's judgments of wreck commissioners.

818. Spinks, T. Reports of cases decided during the present war in the Admiralty Prize Court and the Court of Appeal, 1854-56. London, 1855-56. 1 v.

Reprinted: English reports; Microfilm: Dobbs Ferry, Oceana.

Mercantile Law

See also Bankruptcy

819. The accountant law reports, 1874-1941. London, 1874-1941. 85 v. v. 1-14 published in The accountant.

820. Butterworths company law cases, 1983- . London, Butterworths, 1984- .

Data base: LEXIS.

821. Commercial law reports, 1976-83. London, Oyez Publishing, 1981-83. 3 v.

Data base: LEXIS.

822. Consumer credit law reports, 1978- . London, Oyez Longman, 1980- . 1 v.

Originating in: Bennion, F.A.R. Consumer credit control. Includes Scottish cases.

823. Cox, E.W. Reports of all the cases decided by the superior courts of law and equity, relating to the law of joint-stock companies, 1864-72. London, 1867-73. 5 v.

Also known as: Cox's joint stock companies cases.

824. Cox, E.W. Reports of cases argued and determined in all the courts of law and equity relating to the law of joint-stock companies, 1848-49. London, 1849. 1 v.

Issued as a supplement of Joint-stock companies' law journal.

825. Cox, E.W. Reports of cases decided by the superior courts of law and equity on mercantile law, 1860-61. London, 1861. 1 v.

Pt. 1 only published. Reprinted from The law times 'law reporter'.

826. Danson, F.M. and Lloyd, J.H. Mercantile cases. Reports of cases relating to commerce, manufactures, etc., determined in the courts of common law, at Nisi Prius and in Banc, 1828-29. London, 1830. 1 v.

Microfilm: Dobbs Ferry, Oceana.

Continued by: Lloyd and Welsby. Mercantile cases.

827. Duncan, J.A. The annual review of mercantile cases, being a digest of the decisions of the English, Scotch and Irish courts on matters relating to commerce, 1885-86. London, 1886-87. 2 v.

828. Elder, B.S. Appeal cases under the Sale of Food and Drugs Acts, 1875, 1879, and 1899, and the Margarine Act, 1887, 1876-1905. London, 1900. 1 v.

2nd ed. 1905.

829. Insurance law reports, 1955-1985. Harlow, 1982-85. 3 v.

Data base: LEXIS

Each vol. on a separate theme.

830. Leach, A.F. Club cases: with reference to the liabilities and expulsion of members, 1836-79. London, 1879. 1 v.

2nd ed., with the Labouchere case, 1879.

831. Legal decisions affecting bankers, 1879- . London, Professional Books, 1900- . 8 v.

Data base: LEXIS 1945- .

Originally published in the Journal of the Institute of Bankers. Also known as: Paget's Legal decisions affecting bankers, after the editor of v. 1-3.

832. Lloyd, J.H. and Welsby, W.N. Mercantile cases: reports of cases relating to commerce, manufactures; &c., &c., determined by

the courts of common law at Nisi Prius and in Banc, 1829-30. London, 1830. 1 v.

Microfilm: Dobbs Ferry, Oceana.

Continuation of: Danson and Lloyd. Mercantile reports.

833. Lloyd's list law reports, 1919- . London, Lloyds of London, 1919- . 148 v.

Data base: LEXIS 1945- .

Title varies: 1968 - Lloyd's law reports. Also known as: Lloyd's reports.

834. Marrack, R. The European assurance arbitration. (Before Lord Westbury). Oct. 22, 1872 - Aug. 3, 1874. London, 1872-75. 1 v.

Published with The law times. Also known as: Marrack's reports of the decisions of Lord Westbury.

835. Megone, W.B. Reports of cases under the Companies Act, decided in the High Court of Justice, the Court of Appeal, and the House of Lords, 1888-90. London, 1890-91. 2 v.

Microfilm: Dobbs Ferry, Oceana.

836. Reilly, F.S. Albert Life Assurance Company Arbitration Act, 1871. Lord Cairn's decisions, 1871-73. London, 1872-75. 3 v.

Also known as: Reilly's reports of the decisions of Lord Cairns.

837. Reilly, F.S. European assurance arbitration. Lord Westbury's decision, 1872. London, 1873. 1 v.

Also known as: Reilly's reports of the decisions of Lord Westbury. Pt. 1 only published.

838. Reports of commercial cases, 1895-1941. London, 1896-1941. 46 v.

Incorporated in: Times law reports. Also known as: Commercial cases.

839. Ross, G. Leading cases in the commercial law of England and Scotland, 1707-1855. London, Edinburgh, 1853-57. 3 v.

Microfilm: Dobbs Ferry, Oceana.

840. Trading law reports, 1982- . Chichester, Barry Rose, 1983- . 1 v.

v. 1-3 published with Trading law.

Mining Law

841. Bamber, P.G. Report of mining cases decided by the Railway and Canal Commission Court under the Mines (Working Facilities and Support) Act, 1923, 1923-24. London, 1925. 1 v.

Munitions Law

842. [Munitions appeal reports] Appeals from Munitions Tribunals (5 & 6 Geo. 5, c. 54 and c. 99; Munitions Tribunals (Appeal) Rules, 1916), 1916-20. London, 1916-20. 4 v.

Parliament

843. Barron, A. and Arnold, T.J. Reports of cases of controverted elections, 1843-46. London, 1846. 1 v.

Microfilm: Dobbs Ferry, Oceana.

Continuation of: Barron and Austin. Reports in controverted elections.

844. Barron, A. and Austin, A. Reports of cases of controverted elections, 1842. London, 1844. 1 v.

Microfilm: Dobbs Ferry, Oceana.

Continued by: Barron and Arnold. Reports in controverted elections.

845. Blackmore, E.G. Speaker's decisions [v. 1]. The decisions of ... E. Denison ... 1857-72, and of ... Sir H.B.W. Brand ... 1872-84. [v. 2]: The decisions of ... A.W. Peel ... 1884-95. 1857-95. Adelaide, 1892-1900. 2 v.

Previous eds.: all published in Adelaide: 1881 (Denison); 1882-87 (in 4 v., Brand), 1887-90 (in 2 v., Peel).

846. Bohun, W. Collection of debates, reports, orders and resolutions of the House of Commons, touching the right of electing Members to serve in Parliament, 1586-1700. London, [1702]. 1 v.

Microfilm: Dobbs Ferry, Oceana.

Most of the cases reported were determined 1678-1700.

847. Bourke, R. Parliamentary precedents, being decisions of C.S. Lefevre, Speaker of the House of Commons, 1839-57. 2nd ed. London, 1857. 1 v.

1st ed. 1857 (1839-56).

848. Clifford, H. A report of the two cases of controverted elections of the borough of Southwark ... [**and**] An account of the two subsequent cases of the city of Canterbury, 1796-97. London, 1802. 1 v.

Microfilm: Dobbs Ferry, Oceana.

Previous ed.: 1797.

849. Cockburn, Sir A.E. and Rowe, W.C. Cases of controverted elections, 1833. London, 1833. 1 v.

Microfilm: Dobbs Ferry, Oceana.

850. Collection of cases and records concerning privilege of Parliament. London, 1764. 1 v.

851. Corbett, V. and Daniell, E.R. Reports of cases of controverted elections, 1819. London, 1821. 1 v.

Microfilm: Dobbs Ferry, Oceana.

852. Day, S.H. Elections cases in 1892 and 1893: being a collection of the points of law and practice arising out of the Parliamentary election petitions in those years, together with reports of the judgments, 1892-93. London, 1894. 1 v.

Microfilm: Dobbs Ferry, Oceana.

853. Douglas, S., Baron Glenbervie. The history of the cases of controverted elections, 1775-76. 2nd ed. London, 1802. 4 v.

Microfilm: Dobbs Ferry, Oceana.

Previous eds.: 1775-77; Dublin, 1778.

854. Falconer, T. and Fitzherbert, E.H. Cases of controverted elections determined in committees of the House of Commons, 1835-39. London, 1839. 1 v.

Microfilm: Dobbs Ferry, Oceana.

855. Fraser, S. Reports of the proceedings before Select Committees of the House of Commons in ... cases of controverted elections, 1790-92. London, 1793. 2 v.

Microfilm: Dobbs Ferry, Oceana.

856. Glanville, J. Reports of certain cases determined and adjudged by the Commons in Parliament, 1623-24. London, 1775. 1 v.

Microfilm: Dobbs Ferry, Oceana.

857. Hatsell, J. Precedents of proceedings in the House of Commons. New ed., 1290-1815. London, 1818. 4 v.

Previous eds. (in 3 v.) 1781, 1785, 1796; (in 4 v.) 1796; Dublin (in 3 v.), 1786. Also known as: Hatsell's Parliamentary precedents. In 1776 Hatsell published 'A Collection of Cases of Privilege'; this is included, with additions, in v. 1 of his 'Parliamentary Precedents'.

858. Knapp, J.W. and Ombler, E. Cases of controverted elections, 1834-35. London, 1837. 1 v.

Microfilm: Dobbs Ferry, Oceana.

859. Luders, A. Reports of the proceedings in Committees of the House of Commons, upon controverted elections, 1784-87. London, 1788-90. 3 v.

Reprinted: v. 1, 1808; Microfilm: Dobbs Ferry, Oceana.

860. [O'Malley and Hardcastle's election cases] O'Malley, E.L. and Hardcastle, H. Reports of the decisions of the judges for the trial of election petitions in England and Ireland, pursuant to the Parliamentary Elections Act, 1868, 1869-1929. London, 1870-1929. 7 v.

3 parts only of v. 7 issued. v. 4 is by J.S. Sanders and A.P. Keep, v. 5 by J.S. Sanders, v. 6-7 by H. Cohen.

861. Peckwell, R.H. Cases of controverted elections, 1803-05. London, 1805-06. 2 v.

Microfilm: Dobbs Ferry, Oceana.

Also includes eleven cases 1771-97, not before published.

862. Perry, H.J. and Knapp, J.W. Cases of controverted elections, 1833. London, 1833. 1 v.

863. Philipps, J. Election cases determined ... by Committees of the House of Commons, 1780-81. London, 1782. 1 v.

864. Power, D., Rodwell, H. and Dew, E.L'. Reports of the decisions of Committees of the House of Commons in the trial of controverted elections, 1848-56. London, 1853-57. 2 v.

Microfilm: Dobbs Ferry, Oceana.

865. Tomlins, Sir T.E. Cases explanatory of the rules of evidence before Committees of Election of the House of Commons. Compiled from the reports of trials of controverted elections, 1689-1795. London, 1796. 1 v.

Microfilm: Dobbs Ferry, Oceana.

866. Wolferstan, F.S.P. and Bristowe, S.B. Reports of the decisions of Election Committees, 1859-64. London, 1865. 1 v.

Microfilm: Dobbs Ferry, Oceana.

867. Wolferstan, F.S.P. and Dew, E.L'. Reports of the decisions of Committees of the House of Commons in the trial of controverted elections, 1857-58. London, 1859. 1 v.

Microfilm: Dobbs Ferry, Oceana.

Entitled: v. 1. No more published.

868. Wollaston, G.W. Coronation claims. Containing a full report of all the cases argued before the Court of Claims at the Coronation of King Edward VII, with other matters relating to Coronation services in general, 1901-10. 2nd ed. London, 1910. 1 v.

1st ed. 1903. Supplement to the second edition, contains a report of the cases before the Court of Claims at the Coronation of King George V. London, 1936.

Practice

See also nos. 425, 431, 510

869. Bittleston, A.H. Reports in chambers, Queen's Bench Division. Arranged alphabetically, according to the subject-matter of the several

cases, under the rules of court respectively applicable, and with notes of other recent decisions, 1883-84. London, 1884. 1 v.

Microfilm: Dobbs Ferry, Oceana.

Also known as: Bittleston's chamber cases, Bittleston's reports in chambers, Q.B.

870. [Bittleston's chambers reports] Bittleston, A.H. Practice under the Judicature Acts; being reports of points of practice arising under the Judicature Acts, 1873 and 1875, decided in judges' chambers, 1875-84. London, 1876-84. 2 v.

Title varies: 1883-84 Reports in chambers, Queen's Bench Division.

871. [Charley's chamber cases] Charley, W.T. Reports of cases decided at judges' chambers under the Supreme Court of Judicature Acts (with copious index and marginal notes), 1875-76. London, 1876-77. 2 v.

Microfilm: Dobbs Ferry, Oceana.

Originating in: Charley. Of reports of the cases determined in the Supreme Court of Judicial illustrative of the new system of practice and pleading. v. 2 only has separate title page for the chamber cases.

872. [Charley's practice cases] Charley, W.T. Reports of cases determined in the Supreme Court of Judicature illustrative of the new system of practice and pleading, 1875-78. London, 1876-81. 3 v.

Microfilm: Dobbs Ferry, Oceana.

873. Conroy, J. Custodiam reports; or, a collection of cases relative to outlawries and the grants thereon, 1655-1788. Dublin, 1795. 1 v.

Contains no original reports.

874. New practice cases, together with cases in evidence, stamps, and the law of attorneys and solicitors, 1844-48. London, 1847-48. 3 v.

Microfilm: Dobbs Ferry, Oceana.

v. 3: pts. 1-2 only published. The series is a reprint of cases from The law times.

875. Pleading and practice cases, 1837-38. [184?-?]. 1 v.

Reprinted verbatim from Willmore, Wollaston and Hodges, Arnold and Horn and Hurlstone.

876. The Practical Register of the Common Pleas, containing select cases or determinations in points of practice in that court, 1705-42. London, 1743. 1 v.

877. [Select cases relating to evidence] A collection of select cases relating to evidence. By a late barrister-at-law, 1698-1732. London, 1754. 1 v.

Microfilm: Dobbs Ferry, Oceana.

Suppressed because of its supposed interference with Strange (first published 1755), from which some of the cases were extracted. Published in 8 v. Also known as: Octavo Strange.

Registration Cases

See also no. 1419

878. Coltman, F.J. Registration cases. Reports of cases determined on appeal from the decisions of the revising barristers on the Common Pleas and Queen's Bench Divisions of the High Court of Justice, and on appeal therefrom to the Court of Appeal, 1879-85. London, 1886. 1 v.

Microfilm: Dobbs Ferry, Oceana.

Continuation of: Hopwood and Coltman. Registration cases. Continued by: Fox and Smith. Registration cases.

879. Cox, E.W. and Atkinson, H.T. Registration appeal cases, 1843-46. London, 1845-46. 1 v.

Microfilm: Dobbs Ferry, Oceana.

v. 1: pts. 1-2 only published.

880. Delane, W.F.A. A collection of decisions in the courts for reviewing the lists of electors. 2nd ed., 1832-35. London, 1836. 1 v.

Microfilm: Dobbs Ferry, Oceana.

1st ed. 1834.

881. Fox, J.S. and Smith, C.L. Registration cases. Reports of cases argued and determined on appeal from the decisions of the revising barristers in the Queen's Bench Division of the High Court of Justice,

and on appeal therefrom in the Court of Appeal, 1886-95. London, 1895. 1 v.

Microfilm: Dobbs Ferry, Oceana.

Continuation of: Coltman. Registration cases. Continued by: Smith. Registration cases.

882. Hopwood, C.H. and Coltman, F.J. Registration cases. Reports of cases argued and determined in the Court of Common Pleas, on appeal from the decisions of the revising barristers, ... 1868-78. London, 1873-79. 2 v.

Microfilm: Dobbs Ferry, Oceana.

Continued by: Coltman. Registration cases.

883. Hopwood, C.H. and Philbrick, F.A. Registration cases: reports of cases argued and determined in the Court of Common Pleas, on appeal from the decisions of the revising barristers, 1863-67. London, 1868. 1 v.

884. Keane, D.D. and Grant, J. Registration cases. Reports of cases argued and determined in the Court of Common Pleas, 1854-62. London, 1863. 1 v.

Microfilm: Dobbs Ferry, Oceana.

885. The law reports. Registration cases, 1868-71. London, 1869-71. 1 v.

3 pts. only published. Reprinted from L.R. 4-6 C.P.

886. Lutwyche, A.J.P. Reports of cases argued and determined in the Court of Common Pleas, on appeal from the decisions of the revising barristers, 1843-53. London, 1847-54. 2 v.

Microfilm: Dobbs Ferry, Oceana.

887. Manning, W.M. Proceedings in Courts of Revision in the Isle of Wight, before James Manning, Esq., revising barrister: to which are added cases decided in South Hants. in 1835 ... , 1832-35. London, 1836. 1 v.

Microfilm: Dobbs Ferry, Oceana.

888. Pigott, G. and Rodwell, H. Reports of cases decided in the Court of Common Pleas on appeal from the decisions of the revising barristers, 1843-45. London, 1846. 1 v.

Microfilm: Dobbs Ferry, Oceana.

889. Smith, C.L. Registration cases. Reports of cases argued and determined on appeal from the decisions of the revising barristers in the King's Bench Division of the High Court of Justice, and on appeal therefrom in the Court of Appeal, 1895-1915. London, 1906-15. 3 v.

Continuation of: Fox and Smith. Registration cases. v. 3: pt. 1 only published.

Revenue Law

890. The annotated tax cases, 1922-75. London, 1922-75. 54 v.

Published with The accountant. Title varies: v.1-5 The accountant tax cases. From 1976-81 incorporated in Taxation reports.

891. British tax cases, 1982- . Bicester, CCH Editions, 1983- . 1 v.

892. Butterworths' rating appeals ... Reports of rating appeals heard before the London and other quarter sessions, the King's Bench Division, the Court of Appeal, and the House of Lords, 1913-31. London, 1925-32. 4 v.

Continuation of: Konstam and Ward. Rating appeals. From 1926 includes Chancery Division.

893. Capital transfer tax cases. Appeals to the High Court, etc., 1978-79. London, [H.M.S.O.], 1979. 4 pts.

Leaflet form.

894. Chambers, T.G. and Pretty, A.H.F. Finance (1909-10) Act, 1910. Reports of cases before referees and in the High Court, on the interpretation of Part 1 of the Act, 1911-14. London, 1913-14. 2 v.

Also known as: Appeals concerning taxes on land values. Includes some Scottish cases.

895. CTT [Capital Transfer Tax] reports, 1978-82. London, 1978-82. 2 v.

Merged with CTT news to form: CTT news and reports.

896. Davies, C.E. Reports of land valuation appeals in Referee's Courts, High Court, and House of Lords, 1910-14. London, 1913-14. 3 v.

Also known as: Davies' Land valuation appeals.

897. De-rating appeals. English and Scottish appeals, 1932-61. London, 1934-62. 29 v.

Data base: LEXIS 1945- .

Continuation of: Rowe and Stanton. English de-rating appeals. Superseded by: Rating appeals. Title varies: 1935-61 De-rating and rating appeals, English and Scottish.

898. Excess profits levy. Appeals to the High Court, etc., 1958-65. London, [1959-65]. 4 pts.

Leaflet form.

899. Income tax. Appeals to the High Court, etc., 1918-20. London, 1919-20. 15 pts.

Continued by: Tax cases. Appeals to the High Court, etc. Issued in leaflet form.

900. Excess profits tax. Appeals to the High Court, etc., 1942-61. London, 1942-61. 112 pts.

Leaflet form.

901. Konstam, E.M. Reports of rating appeals heard before the London and other quarter sessions, the King's Bench Division, the Court of Appeal, and the House of Lords, 1904-08. London, 1909-12. 2 v.

Continuation of: Ryde and Konstam. Rating appeals. Continued by: Konstam and Ward. Rating appeals.

902. Konstam, E.M. and Ward, H.R. Reports of rating appeals heard before the London and other quarter sessions, the King's Bench Division, the Court of Appeal, and the House of Lords, 1909-12. London, 1912. 1 v.

Continuation of: Konstam. Rating appeals. Continued by: Butterworth's rating appeals.

903. [Lands Tribunal rating appeals] A selected list of Lands Tribunal rating appeals, 1950-61. London, 1952-62. 11 v.

Continued by: Rating appeals.

904. National Defence Contribution. Appeals to the High Court, etc., 1941-48. London, 1941-48. 12 v.

At head of title: For official use.

905. Profits tax. Appeals to the High Court, etc., 1950-71. London, 1950-[71]. 58 pts.

At head of title: For official use. Issued in leaflet form.

906. Rating and income tax, 1924-60. London, 1924-60. 58 v.

Continued by: Rating and valuation reporter.

907. Rating and valuation reporter, 1961- . London, Rating Publishers, [1961]- . 21 v.

Continuation of: Rating and income tax.

908. Rating appeals, 1962- . London, Rating Publishers, 1963- . 21 v.

Data base: LEXIS.

Continuation of: De-rating appeals **and** Lands Tribunal rating appeals. 1962-70 cases originally published in Rating case notes. Published with: Rating and valuation reporter.

909. Rating case notes, 1962-70. London, [1962]-71. 8 v.

Nothing issued 1968.

910. Reports of tax cases under the Act 37 Vict. cap. 16. and under the Taxes Management Act, 1875- . London, H.M.S.O., 1884- . 53 v.

Data base: LEXIS 1875- .

Title varies: v. 2 - Reports of tax cases. Also known as: Tax cases.

911. Rowe, M.E. and Stanton, J. English de-rating appeals heard under the Rating and Valuation (Apportionment) Act, 1928 in the Divisional Court of the King's Bench and the Court of Appeal [and the House of Lords], 1930-32. London, 1930-33. 3 v.

Continued by: De-rating appeals.

912. Ryde, W.C. and Konstam, E.M. Reports of rating appeals heard before the London and other quarter sessions, the Queen's and King's Bench Division, the Court of Appeal, and the House of Lords, 1894-1904. London, 1904. 1 v.

Continuation of: Ryde's rating appeals. Continued by: Konstam. Rating appeals.

913. [Ryde's rating appeals] Ryde, E. and Ryde, A.L. Reports of appeals heard before the Court of General Assessment Sessions ... by E. Ryde and A.L. Ryde. The fourth edition brought down to the present date, with an introduction to the Valuation (Metropolis) Act, 1869, and an appendix. By W.C. Ryde, 1871-93. London, 1885-93. 3 v.

1st-3rd eds. published as: Metropolitan rating. London, 1873-81. Continued by: Ryde and Konstam. Rating appeals.

914. Ryde's rating cases, 1956-79. London, 1957-79. 21 v.

Data base: LEXIS.

References to Ryde on rating given. Series intended to update that work.

915. Simon's tax cases, 1975- . London, Butterworths, 1976- . 8 v.

Data base: LEXIS.

Issued as part of Simon's weekly tax service.

916. Stamp duty cases, 1921-78. London, [1943-78]. 71 pts.

At head of title: For official use. In leaflet form.

917. Tax cases. Appeals to the High Court, etc., 1920- . London, H.M.SO., 1920- . 2903 pts.

Data base: LEXIS.

Continuation of: Income tax. Appeals to the High Court, etc. In leaflet form.

918. Taxation reports, 1939-81. London, 1940-81. 42 v.

Incorporating Annotated tax cases, 1976-81.

919. Value Added Tax Tribunals reports, 1973- . London, H.M.S.O., 1974- . 10 v.

Data base: LEXIS.

Published under the direction of the President of the Value Added Tax Tribunals.

Social Security

920. Archbold, J.F. An abridgment of cases upon poor law, vol III, 1842-58. London, 1858. 1 v.

Continuation of: Lumley. Abridgment of poor law cases. Continued by: Paterson. Abridgment of poor law cases.

921. Bott, E. The laws relating to the poor, including the collections originally made by E. Bott and afterwards edited by F. Const, 1560-1827. 6th ed. by J.T. Pratt. London, 1827-33. 2 v.

Previous eds.: 1771 (in 1 v., anonymous); 2nd ed. 1773 (in 1 v.); 3rd ed. 1793 (in 2 v., Const); 4th ed. 1800 (in 3 v., Const); 5th ed. 1807 (Const) with supps. 1815, 1820.

922. Decisions of the courts relating to supplementary benefits and family income supplements legislation, 1972-80. London, 1980-81. [loose leaf] 1 v.

923. Foley, R. Laws relating to the poor ... with cases adjudged in the Court of King's Bench. 4th ed., 1680-1731. London, 1756. 1 v.

1st ed. 1739; 2nd ed. 1743; 3rd ed. 1751.

924. Griffith, E. Cases of supposed exemption from poor rates, claimed on the ground of extra-parochiality, 1821-31. London, 1831. 1 v.

Microfilm: Dobbs Ferry, Oceana.

925. Lumley, W.G. An abridgment of the cases upon the subject of the poor law, 1834-42. London, 1840-43. 2 v.

Continued by: Archbold. Abridgment of poor law cases.

926. Paterson, J. An abridgment of cases upon poor law, vol IV, 1857-63. London, 1864. 1 v.

Continuation of: Archbold. Abridgment of poor law cases.

927. Reported decisions of the Commissioner under the National Insurance Acts, 1948- . London, H.M.S.O., 1955- . 8 v.

The decisions are issued in 8 benefit series, details of which are in the front of the last volume. Title varies: 1977 - ... under the Social Security and Child Benefit Acts. Issued in series covering various benefits.

928. Reported decisions of the Commissioner under the National Insurance (Industrial Injuries) Acts, 1948/52-1973/76. (... under the Social Security and National Insurance (Industrial Injuries) Acts in volume 7). London, 1955-78. 7 v.

Continued by: Reported decisions of the Commissioner under the Social Security and Child Benefit Acts.

929. Reports of decisions on appeals and applications under Section 67 of the National Insurance Act, 1911, and Section 27 of the National Insurance Act, 1913, 1913-18. London, 1915-19. 5 v.

Decisions of the National Health Insurance Commissioners.

930. Reports of inquiries and appeals under the National Health Insurance (Medical Benefit) Regulations (England) 1913, 1913-24. London, 1917-24. 3 v.

At head of title: National Health Insurance Commission (England).

931. [Unemployment insurance. Decisions of the Umpire - claims to benefit (1912-21)]. Decisions given by the Umpire respecting claims to benefit ... National Insurance Act, 1911, Part II: Unemployment insurance, 1912-21. London, 1914-21. 4 v.

Continued by: Unemployment Insurance Acts ... Decisions given by the Umpire respecting claims to benefit. Selected decisions.

932. [Unemployment insurance. Decisions of the Umpire - demarcation of trades] Decisions given by the Umpire respecting demarcation of trades ... National Insurance (Unemployment) Acts, 1911 to 1916, 1912-17. London, 1918. 1 v.

933. Unemployment Insurance Acts ... Decisions given by the Umpire respecting claims to benefits. Selected decisions, 1922-48. London, 1922-48. 21 v.

Continuation of: Unemployment insurance. Decisions of the Umpire - claims to benefit (1912-21). In leaflet form.

Tithes

934. Eagle, F.K. and Younge, E. A collection of the reports of cases ... relating to tithes, 1204-1825. London, 1826. 4 v.

Microfilm: Dobbs Ferry, Oceana.

935. Gwillim, Sir H. A collection of Acts and records of Parliament with reports of cases argued and determined in the courts of law and equity respecting tithes, 1224-1824. 2nd ed. by C. Ellis. London, 1825. 4 v.

Microfilm: Dobbs Ferry, Oceana.

1st ed. 1801.

936. Rayner, J. Cases at large concerning tithes, 1575-1782. London, 1783. 3 v.

Microfilm: Dobbs Ferry, Oceana.

937. Western, T.G. Cases relating to tithes of the City of London ... , 1592-1822. London, 1823. 1 v.

Microfilm: Dobbs Ferry, Oceana.

938. Wood, H. A collection of decrees by the Court of Exchequer in tithe-causes, 1650-1798. London, 1798-99. 4 v.

Microfilm: Dobbs Ferry, Oceana.

Tort

See no. 1691.

Transport

See also no. 331

939. Beavan, E. and Walford, F. Parliamentary cases relating to railways, 1846. London, 1847. 1 v.

Microfilm: Dobbs Ferry, Oceana.

940. Oxley, J.S. Light railways, procedure, reports and precedents, 1897-1903. London, 1901-03. 2 v.

941. [Railway and canal cases] Cases relating to railways and canals, argued and adjudged in the courts of law and equity, 1835-54. London, 1840-55. 7 v.

Microfilm: Dobbs Ferry, Oceana.

Title varies: v. 7 Cases relating to railway, canal and joint stock companies. Also known as: Nicholls, Hare and Carrow.

942. [Railway and canal traffic cases] A collection of cases decided under the 2nd sect. of the Railway and Canal Traffic Act, 1854, and reports of cases decided by the Railway Commissioners under the Regulation of Railways Act, 1873; with the statutes and notes. Also a digest of cases on railway and canal traffic, 1855-1933. London, 1874-1934. 21 v.

Continued by: Traffic cases. Title varies: v. 2-6 Reports of cases decided by the Railway Commissioners; v. 7-16 Reports of cases decided by the Railway and Canal Commissioners; v. 17-19 Reports of cases decided by the Railway and Canal Commissioners and the Railway Rates Tribunal; v. 20-21 Reports of cases decided under the Railway and Canal Traffic Acts and the Railway Act.

943. Road haulage cases (England and Wales). Selected decisions given by the Tribunal for the settlement of questions arising in connection with compulsory acquisitions of road haulage undertakings under the above mentioned Act, 1950-53. London, 1950-52. 16 pts.

Continued by: Transport Tribunal appeals. At head of title: Transport Arbitration Tribunal. Transport Act, 1947, 10 & 11 Geo. 6 ch. 49.

944. Road traffic reports, 1970- . Homewell, Havant, Kenneth Mason, 1970- . 13 v.

Data base: LEXIS.

945. Traffic cases: reports of cases decided under the Railway and Canal Traffic Acts, Railways Act and the Road and Rail Traffic Act, 1934-75. London, 1935-76. 12 v.

v. 30 - New series. Continuation of: Railway and canal traffic cases.

946. [Transport Tribunal appeals] [Appeals] in the Court of the Transport Tribunal, 1955- . London, H.M.S.O., 1955- . ca 450 pts.

946 ENGLAND AND WALES

Continuation of: Road haulage cases. In typescript.

War Compensation

947. War Compensation Court. Reports, 1920-28. London, 1921-28. 77 pts.
Known as the Defence of the Realms Losses Commission from 1916-1920. The Commission issued 5 reports which contain a few decisions in the appendices.

Typescript leaflets.

F I J I

In 1987 Fiji left the Commonwealth.

948. Fiji gazette. [Supplement containing reports of the Supreme Court], 1874- . Suva, Government Printer, 1874- . c.109 v.

Title varies: 1875-1970 Fiji Royal gazette. Decisions of the Supreme Court published occasionally as a supplement.

949. Fiji law reports: cases determined by the Supreme Court of Fiji, 1875- . Suva, Government Printer, 1903- . 20 v.

Includes cases in the High Commissioner's Court for the Western Pacific until 1952.

G A M B I A

See nos. 7, 8

SUBJECT REPORTS

Mercantile Law

See no. 1.

G H A N A

To 1957, two territories called Gold Coast and Togoland

See also nos. 7, 8, 1521

950. Earnshaw, A. Gold Coast judgments. Reports of 18 cases decided. Judgments delivered at Cape Coast Castle, Gold Coast Colony, 1909-10. London, [1910], 1 v.

951. The Ghana law reports: cases determined by the High Court of Justice and on appeal therefrom in the Court of Appeal, 1959-66; 1971- . Accra, Council for Law Reporting, 1974- . 19 v.

952. Griffith, W.B. Digest and index to the reports of cases decided in the Supreme Court of the Gold Coast Colony, 1844-1931. Accra, 1935. 1 v.

953. Judgments of the Full Court, 1919-26/29. Accra, 1919-31. 5 v.

Title varies: v. 5-6 Selected judgments ... Titles include various details of court locations. v. 6 also includes judgments in 1898 and 1914.

954. Judgments of the Judicial Committee of the Privy Council on appeal from the Gold Coast Colony, 1874-1928. Accra, 1929. 1 v.

955. King-Farlow, S. Some Gold Coast judgments, ... 1915-17 and the Masai case in the Court of Appeal for Eastern Africa 1913. Accra, 1917. 1 v.

956. Selected judgments of the divisional courts of the Gold Coast Colony, 1921/25-1931/37. Accra, London, [1926]-39. 4 v.

957. Some judgments of divisional and full courts held in the Gold Coast Colony, 1911-16. [Accra], 1919. 1 v.

SUBJECT REPORTS

Customary Law

958. Cases in Akan law, decisions delivered by Sir Ofori Atta with introduction, synopses and notes ... , 1912-16. London, 1928. 1 v.

959. Sarbah, J.M. Fanti customary laws ... with a report of some cases thereon decided in the law courts, [1845-95]. 3rd ed. London, 1968. 1 v.

1st ed. 1897. 2nd ed. 1904. Subtitle varies: Additional vol: Fanti law report of cases on Fanti customary law: second selection [1845-1903]. 1904.

Mercantile Law

See no. 1.

G I B R A L T A R

960. Gibraltar law reports, 1812/77- . Gibraltar, Government Printer, [1979-]. 3 v.

From 1978 issued annually as supplements to the Gibraltar Gazette.

G R E N A D A

See no. 1863.

G U Y A N A

To 1966 called British Guiana.

See also no. 1862.

961. Abrahams, E.A.V. A digest of cases decided in the Review Court of British Guiana, 1856-91. Demerara, 1892. 1 v.

962. Alves, J., Dampier, F.E. and Maxwell, B. Collection of cases decided in the Court of Review, 1856-73. Demerara, 1873-74. 2 v.

963. [British Guiana Court of Review reports] Cases determined by the Supreme Court in appeal from magistrates' decisions, 1879-93. Georgetown, [1879?]-94. 16 v.

Also known as: Review Court judgements. Printed for circulation to magistrates and judiciary only.

964. [British Guiana law reports. New series] The law reports of British Guiana, 1890-97. Georgetown, 1892-94; 1916-18. 7 v.

Material compiled for v. 4, 1894 (probably published in 1895) was utilized with minor alterations in v. 4, 1894 published in 1916.

965. [British Guiana law reports. Old series] The law reports of British Guiana, edited by E.M.V. Abrahams, 1855-65. Demerara, 1893-96. 2 v.

966. [British Guiana law reports] Reports of decisions of the Supreme Court of British Guiana, 1914-65. Georgetown, 1915-72. 46 v.

Continued by: Guyana law reports. Title varies: 1958-65 Law reports of British Guiana. Includes cases in the West Indian Court of Appeal and its successors.

967. Erskine, R.H. Digest of decisions of the Privy Council under Roman Dutch law, 1829-69. Demerara, 1870. 1 v.

Reprinted: 1882.

968. Guyana law reports, 1966- . Ruimveldt, Government Printer, 1977- . 4 v.

Continuation of: British Guiana law reports. 1966 volume includes the Law reports of British Guiana for the period January 1, 1966 to May 25, 1966 (i.e. independence).

969. Judgements. Supreme Court of British Guiana. Appellate jurisdiction, 1894-98. Georgetown, 1895-98. 5 v.

970. Official gazette. [Reports], 1881-1952. Demerara, 1881-1952. 72 v.

Reports 1901-13 reprinted as Supreme Court judgements.

H O N G K O N G

971. District Court law reports, 1953- . Hong Kong, Government Printer, [1956]- . 28 v.

Published as an independent series in 3 vols., 1953-57, then as a separately published supplement to the Hong Kong law reports. Incorporates the Hong Kong Lands Tribunal law reports from 1981.

972. Hong Kong law reports, 1905-38; 1946- . Hong Kong, Government Printer, 1906-1939; 1949- . 66 v.

Reprinted v. 1-30, Government Printer, 1958-63.

Has separately paginated supplement: District Court law reports.

SUBJECT REPORTS

Land Law

973. Hong Kong Lands Tribunal law reports, 1977- . Hong Kong, Government Printer, 1977- . 3 v.

Incorporated with the District Court law reports from 1981.

Revenue Law

974. Hong Kong Inland Revenue Board of Review decisions, 1968- . Hong Kong, Government Printer, [1972]- . 11 v.

Second and subsequent volumes appear as numbered supplements to the first volume and continue the pagination.

975. Hong Kong tax cases, 1949- . Hong Kong, Government Printer, [1967]- . 13 v.

Second and subsequent volumes appear as numbered supplements to the first volume and continue the pagination.

976. Inland Revenue Board of Review decisions, 1972-73. Hong Kong, 1972-74. 2 v.

Published with District Court law reports as a supplement to the Hong Kong law reports.

I N D I A

Before Aug. 1858, the British courts were under the jurisdiction of the East India Company.

977. All India reporter, 1914- . Nagpur, V.V. Chitaley, n.d. 69 v. in 452.

Covers Supreme Court (1950-), Federal Court (1939-50) Privy Council (1914-50) and states and court jurisdictions in over 37 separate sections issued in multiple vols. p.a.

978. Dave, B.R. Privy Council judgments in cases, heard and determined on appeal from India which are not reported in the Indian Law Reports, 1876-97. Allahabad, 1897. 1 v.

Details of a collateral reprint given in no. 985.

979. Dominion law reporter, ... 1947-53. Nagpur, 1947-53. 37 v.

980. Federal Court reports, containing cases determined by the Federal Court of India and the Judicial Committee of the Privy Council on appeal, 1939-50. Delhi, 1939-50. 11 v.

Continued by: Supreme Court reports.

981. Federal law journal of India [containing reports of cases heard in the Federal Court], 1937-49. Madras, 1937-51. 14 v.

Continued by: Supreme Court journal.

982. The Full Bench decisions containing full reports of full bench decisions of all superior courts in British India, 1930-34. Mylapore, Madras, 1930-34. 5 v.

Frequently bound with: Privy Council decisions.

983. Indian appeals decided by the Judicial Committee of the Privy Council. March 1872-July 1873. Madras, 1878. 1 v.

Details of a collateral reprint given in no. 985.

984. Indian cases. Full reports of cases decided by all the superior Indian courts and Privy Council, 1909-47. Lahore, 1909-47. 231 v.

985. Indian decisions (new series) being a re-print of all the decision of the Privy Council on appeals from India and of the various High Courts and other superior courts in India reported both in the official and non-official reports, 1875-1900. Trichinopoly, Madras, 1912-22. 43 v.

Reprint of Indian law reports series, with a table showing where cases reported in other series can be found in I.L.R. Published in 4 series covering Allahabad, Bombay, Calcutta and Madras with separate vol. numbering for each. Allahabad series v. 1-4 originally published 1911 with all cases in chronological order. Subsequently withdrawn for copyright reasons and replaced. Later vols. seriatim reprints.

986. Indian decisions [o.s.] being a verbatim re-print of the reports of cases decided by the late Supreme Courts and the Sudder Dewanny Adawluts in India, 1774-1858. Madras, 1911-16. 17 v.

987. Indian Full Bench reports, full bench cases of all the High Courts in India, 1939- . Allahabad, M.L. Kharbanda, 1939- . 1 v.

988. Indian High Court reports: being a re-print of all the cases of the Privy Council on appeal from India and of all the High Courts in India, 1901-13. Calcutta, 1901-13. 25 v.

989. Indian jurist, 1862-63. Calcutta, 1862-63. 2 v.

Continued by: Indian jurist, n.s.

990. Indian jurist [new series], 1866-67. Calcutta, 1867. 2 v.

Continuation of: Indian jurist.

991. Indian rulings containing full reports of all reportable decisions, 1929-? Lahore, 1929-? 8v. to 1935.

Published in several different series representing different courts. Title varies: pts. 1-4 Indian decisions.

992. Knapp, J.W. Reports of cases determined before the committee of H.M.'s Most Honourable Privy Council, 1829-36. London, 1831-[36]. 3 v.

993. The law reports. Indian appeals, being cases in the Privy Council on appeal from the East Indies, 1873/74-1945/50. London, 1874-1950. 77 v.

1873-1930 reprinted: India, n.d.; Allahabad, Law Publishers (India), 1988.

Includes supplemental volume (March 1872-Nov. 1873) 1880. Contains cases not reported in Moore. Details of collateral reprint given in no. 985.

994. Law reports of British India. A verbatim reprint of the Indian law reports, 1876-1900. Madras, 1914-20. 41 v.

Published in 4 series - Allahabad, Bombay, Calcutta and Madras.

995. Moore, E.T. Reports of cases determined by the Judicial Committee and Lords of H.M.'s Most. Hon. Privy Council on appeal from the Supreme and Sudder Dewanny Courts in the East Indies, 1836-72. London, 1836-73. 14 v.

Reprinted: English reports; Indian reports, Madras, 1909-11; Allahabad, Law Publishers (India), 1988. Microfilm: Dobbs Ferry, Oceana.

Also known as: Moore's Indian appeals.

996. The Privy Council decisions containing full reports of the decisions of the Judicial Committee of the Privy Council, 1930-34. Mylapore, Madras, 1930-34. 5 v.

Frequently bound with: Full bench decisions.

997. The revised cases being the 'live' case law of a century, containing full reports of all 'live' cases decided by the courts

in England, the Privy Council, Adawlut courts and the chartered and non-chartered High Court in India and Burmah, 1809-1909. Madras, 1910. 1 v.

998. Saraswati, P.N. [and others]. Privy Council judgments on appeals from India, 1825-1910. Bhowanipore, 1880-[1910]. 9 v.

Details of collateral reprint given in no. 985.

999. Sevestre, A.A. Reports of cases heard and determined by the ... Judicial Committee ... on appeal from the Supreme and Sudder Dewanny courts of Calcutta, Madras and the Northwestern Provinces, 1860-63. London, Calcutta, 1863. 1 v.

Also known as: v. 7 of the author's cases in the S.D.A. Nos. 1103 and 1104 are vols. 1-6 and 8-12 of this series.

1000. Supreme Court cases, ... 1969- . Lucknow, Eastern Book Company, 1969- . 52 v.

1001. Supreme Court journal, 1950- . Madras, Supreme Court Journal, 1950- . 67 v.

1002. Supreme Court reports, containing cases determined by the Supreme Court of India, 1950- . Delhi, Supreme Court, 1950- . 97 v.

1003. Supreme Court weekly reporter, ... 1963-79. Ernakulam, 1963-79. 33 v.

1004. Sutherland, D. Judgments of the Privy Council on appeals from India, 1831-80. Calcutta, 1867-80. 3 v.

Details of a collateral reprint given in no. 985.

1005. Uchcha Nyayalaya Nirnaya Patrika [High Courts side reports] ... 1969- . New Delhi, Ministry of Law, 1969- . 53 v. In Hindi.

1006. Uchchatam Nyalaya Nirnaya Patrika [Supreme Court side reports] ... 1968- . New Delhi, Ministry of Law, 1968- . 52 v. In Hindi.

1007. Unreported judgments (S.C.), 1969- . Jodhpur, 1969- . 14 v.

1008. Wigram, H. Selections from Judicial Committee of the Privy Council, [on appeals from India], 1836-87. Madras, 1888. 1 v.

Reprinted: 1928, 1934.

Previous ed.: 1881.

SUBJECT REPORTS

Criminal Law

1009. All India criminal reports, 1924-? Allahabad, 1924-? 21 v. to 1935.

1010. Consolidated Supreme Court criminal rulings, a full text reporter of decisions made by the Supreme Court of India on every branch of criminal law, 1950- . Allahabad, Supreme Court Criminal Rulings Office, 1970- . 12 v.

Reprinted: 1984.

1950-70 issued in 4 vols.; one vol. p.a. thereafter.

1011. Cranenburgh, D.E. A handbook of criminal cases containing a verbatim reprint of all criminal cases reported in the Indian law reports, 1876-1899. Calcutta, 1901. 5 v.

Published in four series covering the High Courts of Allahabad, Bombay, Calcutta (2 vols) and Madras. Previous eds.: 1890, Madras; 1891, Bombay; 1892, Calcutta. Continued by: Desai. Criminal cases.

1012. Criminal appeal reporter (Supreme Court), 1969- . Meerut, 1969- . 16 v.

1013. Criminal cases, containing full reports of all reportable criminal judgments of all superior courts of India and Burma and of the Privy Council, 1929-36. Nagpur, 1929-36. 8 v.

1014. Criminal law journal of India, 1904- . Nagpur, All India Reporter, 1904- . 88 v.

1015. Desai, B.R. Handbook of criminal cases being a verbatim reprint of all criminal cases reported in the Indian law reports, 1900-11. Baroda, 1907-12. 3 v.

Continuation of: Craneburgh. Criminal cases. Continued by: Ganatra. Criminal cases.

1016. Ganatra, L.N. A handbook of criminal cases reprinted verbatim from the Indian law reports, 1912-27. Rajkot, 1915-27. 5 v.

Continuation of: Desai. Criminal cases.

1017. Law weekly (criminal), ... 1966- . Madras, Law Weekly Office, 1966- . 17 v.

1018. The revised law reports, criminal rulings, being a re-publication of all such criminal cases decided by the High Courts, 1862-75. Calcutta, 1899-1900. 4 v.

1019. Sanyal, R.G. The record of criminal cases between natives and Europeans, 1796-1895. Calcutta, 1896. 1 v.

1020. Supreme Court criminal rulings, 1970- . Allahabad, 1970- . 13 v.

Dancing Girls

1021. Ramachendrier, C. Collection of the decisions of the High Courts and the Privy Council on the law of succession, maintenance, etc. applicable to dancing girls ... to 1891. Madras, 1892. 1 v.

Food and Drugs

1022. All India prevention of food adulteration cases [determined in the High Courts and Supreme Court of India on appeal], 1972- . Delhi, International Law Book Company, 1972- . 19 v.

Hindu Law

1023. All India Hind law reporter, ... 1975- . Delhi, J.S. Chawla, 1975- . 8 v.

1024. Norton, J.B. Selection of the leading cases of the Hindoo law of inheritance to 1871. Madras, 1870-71. 2 v.

1025. Pershad, H.M. Precedents of Hindoo law: being a collection of the judgments by H.M. Privy Council on questions of Hindoo law, 1829-69. Allahabad, 1870? 1 v.

1026. Ramachendrier, C. A collection of the decisions of the High Courts and the Privy Council on the Hindu law of adoption - 1893. Nellore, 1893. 1 v.

Previous ed.: 1892.

1027. Ramachendrier, C. Collection of the decisions of the High Courts and the Privy Council on the Hindu law of marriage. Madras, 1891. 1 v.

1028. Rattigan, W.H. Select cases in Hindu law decided by H.M.'s Privy Council and the superior courts of India. Lahore, 1869-71. 2 v.

Industrial Law

1029. All India services law journal, 1973- . Delhi, All India Services Law Journal, 1973- . 12 v.

1030. Indian factories and labour reports, [of cases determined in the Labour Courts, High Courts and Supreme Court of India on appeal], 1960- . Allahabad, Law Publishing House, 1960- . 45 v.

1031. Indian factories journal ... 1949- . Madras, Laws of India, 1949- . 61 v.

1032. Labour and industrial cases [determined by the Labour Appeal Tribunal, the High Courts and Supreme Court of India on appeal], 1968- . Nagpur, All India Reporter, 1968- . 15 v. in 30.

1033. Labour appeal cases. Decisions of the Labour Appellate Tribunal and of the Supreme Court on appeal, 1954-60. Delhi, 1954-60. 7 v.

1034. Labour law journal, ... 1949- . Madras, Labour Law Journal, 1949- . 66 v.

1035. Mines & factories journal, ... 1967-70. Patna, 1967-70. 6 v.

1036. Service law reporter, 1967- . Chandigarh, J.S. Chawla, 1967- . 31 v.

1037. Services law cases, containing recent judgments of all the High Courts in the country and Supreme Court of India, 1973- . Delhi, International Law Book Company, 1973- . 10 v.

1038. Supreme Court cases (labour and services), ... 1973- . Lucknow, Eastern Book Company, 1973- . 10 v.

Land Law

1039. All India land law reporter, ... 1979- . Chandigarh, Punjab Law Agency, 1979- . 4 v.

Covers the Punjab, Haryana and Himachal Pradesh.

Local Government

1040. Municipalities and corporation cases, [decided in the High Courts and Supreme Court of India], 1973- . Delhi, International Law Book Company, 1973- . 9 v.

Mercantile Law

1041. Company law journal, 1963-70; 1981- . Madras, Madras Law Journal Office, 1963-70; 1981- . 16 v.

1042. Mercantile law reporter, [containing cases determined by the High Courts and Supreme Court of India], 1969-73. Delhi, 1969-73. 5 v.

1043. Reports of company cases, 1931- . Madras, Company Law Institute of India, 1931- . 52 v.

Parliament

1044. Election law reports. Official reports of cases on election law decided by the Supreme and High Courts, with opinions of the Election Commissioner and important decisions of election tribunals, 1951- . Delhi, Govt. of India, 1951- . 55 v.

1045. Hammond, R.F. Reports of the Indian election petitions, 1920-23. Allahabad, [1920-23]. 3 v.

1046. Narain, J. Reports of Indian election petitions, 1920-33. Allahabad, [1920-33]. 4 v.

1047. Reports of municipal and election cases ... 1934- . Madras, Company Law Institute of India, 1934- . 2 v.

Practice

1048. Broughton, L.P.D. Notes of cases decided upon points of civil procedure to 1886. Calcutta, 1884-86. 2 v.

Rent

1049. All India rent control journal, [containing cases determined by the High Courts and Supreme Court of India], 1969- . Delhi, Vinod Publications, 1969- . 20 v.

1050. Rent control reporter, [containing cases determined by the High Courts and Supreme Court of India], 1969- . Chandigarh, J.S. Chawla, 1969- . 20 v.

1051. Rent law reporter, [containing cases determined by the High Courts and Supreme Court of India], 1977- . Chandigarh, J.S. Chawla, 1977- . 10 v.

1052. Supreme Court rent cases, ... 1981- . Nasik, 1981- . 2 v.

Revenue Law

1053. Current tax reporter: tax cases decided by the Supreme Court, 1972- . Jodhpur, Current Tax Reporter, 1972- . 31 v.

1054. Excise law times, ... 1977- . Delhi, Central Law Office, 1977- . 10 v.

1055. Hari Rao, P. The Indian income-tax decisions being a complete collection of all the judgments of the several High Courts, 1919-25. Madras, 1926. 1 v.

The author's real name is Hari G.P. Rao Gharpurey.

1056. Income tax gazette, 1941- . Delhi, Income-Tax Law Publishing House, 1941- . 5 v. to 1945.

Contains reports of cases.

1057. Income tax journal, ... 1963- . Madras, Madras Law Journal, 1963- . 40 v.

1058. Income tax reports. A journal ... with reports of Indian and select English cases, 1933- . Madras, Company Law Institute of India, 1933- . 16 v. to 1948.

1059. Sales tax cases, ... 1938- . Madras, Commercial Laws of India, 1938- . 51 v.

1060. Sales tax intepretations, ... 1976- . Ghaziabad (U.P.), Law & Management House, 1976- . 7 v.

1061. Srinivasan, P.R. Reports of income tax cases, decided in the High Courts of Judicature and Chief Courts in British India, 1886/1925-1935/37. Mylapore, Madras & Sripuram, 1886-1937. 10 v.

1062. Supreme Court cases (taxation), ... 1973- . Lucknow, Eastern Book Company, 1973- . 10 v.

1063. Tax gazette, ... 1973- . Jammu, Indira Dutta, 1973- . 12 v.

1064. Tax law review, ... 1976- . Jullundur (Punjab), Intax Publications (P), 1976- . 13 v.

1065. Taxation, ... 1947- . New Delhi, Taxation, 1947- . 67 v.

1066. Taxation law reports, ... 1971- . Nagpur, All India Reporter, 1971- . 12 v.

1067. Taxman, ... 1978- . Delhi, 1978- . 10 v.

Tort

1068. Accidents claims journal, ... 1966- . Delhi, Pankaj Dhawan, 1966- . 17 v.

Transport Law

1069. Hari Rao, P. [Reports of railway cases], 1928. Madras? [1929]. 1 v.

See no. 1055 for author's real name.

1070. Teruvenkatachariar, M. High Court decisions of Indian railway cases ... , 1864-1911. Trichinopoly, 1912. 1 v.

Previous ed.: 1901. Supplement, 1907.

ANDRHA PRADESH

See also the following series of no. 977: (Hyderabad) 1950-57; (Andhra Pradesh) 1954-

1071. Andhra law times. [Containing reports of cases in the High Court of Andhra Pradesh], 1954- . Hyderabad, Andhra Law Times, 1954- . 50 v.

1072. Andhra Pradesh law journal, [containing reports of cases in the High Court of Andhra Pradesh and on appeal in the Supreme Court of India], 1969- . Hyderabad, A.P. Law Publishers, 1969- . 28 v.

1073. Andhra weekly reporter, [containing cases in the High Court of Andhra Pradesh and on appeal to the Supreme Court of India], 1955- . Madras, Andhra weekly reporter, 1955- . 54 v.

1074. Indian law reports: Andhra Pradesh series, containing cases determined by the High Court of Andhra Pradesh at Hyderabad-Dn, 1954- . Hyderabad-Dn, Govt. of Andhra Pradesh, 1954- . 29 v.

Continuation of: India law reports: Hyderabad series.

1075. Indian law reports: Hyderabad series, [containing cases decided by the Hyderabad High Court], 1951-56. Hyderabad, 1951-56. 6 v.

Continued by: Indian law reports: Andhra Pradesh series.

ASSAM

See also the following series of no. 977: (Assam) 1949-63, (Manipur) 1952-53; (Assam and Nagaland) 1964-71; (Gauhati) 1972- .

1076. Assam law reports, [containing reports of cases determined by the High Court of Assam], 1969-77. Gauhati, 1966-77. 10 v.

Continued by: Gauhati law reports. Covers Manipur, Meghalaya, Nagaland and Tripura States.

1077. Gauhati law reports, [containing cases determined by the High Court of Assam], 1978- . Gauhati, 1978- . 5 v.

Continuation of: Assam law reports. Covers Assam, Manipur, Meghalaya, Nagaland and Tripura States.

1078. Indian law reports: Assam and Nagaland series. [Cases decided by the High Court of Assam and by the Supreme Court on appeal], 1964-73. [Shillong], 1964-73. 10 v.

1078 INDIA

Continuation of: Indian law reports: Assam series.

1079. Indian law reports: Assam series. Cases decided by the Assam High Court and by the Supreme Court on appeal, 1949-63. Shillong, 1949-63. 15 v.

Continued by: Indian law reports: Assam and Nagaland series.

BENGAL

For series continuing or commencing post Aug. 1947 **see** West Bengal

See also Calcutta series of nos. 987, 988, 991, 1018

1080. Bengal law reports. Decisions of the High Court at Fort William (civil and criminal), in its original and appellate jurisdictions, Privy Council decisions on Indian appeals [etc.], 1868-75. Calcutta, 1869-75. 15 v.

Reprinted: Bangalore, 1868-75 in 15 v.; see also no. 1119.

Continued by: Indian law reports, Calcutta series. For supplement see no. 1081.

1081. [Bengal law reports] Full Bench rulings of the High Court at Fort William, 1862-75. Calcutta & London, 1862-75. 12 v.

Reprinted: see no. 1119.

Supplemental series, edited by L.A. Goodeve and J.V. Woodman, to Bengal law reports, 1868-75.

1082. Bignell, M.A. Reports of cases in the Supreme Court of Judicature at Fort William in Bengal, 1830-31. Calcutta, 1831. 1 v.

Reprinted: Indian decisions (o.s.), Madras, 1911-16.

v. 1 pt. 1 only issued.

1083. Boulnois C. Reports of cases decided in the Supreme Court of Judicature at Fort William in Bengal, 1856-59. Calcutta, 1859. 2 v.

Reprinted: Indian decisions (o.s.), Madras, 1911-16.

1084. Bourke, W.M. Reports of cases heard and determined ... in the High Court of Judicature at Fort William in Bengal and in appeal therefrom, 1864-66. Calcutta, 1867. 1 v.

1085. Calcutta law reports. Cases decided by the High Court of Calcutta, edited by P. O'Kinealy and G.S. Henderson, 1877-82. Calcutta, 1877-82. 10 v.

Details of collateral reprint given in no. 985.

1086. Carrau, J. Reports of summary cases determined in the Presidency Sudder Court, 3rd ed., 1834-52. Calcutta, 1853. 1 v.

Previous eds.: 1841, 1849 published anonymously.

1087. Collier, G. Reports of proceedings of the Supreme Court of Judicature at Fort William in Bengal in its Admiralty jurisdiction in the case of George Collier v. The Cutter Dispatch, 4 Feb. 1817. Calcutta, 1817. 1 v.

1088. Coryton, J. Reports of cases argued and decided in the High Court of Judicature at Fort William in Bengal, 1864-65. Calcutta, 1864-65. 1 v.

1089. Decisions of civil causes decided by the Appellate side of the High Court of Judicature at Fort William in Bengal on appeals from the judgments of courts not established by royal charter, 1862-63. Calcutta, 1862-63. 1 v.

Also known as: Hay's reports, after the publisher.

1090. Decisions of Sudder Dewanny Adawlut, recorded in English, in conformity to Act III of 1843, 1845-60. Calcutta, 1846-61. 18 v.

1091. Decisions of Zillah Courts, Lower Provinces, 1846-61. [Calcutta], [1846-61?].

From 1843 the courts had a statutory obligation to publish monthly reports. Not arranged or digested and paged irregularly. Concern mainly oriental law.

1092. East, E.H. Notes of cases decided in the Supreme Court of Judicature at Fort William in Bengal, 1785-1821. London, 1849. 1 v.

Reprinted: Indian decisions (o.s.), Madras, 1912.

Published as part of Morley, W.H. An analytical digest of all the reports ..., appendix, v. 2.

1093. Fulton, J.W. Reports of cases determined in the Supreme Court of Judicature at Fort William in Bengal, 1842-44. Calcutta, 1845. 1 v.

Reprinted: Indian decisions (o.s.), Madras, 1911, 1905.

v. 1 only issued.

1094. Gasper, N.M. Reports of cases, Supreme Court of Calcutta, on reference from the Calcutta Court of Small Causes and by the High Court in its ordinary, original civil jurisdiction, 1850-62. Calcutta, 1867. 1 v.

Details of collateral reprint given in no. 985.

1095. Hyde, E. Reports of cases argued and determined ... in the High Court of Judicature at Fort William in Bengal ... and on appeal therefrom, 1862-64. Calcutta, 1864-65. 2 v.

Reprinted: Indian decisions (o.s.), Madras, 1911-16; 1897; 1912.

1096. Marshall, W. Reports of cases on appeal in the High Court of Judicature at Fort William in Bengal, 1862/3. Calcutta, 1864. 1 v.

Reprinted: 1903.

Also known as: Marshall and Sevestre, v. 1.

1097. Montriou, W.A. Reports of cases determined in the Supreme Court of Judicature at Fort William in Bengal, 1846. Calcutta, 1850. 1 v.

Reprinted: Indian decisions (o.s.), Madras, 1911-16.

1098. Morton, T.C. Decisions of the Supreme Court of Judicature at Fort William in Bengal, 1774-1841. Calcutta, 1841. 1 v.

Reprinted: Indian decisions (o.s.), Madras, 1911-16.

2nd ed. 1851, has supplement with added cases, 1789-1803, edited by Montriou; 3rd ed. 1853.

1099. Reports in the Sudder Dewanny Adawlut ... previous to, and in 1805 and to the end of 1811. Calcutta, 1812. 2 v.

1100. Reports of cases in the Court of Sudder Dewanny Adawlut, Calcutta, approved by the court, 1791/1811-1841/48. Calcutta, 1827-49. 7 v.

Reprinted: Calcutta, 1867-74 in 6 v.; Indian decisions (o.s.), Madras, 1911-16.

v. 1-4 (W.H. MacNaghten); v. 5 (J.C.C. Sutherland). Also known as: Select cases; Select reports.

1101. Reports of summary cases determined in the Court of Sudder Dewanny Adawlut, 1834-48. Calcutta, 1849. 1 v.

1102. Revenue civil and criminal reporter, 1866-68. Calcutta, 1866-68. 5 v.

v. 6, pt. 1 sometimes known as Wyman's reports.

1103. Sevestre, A.A. Report of summary cases determined in the Court of Sudder Dewanny Adawlut, 1834-?62. Calcutta, 1841-?62. 6 v.

Title varies: From v. 2 pt.3 adds: on appeal from the Zillah and city courts, with other variants from v. 3 onwards. Nos. 999 and 1104 are vols. 7 and 8-12 of this series.

1104. Sevestre, A.A. Reports of cases heard and determined by the Calcutta High Court, Appellate Jurisdiction, on appeal from the lower courts in Bengal on points of law and practice, 1864-73. Calcutta, London, 1866-73. 5 v.

Title varies: From v. 9 pt. 2: Reports of select cases. Nos. 999 and 1103 are vols. 7 and 1-6 of this series.

1105. Sevestre, A.A. Reports of cases on appeal from the lower courts in Bengal to the High Court of Judicature at Calcutta. In continuation of Marshall's official reports. 1863-64. Calcutta, 1866. 1 v.

Also known as: Marshall and Sevestre, v. 2, and Sevestre's Appeal cases.

1106. No entry.

1107. Shome, J.G. The law reporter, containing the civil and criminal judgments of the Calcutta High Court ... of the Privy Council, leading cases on Hindoo law, 1878-81. Calcutta, 1879-82. 4 v.

Details of a collateral reprint given in no. 985.

1108. Smoult, W.H. and Ryan, S.B. Collection of orders made and passed by the Supreme Court at Fort William, including decisions of the Court, 1774-1798. Calcutta, 1834. 1 v.

1109. Sutherland, D. Privy Coucil judgments [from] the Weekly reporter, 1864-71. Calcutta, 1867-71? 1 v.

1110. Sutherland, D. Rulings by the Sudder court and Appellate High Court ... on reference from the Mofussil small cause courts, to 1861. Calcutta, 1865. 1 v.

1111. Sutherland, D. Weekly reporter, containing decisions of the Appellate High Court, 1864-June 1876. 1864-76. 26 v.

Reprinted twice.

Includes 1 supplementary vol. (Jan-July 1864) 1867, known as the 'Gap Number'. Details of a collateral reprint given in no. 985.

1112. Sutherland, D. Weekly reporter. Supplement volumes, June 1868-July 1875. Calcutta, 1887. 3 v.

Reprinted: 1909-10.

Containing cases in Bengal law reports not printed in the Weekly reporter.

1113. Sutherland, D. Weekly reporter special number [1862] containing Full Bench rulings, July 1862-July 1864. Calcutta, 1886. 1 v.

Reprinted thrice.

1114. Taylor, G. Reports of cases determined in the Supreme Court of Judicature at Fort William in Bengal, 1847-1848. Calcutta, 1851. 1 v.

1115. Taylor, G. and Bell, J.D. Reports of cases determined in the Supreme Court of Judicature at Fort William in Bengal, 1849-1851. Calcutta, 1853-[54]. 2 v.

SUBJECT REPORTS

Criminal Law

1116. Cranenburgh, D.E. Criminal cases, [determined in the High Court], 1864-76. Calcutta, 1891-92. 2 v.

Reprinted from Sutherland. Weekly reporter.

1117. Cranenburgh, D.E. Handbook of criminal cases reprinted verbatim from the Bengal law reports and supplement, 1868-75. Calcutta, 1889. 2 v.

1118. Reports of cases determined in the Court of Nizamut Adawlut, 1805-50. Calcutta, 1827-52. 6 v.

Also known as: Select cases. v. 1-3 by W.H. MacNaghten. Continued by: Reports of cases ... , new series.

1119. Reports of cases determined in the Court of Nizamut Adawlut, new series, 1851-59. Calcutta, 1851-59. 9 v.

Continuation of: Reports of cases determined in the Court of Nizamut Adawlut.

1120. Reports of criminal cases adjudged by the Court of Nizamut Adawlut, 1855. Calcutta, 1806? 1 v.

Hindu Law

1121. Montriou, W.A. Cases of Hindu law before H.M. Supreme Court of Judicature at Fort William in Bengal, 1779-1840. Calcutta, 1853-61. 2 v.

Paged continuously with Morton, 2nd ed. 1851.

Mercantile Law

1122. Reports of the principal commercial cases heard and determined in the Supreme Court of Judicature ... and Calcutta Court of Small Causes, 1851-60. Calcutta, 1863. 1 v.

Reprinted: Indian decisions (o.s.), Madras, 1911-16.

Rent

1123. Decisions under the rent laws of the Court of Sadr Dewani Adalat and the High Court of Justice at Fort William in Bengal, 1861-66. Calcutta, 1866. 3 v.

BIHAR

1912-36 united with Orissa.

See also the following series of no. 977: (Patna) 1914-

1124. Bihar Bar Council journal, [containing cases determined in the High Court of Bihar and in the Supreme Court of India], 1973- . Patna, State Bar Council, 1973- . 10 v.

1125. Bihar law journal reports, [containing reports of cases decided in the High Court of Bihar and in the Supreme Court of India], 1953- . Allahabad, Allahabad Law Journal Company, 1953- . 30 v.

1126. Bihar reports, [containing reports of cases determined in the High Court of Bihar], 1934-46. Lahore, c. 1934-46. 12 v.

1127. Indian law reports: Patna series, containing cases determined by the High Court at Patna and by the Judicial Committee of the Privy Council on appeal, 1922- . Patna, Govt. of Bihar, 1922- . 59 v. to 1980.

P.C. appeals ceased in 1949.

1128. [Patna High Court reports] Supplement to the Calcutta weekly notes. Patna High Court cases, 1917-26. Calcutta, 1917-26. 10 v.

1129. Patna law journal containing cases determined by the High Court at Patna and on appeal in the Supreme Court of India, 1916-21. [Patna], 1916-21. 6 v.

1130. Patna law journal reports. [Cases determined in the High Court at Patna and on appeal in the Supreme Court of India], 1968-80. Patna, 1968-80. 13 v.

1131. Patna law reporter [containing reports of cases determined in the High Court], 1923-25. Patna, 1923-25. 3 v.

1132. Patna law times [containing cases determined in the High Court at Patna], 1920-49. Patna, 1920-49. 30 v.

1133. Patna weekly notes [of cases determined in the High Court], 1936- . [Patna], 1936- .

SUBJECT REPORTS

Criminal Law

1134. Patna criminal reports, 1938- . Patna, Bihar Publishers, c. 1938- . 8 v. to 1945.

DELHI TERRITORY

See also the following series of no. 977: (Delhi) 1967-

1135. Delhi law times [containing cases decided by the High Court of Delhi and on appeal by the Supreme Court], 1965- . Delhi, Delhi Law Times, 1965- . 22 v.

1136. Indian law reports: Delhi series, [containing cases determined by the High Court of Delhi], 1968- . Delhi, Govt. of India, Publications Dept., 1968- . 29 v.

1137. Rajdhani law reporter [containing reports of cases determined by the High Court of Delhi and by the Supreme Court on appeal], 1971- . New Delhi, K.K. Gujral, 1971- . 12 v.

GUJARAT

See also the following series of no. 977: (Kutch) 1949-56; (Saurashtra) 1950-56; (Gujarat) 1960-

1138. Baroda High Court reports, 1877-91. Baroda, 1893. 3 v.

1139. Baroda law reports [being reports of cases determined in the High Court of Baroda]. 1881/2-1948/9. Baroda, 1882-1949. 58 v. Some judgments in Gujarati.

1140. Gujarat law herald [containing decisions on the High Court of Gujarat and of the Supreme Court of India on appeal], 1981- . Ahmedabad, Bar Council of Gujarat & the Ahmedabad Lawyers Benevolent Fund, 1981- . 2 v.

1141. Gujarat law reporter [containing reports of cases determined by the High Court of Gujarat and by the Supreme Court of India on appeal], 1960- . Ahmedabad, C.C. Vora, 1960- . 24 v.

1142. Gujarat law times [containing reports of cases determined by the High Court and by the Supreme Court of India on appeal], 1964/65-1966/67. Ahmedabad, Gujarat Law Reporter Office, 1964-67. 4 v.

1143. Hak patrak decisions of the Rajasthanik Court [of Kathiawar], 1877-99. Rajkot, 1884-1935. 8 v.

1144. Indian law reports: Gujarat series [containing cases determined by the High Court of Gujarat], 1960-74. Gandhi Nagar, 1960-74. 15 v.

1145. Kathiawar law reports [containing reports of cases determined in the High Court of Kathiawar], 1891-1923. Limbdi, 1891-1923. 33 v.

Continued by: Western States Agency law reports.

1146. Western States Agency law reports [containing decisions of cases determined in the High Court of Kathiawar], 1924-? 1924-? 10 v. to 1934.

Continuation of: Kathiawar law reports. v. 1 also numbered 'Old vol. 34'.

HIMACHAL PRADESH

See also the following series of no. 977: (Bilaspur) 1952-54; (Himachal Pradesh) 1949-67, 1971-

1147. Indian law reports: Himachal Pradesh series [containing cases decided by the High Court of Himachal Pradesh], 1971- . Simla, Govt. of Himachal Pradesh, 1971- . 12 v.

JAMMU AND KASHMIR

See also the following series of no. 977: (Jammu and Kashmir) 1951- **and** no. 1220

1148. Jammu and Kashmir law reporter [containing reports of cases in the High Court of Jammu and Kashmir], Dec. 1970- . Jammu, Jammu and Kashmir High Court, 1970- . 5 v. to 1974.

1149. Kashmir law journal, ... 1962- . Jammu, Chand Mohan Gupta, 1962- . 21 v.

A single volume with same title was issued in two pts. for 1929 in 1929.

1150. Srinagar law journal, ... 1979- . Srinagar, Hakim Ishtaq, 1979- . 4 v.

Containing reports of High Court cases.

KARNATAKA

Until 1973 called Mysore

See also the following series of no. 977: (Mysore) 1950-74; (Karnataka) 1974-

1151. Indian law reports: Karnataka series [containing cases decided in the High Court of Karnataka], 1973- . Bangalore, Govt. of Karnataka, 1973- . 16 v.

1152. Indian law reports: Mysore series, containing cases decided by the High Court of Mysore and by the Supreme Court of India on appeal, 1959-67. Bangalore, 1959-67. 9 v.

1153. Karnataka law journal [containing cases decided in the High Court of Karnataka and on appeal in the Supreme Court of India], 1974- . Bangalore, Karnataka Law Journal, 1974- . 18 v.

Continuation of: Mysore law journal.

1154. Mysore Chief Court reports, 1896-1923. Bangalore, 1898-1924. 28 v.

Reprinted: Mysore reports. Bangalore, 1926.

1155. Mysore High Court reports, ... 1931-50. Bangalore, 1931-50. 55 v.

1156. Mysore law journal [containing cases decided by the High Court of Mysore and by the Supreme Court of India on appeal], 1957-73. Bangalore, 1957-73. 17 v.

Continued by: Karnataka law journal.

1157. Mysore law reports, containing cases determined by the Court of the Justiciary Commissioner of Mysore and Coorg which, since March 1881, is called the Chief Court of Mysore and the Court of the Justiciary Commissioner of Coorg, on appeal from all other courts in Mysore and Coorg, 1878-95. Bangalore, [1883]-97. 18 v.

Reprinted: Mysore reports. Bangalore, 1926.

KERALA

Until 1956 called Travancore-Cochin

See also the following series of no. 977: (Travancore-Cochin) 1950-57; (Kerala) 1957-

1158. Aiyar, T.S. Unreported decisions [of cases determined in the High Court of Travancore-Cochin], 1875-1909. [Ernakulam], 1913-28. 4 v.

1159. Cochin law reports. [Reports of cases determined in the Chief Court of Cochin], 1909-47. Ernakulam, 1909-47. 40 v.

1160. Indian law reports: Kerala series containing cases determined by the High Court of Kerala and by the Supreme Court of India on appeal, 1957-. Ernakulum, Govt. of Kerala, 1957- . 48 v.

Continuation of: Indian law reports: Travancore-Cochin.

1161. Indian law reports: Travancore-Cochin containing cases determined by the High Court of Travancore-Cochin, 1950-56. Ernakulam, 1950-56. 5 v.

Title varies: 1950 Travancore-Cochin law reports.

1162. Kerala law journal [containing cases decided in the Kerala High Court], 1957- . Cochin, V. Bhaskare Menon, 1957- . 26 v.

1163. Kerala law reporter [containing reports of cases determined in the High Court of Kerala and on appeal to the Supreme Court of India], 1959-73. Ernakulam, 1959-73. 15 v.

1164. Kerala law times [containing reports of cases decided in the Kerala High Court and in the Supreme Court on appeal], 1951- . Ernakulam, Kerala law times, 1951- . 32 v.

1165. Malabar law quarterly [containing cases determined in the High Court of Travancore], 1905-06. Ernakulam, 1905-06. 1 v.

In three parts separately paginated, (1) journal, (2) Cochin law reports, (3) Travancore law reports.

1166. Pillai, P.V.K. The important unreported Travancore decisions, 1897-1909. Trivandrum, 1909-10. 1 v.

Reprinted: 1930.

1167. Select decision of cases determined in the Appeal Court, 1894-1908. Ernakulam, 1898-1920. 4 v.

Title varies: v. 1 Cochin law reports.

1168. Travancore law journal [containing decisions of cases in the High Court of Travancore], 1910-45. Trivandrum, 1911-45. 35 v.

1169. Travancore law reports [cases determined in the High Court of Travancore], 1884-? Trivandrum, 1884-[?1947]. 50 v. to 1935.

1170. Travancore law times [containing reports of cases in the High Court of Travancore], 1926-46. Trivandrum, 1926-46. 10 v. to 1935.

MADHYA PRADESH

Until 1950 known as the Central Provinces and Berar

See also the following series of no. 977: (Bhopal) 1951-56; (Madhya Barat) 1950-57; (Vindhya Pradesh) 1951-56; (Madhya Pradesh) 1957-

1171. Central Provinces law reports [containing reports of cases determined by the Court of the Judicial Commissioner], 1886-1904. Nagpur, 1886-1904. 17 v.

1172. Indian law reports: Madhya Bharat series, containing cases decided by the High Court of Madhya Barat and by the Supreme Court on appeal, 1952-56. Indore, 1952-56. 5 v.

1173. Indian law reports: Madhya Pradesh series, containing cases determined by the High Court of Madhya Pradesh, at Jabalpur, 1957- . Bhopal, Controller, Printing and Stationery, Madhya Pradesh, 1962- . 26 v.

1174. Jabalpur law journal [containing cases determined by the High Court of Madhya Pradesh at Jabalpur and by the Supreme Court of India on appeal], 1957-82. Gwalior, 1957-82. 31 v.

1175. Madhya Pradesh law journal [containing cases determined in the High Court and in the Supreme Court of India on appeal], 1956- . Nagpur, Central Law House Journal Publications, 1956- . 27 v.

1176. Nagpur law notes, ... 1938-39. Nagpur, 1938-39. 1 v.

SUBJECT REPORTS

Revenue Law

1177. Central Provinces and Berar revenue rulings [determined by the Court of the Judicial Commissioner], 1895-1949. Nagpur, 1895-49. 16 v.

1178. Revenue law reports, Central Provinces and Berar, to 1917. [Nagpur], [1917]. 1 v.

1179. Rulings under the Berar Patels and Patwaris law, 1903-1949? Nagpur, Government Printing, 1909-49? 69 pts. to 1939.

Issued in numbered parts, each with separate pagination.

MAHARASHTRA

Until May 1960 known as Bombay

See also the following series of no. 977: (Nagpur) 1914-58; (Bombay) 1914- **and** Bombay series of nos. 987, 988, 991, 1018

1180. Bellasis, A.F. Reports of civil causes determined in the Court of Sudder Dewanee Adawlut, 1840-48. Bombay, 1850. 1 v.

Continuation of: Reports of selected cases (1820-40).

1181. Bombay High Courts reports. Reports of cases decided in the High Court of Bombay, 1862-75. Bombay, 1862-79. 12 v.

Reprinted: Revised law reports; criminal rulings, Bombay series, Calcutta, 1902.

Previous eds.: 1862-75; 1865-79. Continued by: Indian law reports, Bombay series.

1182. Bombay law journal [containing reports of cases in the High Court at Bombay], 1923-46. Bombay, 1923-46. 24 v.

1183. Bombay law reporter [containing reports of cases in the Bombay High Court and Supreme Court on appeal], 1899- . Bombay, Bombay Law Reporter, 1899- . 84 v.

Details of a collateral reprint given in no. 985.

1184. Borrodaile, H. Reports of civil causes adjudged by the Court of Sudur Udulut for the Presidency of Bombay, 1800-24. Bombay, 1825. 2 v.

1185. Chitty, C.W. and Patell, R.M. Causes referred from the Bombay Court of Small Causes for the opinion of the High Court of Bombay, 1861-99. Bombay, 1900. 1 v.

Details of a collateral reprint given in no. 985.

1186. Dadyburjor, S.B. Cases referred from the Bombay Court of Small Causes for the opinion of the High Court of Bombay, 1899-1927. Bombay, 1929. 1 v.

1187. Indian law reports: Bombay series, containing cases determined by the High Court at Bombay and by the Judicial Committee of the Privy Council on appeal, 1876/77- . Bombay, Govt. of Maharashtra, 1876- . 60 v. to 1936.

1876-1900 reprinted: Indian decisions (n.s.), Madras, 1912-22; **see also** nos. 985, 994, 1011, 1015, 1016, 1018.

Continuation of: Bombay High Court reports. P.C. appeals ceased in 1949.

1188. Indian law reports: Nagpur series. Cases determined by the High Court of Nagpur and by the Judicial Committee of the Privy Council on appeal, 1935-66. Nagpur, 1936-56. 21 v.

Continuation of: Nagpur law reports. P.C. appeals ceased in 1949.

1189. Maharashtra law journal [containing reports of cases in the Bombay High Court and Supreme Court on appeal], 1963- . Nagpur, Manohar Chandurkar, 1963- . 20 v.

1190. Morris, J. Selected decisions of the Court of Sudder Dewanee Adawlut of Bombay, 1848-53. Bombay, 1853-54. 1 v.

Issued in three parts, each separately paginated.

1191. Morris, J. and Harrington, E. Cases disposed of by the Sudder Dewanee Adawlut of Bombay, 1854-62. Bombay, 1854-62. 9 v.

v. 1-4 (Morris); v. 7-9 (Harrington).

1192. Nagpur law journal [containing reports of cases in the High Court of Nagpur], 1918-62. Nagpur, 1918-62. 49 v.

1193. Nagpur law reports. Cases determined by the Court of Justiciary Commissioners at Nagpur and by the Privy Council, Aug. 1904-July 1935. Nagpur, [1905]-1938. 31 v.

Continued by: Indian law reports, Nagpur series.

1194. Perry, Sir E. Cases illustrative of oriental life on the application of English law to India, decided in H.M.'s Supreme Court at Bombay, 1843-52. Bombay, 1853. 1 v.

1194 INDIA

Reprinted: Indian decisions (o.s.), Madras, 1911-16.

1195. Perry, Sir E. Notes of cases decided in the Recorders' Court and in the Supreme Court of Judicature at Bombay, 1826-47. London, 1849. 1 v.

Reprinted: Indian decisions (o.s.), Madras, 1911-16.

Published as part of Morely, W.H. An analytical digest of all the reports ... , appendix, v. 2.

1196. Printed judgments of the Bombay High Court, appellate side, 1866-1900. Bombay, 1868-1900. 30 v.

1197. Reports of selected cases decided by the Sudder Dewanee Adawlut, Bombay, March 1820-40. Bombay, 1843. 1 v.

Reprinted: Bombay, 1862.

Continued by: Bellasis. Reports of civil causes.

1198. Selections from proceedings of the Court of Oyer and Terminer, 1726-45. Bombay, 1877. 1 v.

1199. Unreported printed judgments of the High Court of Bombay, 1868-98. Rajkot, 1910-14. 9 v.

For details of a collateral reprint see no. 985.

SUBJECT REPORTS

Criminal Law

1200. Bellasis, A.F. Reports of criminal causes determined in the Court of Sudder Foujdaree Adawlut, 1827-46. Bombay, 1849. 1 v.

1201. Bombay High Court criminal ruling, ... 1869-1907. Bombay, 1869-1907. 13 v.

1202. The criminal cases of the Bombay High Court, 1911/12- . Bombay, Bombay Law Reporter, 1912- . 13 v. to 1935.

Reprinted from Bombay law reporter.

1203. Harrington, E. Cases disposed of by the Sudder Foujdaree Adawlut of Bombay, 1861-62. Bombay, 1861-62. 4 v.

1204. Morris, J. Cases disposed of by the Sudder Foujdaree Adawlut of Bombay, 1854-58. Bombay, 1854-58. 10 v.

1205. Ranchhoddas, R. Unreported criminal cases of the Bombay High Court, 1862-99. Bombay, 1901. 1 v.

Industrial Law

1206. Industrial Court reporter, ... 1948-67. Bombay, 1948-67. 20 v.

Revenue Law

1207. Selected decisions of the Revenue Tribunal, 1939- . c. 1940- 1 v. to 1945.

ORISSA STATE

1912-32 united with Bihar

See also the following series of no. 977: (Orissa) 1949-

1208. Cuttack law times [containing reports of cases in the Orissa High Court and Supreme Court on appeal], 1935- . Cuttack, Law Times Press, 1935- . 54 v.

1209. Cuttack weekly reporter [containing cases in the Orissa High Court], 1970-77. Cuttack, 1970-77. 14 v.

1210. Indian law reports: Cuttack series, containing cases determined by the High Court of Orissa and by the Supreme Court of India on appeal, 1949-75. Cuttack, 1949-75. 34 v.

1211. Orissa judicial decisions [of cases determined by the High Court of Orissa], 1959-60. Cuttack, 1959-60. 2 v.

PUNJAB STATE

See also the following series of no. 977: (Lahore) 1914-50; (East Punjab) 1948-50; (Pepsu) 1950-57; (Punjab) 1951-56; (Punjab and Haryana) 1967- .

1212. Current law journal [containing decisions of the High Court and Supreme Court on appeal], 1961- . Chandigarh, Current Law Journal 1961- . 22 v.

1213. Indian law reports: Lahore series, containing cases determined by the High Court at Lahore and by the Judicial Committee of the Privy Council on appeal, 1920-47. Lahore, 1920-47. 28 v.

Continued by: Pakistan law reports, Lahore series.

1214. Indian law reports: Patiala series [containing cases determined by the High Court of Patiala and East Punjab States Union], 1952-55. Patiala, 1952-55. 4 v.

1215. Indian law reports: Punjab and Haryana series, containing cases determined by the High Court of the Punjab and Haryana, 1948- . Chandigarh, Govt. of East Punjab, 1948- . 35 v.

Title varies: v. 1-2 I.L.R. East Punjab series; v. 3-4 I.L.R. Punjab series but subtitle ... East Punjab; v. 5-20 correctly subtitled; v. 20 pt. 1 I.L.R. Punjab and Haryana series. Appeals to Federal Court and Privy Council cease after v. 3, to Supreme Court, India for v. 4, 5.

1216. Johnstone, Sir D.C. Reprinted selections from reports on civil cases in the Punjab record, 1866-1900. Lahore, 1915. 3 v.

1217. Lahore law journal [containing decisions of the High Court at Lahore], 1919-30. Lahore, 1919-30. 12 v.

1218. Lahore law times [containing decisions of the High Court], 1922- . Chandigarh, Law Times Press, 1922- . 61 v.

Subtitle: v. 26-29 (East Punjab section); v. 30-32 [Punjab (India) Section]. v. 1-29 published Lahore; v. 30-33 published Simla.

1219. Punjab law journal [containing decisions of the High Court of Financial Commissioner], 1957- . Chandigarh, Punjab Law Journal, 1957- . 18 v.

1220. Punjab law reporter [containing cases determined by the Lahore High Court], 1900- . Lahore, Punjab Law Reporter, 1900- . 84 v.

From 1922 included Jammu and Kashmir High Court rulings. 1935-47 in a separate section. Also 4 supplementary vols. 1900-16.

1221. Punjab record, or reference book for civil officers, 1866-1919. [Lahore?], 1866-1919. 54 v.

Issued in two parts p.a., part A containing civil judgments. Details of a collateral reprint given in no. 985.

1222. Punjab weekly reporter [containing cases decided in the Lahore High Court], 1905-23. 1906-23. 19 v.

1912-15 includes Rulings of the Judicial Commissioners, N.W. Frontier Province.

SUBJECT REPORTS

Criminal Law

1223. Broadway, A.B. and Danson, A.L. Reprints of the criminal rulings of the Chief Court of the Punjab, 1866-1919. Lahore, 1911-[20]. 4 v.

Reprinted from the Punjab Record.

Revenue Law

1224. Ashraf, K.M. Revenue decisions of the Punjab, 1900-50. Lahore, n.d. 2 v.

1225. Lahore law times revenue rulings, 1914-31. Lahore, 1914-31. 1 v.

Previous ed.: 1914-20.

RAJASTHAN STATE

See also the following series of no. 977: (Ajmer) 1946-56; (Rajasthan) 1950-

1226. Ajmer-Merwara law journal [containing decisions of the Court of the Judicial Commissioner], 1926-56. Ajmer, 1927-56. 30 v.

1227. Dholpur High Court decisions, 1940. [Dholpur], c. 1941. 1 v.

Now spelt Dhaulpar.

1228. Indian law reports: Rajasthan series [containing cases decided by the High Court of Rajasthan at Jaipur and the Supreme Court of India on appeal], 1951- . Jodhpur, Govt. of Rajasthan, 1951. 30 v.

1229. Marwar law reports [containing decisions of the Court of the Judicial Commissioner], 1930-48. Jodhpur, 1930-48. c.18 v.

1230. Rajasthan law weekly [containing decisions of the High Court of Rajasthan and the Supreme Court on appeal], 1950- . Jodhpur, Rajasthan Law Weekly, 1950- . 33 v.

SIND

For reports starting after August 1947 **see** Pakistan

See also the following series of no. 977: (Sind) 1914-50

1231. Hoonahan, W.R. Reports of the decisions of the Suddur Court of Sindh, 1867-71. Kurrachee, 1870-71. 2 v.

1232. Indian law reports: Karachi series, containing cases determined by the Court of Judicial Commissioner of Sind, by the Federal Court of India and on appeal from all High Courts of British India by the Judicial Committee of the Privy Council, 1939-47. Karachi, 1939-47. 72 v.

Continued by: Law reports. Karachi series. Title varies: 1947, pts. 7, 8 [i.e. after Partition] called Law reports. Karachi series but generally bound with the rest of the 1947 vol.

1233. Leggett, E. Reports of cases decided in the Sudder Court of Sindt by R. West, 1872-73. Kurrachee, 1873. 1 v.

1234. Printed judgments in the Sadar Court of the Province of Sind, 1881-84. Sind, 1885? 2 v.

v. 1 edited H.M. Birdwood; v. 2 edited E.T. Candy.

1235. Selected decisions of the Sind Sadar Court relating to the local laws and customs of the Province of Sind, 1866-1906. Karachi, 1909-10. 2 v.

1236. Sind law reporter [containing decisions of the Judicial Commissioners Court], 1907-38. Karachi?, 1907-38. 32 v.

1237. Sind Sadar Court reports, being the reports of principal civil and criminal cases determined by the Sadar Court of Sindh, 1897-99. Kurachee, 1900. 3 v. in 1.

v. 1-2 edited V. Nihalsing; v. 3 edited N. Gidumal.

TAMIL NADU

See also the following series of no. 977: (Madras) 1914- **and** Madras series of nos. 987, 988, 991, 1018.

1238. Aiyar, A.S.S. and T.S.S. Aiyar. Privy Council decisions and Full Bench decisions, 1930-34. Madras, 1930-34. 5 v.

1239. Chetty, S.V. Rulings of the Court of Sudder Adalut contained in the decisions passed by them, 1850-62. Madras, 1858-65. 2 v.

1240. Decisions of Zillah courts, 1851-55. Madras, n.d. 2 v.

See also note under no. 1091.

1241. Decrees in appeal suits determined in the Court of Sadar Adalut, 1805-47. Madras, 1843-53. 2 v.

1242. No entry.

1234. No entry.

1244. Indian jurist (Madras) [containing cases decided in the Madras High Court], 1877-83. Madras, 1877-83. 7 v.

Continued by: Indian jurist (Madras) n.s. Details of a collateral reprint given in no. 985.

1245. Indian jurist (Madras): new series [containing cases decided in the Madras High Court], 1884-93. Madras, 1884-93. 10 v.

Continuation of: Indian jurist (Madras). Details of a collateral reprint given in no. 985.

1246. Indian law reports: Madras series, containing cases determined by the High Court at Madras and by the Judicial Committee of the Privy Council on appeal, 1876-78- . Madras, Government of Tamil Nadu, 1876- . 129 v.

1876-1900 reprinted: Indian decisions (n.s.), Madras, 1912-22; see also nos. 985, 994, 1011, 1015, 1016, 1018.

P.C. appeals ceased in 1949.

1247. Law weekly [containing decisions of the Madras High Court and of the Supreme Court of India on appeal], 1914- . Madras, Law Weekly, 1914- . 95 v.

1248. The lawyer [containing cases decided in the Madras High Court and by the Supreme Court of India on appeal], 1956- . Madras, Indian Law Institute, Tamil Nadu Branch, 1956- . 27 v.

1249. Madras High Court reports. Reports of cases decided in the High Court of Madras, 1862/63-1874/75. Madras, 1864-75. 8 v.

1250. Madras jurist [containing reports of High Court decisions], 1866-76. Madras, 1866-76. 11 v.

Details of a collateral reprint given in no. 985.

1251. Madras law journal reports [containing cases determined by the High Court and by the Supreme Court on appeal], 1891- . Madras, Madras Law Journal, 1891- . 163 v.

Title varies: v. 1 Madras law journal. 1900-15 some vols. have unusual publication dates due to misprints, late issues, etc. Details of collateral reprint given in no. 985.

1252. Madras law reporter, reports of cases decided in the High Court of Madras, 1876-77. Madras, 1876-77. 1 v.

Details of a collateral reprint given in no. 985.

1253. Madras law times [containing reports of High Court decisions], 1906-28. Madras, 1906-28. 38 v.

Title varies: v. 40 - Indian law times. v. 36-37 never issued.

1254. Madras weekly notes [of cases determined by the High Court], 1910-66. Madras, 1910-66. 56 v.

1255. [Strange, T.A.], Notes of cases determined in the Court of the Recorder and in the Supreme Court of Judicature at Madras, 1798-1816. Madras, 1816-27. 2 v.

Reprinted: Indian cases (o.s.), Madras, 1911-16.

Another ed. 1816.

1256. Sudder Udalat decisions, 1849-62. [Madras], 1858-65. 14 v.

SUBJECT REPORTS

Criminal Law

1257. Arbuthnot, A.J. Select reports of criminal cases determined in the Court of Foujdaree Udalat, 1826-50. Madras, 1851. 1 v.

Reprinted: 1880.

1258. Madras criminal cases [decided by the High Court of Madras], 1924-42. Madras, 1924-42. 19 v.

1259. Madras law journal (criminal) [containing decisions of the Madras High Court], 1957- . Madras, Madras Law Journal, 1957- . 25 v.

Revenue Law

1260. Tatachariar, N.R.K. The decisions of the Board of Revenue under the Madras Estates Act, 1910-18. Mylapore, 1913-19. 2 v.

UTTAR PRADESH

Until August 1947 known as the United Provinces of Agra and Oudh.

See also the following series of no. 977: (Oudh) 1914-49; (Allahabad) 1914- **and** Allahabad series of nos. 987, 988, 991, 1018

1261. [Agra High Court reports] Reports of the High Court of Judicature [at Agra] for the North-Western Provinces, June 1866-June 1868. Agra, 1867-68. 3 v.

Rajkot, 1893. Three other reprints, dates wanting.

1262. Allahabad and Oudh select law reports [of cases determined in the Allahabad High Court], 1942-43. Allahabad, [1942-43], 1 v.

1263. Allahabad law journal [containing cases decided by the Allahabad High Court and the Supreme Court, India (and earlier courts) on appeal therefrom], 1904- . Nagpur, All India Reporter, 1904- . 80 v.

1264. Allahabad law reporter [containing cases decided in the High Court of Allahabad], 1919- . Allahabad, 1919- . 15 v. to 1935.

1265. Allahabad law reports [of cases decided in the Allahabad High Court], 1933-38. Allahabad, [?1933-38]. 5 v.

1266. Allahabad law reports [of cases determined in the High Court at Allahabad and by the Supreme Court of India on appeal], 1975- . Allahabad, Law Publishing House, 1975- . 8 v.

1267. Allahabad law times [containing reports of cases decided in the Allahabad High Court], 1923- . Allahabad, Allahabad Law Times, 1923- . 46 v.

1268. Allahabad law weekly [containing reports of cases decided in the Allahabad High Court and by the Supreme Court, India on appeal], 1933- . Allahabad, 1933- . 12 v. to 1945.

1269. Allahabad weekly cases [Reports of cases decided in the Allahabad High Court], 1975- . Allahabad, Kharbanda Publications, 1975- . 8 v.

1270. Allahabad weekly notes [of cases decided in the Allahabad High Court], 1881-1908. Allahabad, 1881-1908. 28 v.

1881-1900 reprinted: Indian decisions (n.s.), Madras, 1912-22.

Two supplementary vols. issued 1912-14.

1271. Allahabad weekly reporter [containing cases decided in the Allahabad High Court], 1933-47. Allahabad, 1933-47. 15 v.

1272. Decisions of the Sudder Dewanny Adawlut, North-Western Provinces, recorded in English, 1st July 1843-30th April 1846. Agra, 1854. 1 v.

1273. Decisions of the Sudder Dewanny Adawlut, North-Western Provinces, recorded in English, 1846-61. Agra, [1846-61]. 16 v.

1274. Indian law reports: Allahabad series. Cases determined by the High Court of Allahabad and by the Judicial Committee of the Privy Council on appeal, 1876/78- . Calcutta and Allahabad, Superintendent of Printing and Stationery, 1876- . 136 v.

Reprinted: Indian decisions (n.s.), Madras, 1912-22; see also nos. 985, 994, 1011, 1015, 1016, 1018.

P.C. appeals ceased 1949 and Supreme Court appeals substituted.

1275. Indian law reports: Lucknow series, containing cases determined by the Chief Court of Oudh and by the Judicial Committee of the Privy Council on appeal, 1926-48. Allahabad, 1926-48. 23 v.

1276. Lucknow cases [decided in the Chief Court of Oudh], 1926. Lucknow, 1927. 1 v.

A supplement to Oudh weekly notes.

1277. Oudh and Agra law reporter [containing decisions of the Chief Court of Oudh], 1910-25. [Lucknow], [1910-25]. 11 v.

1278. Oudh appeals [cases determined on appeal by the Chief Court of Oudh], 1938-? Lucknow? 1938-? 10 v. to 1945.

1279. Oudh cases, containing cases decided by the Court of the Judicial Commission of Oudh, 1889-1926. Lucknow, 1903-27. 29 v.

1280. Oudh law journal [containing cases decided by the Chief Court of Oudh], 1914-26. Lucknow, 1914-26. 13 v.

1281. Oudh law reports [of cases determined by the Chief Court of Oudh], 1933-46. Lucknow, 1933-46. 8 v.

1282. Oudh select cases [decided by the Court of Judicial Commission, Oudh], 1859-96. Lucknow, 1915. 1 v.

1283. Oudh weekly notes [of cases decided in the Chief Court of Oudh], 1924-48. Lucknow, 1924-48. 25 v.

1284. Rafique, M., and Jackson, G.H. Privy Council decisions on appeals from the Oudh High Court, 1864-1913. Lucknow, 1913. 1 v.

Details of collateral reprint given in no. 985.

1285. Reports of cases heard and determined in the High Court, North-Western Provinces, 1869-75. Allahabad, 1873-76. 7 v.

Reprinted: Rajkot, 1892, 1908.

1286. Selected cases of the Sudder Dewanny Adawlut, North-Western Provinces, recorded in English, 1850-57. Calcutta, 1860-61. 2 v.

1287. United Provinces law reporter [containing decisions of the High Court of Oudh], 1919-22. [Lucknow], [1919-22]. 4 v.

1288. Young, Sir D. Notable judgments of Judge Young, edited by B. Behari and S. Ram, 1929-34. Sapru, 1934. 1 v.

SUBJECT REPORTS

Criminal Law

1289. Allahabad criminal cases and reports, 1928- . Allahabad, Law Publishing House, 1928- . 54 v.

1290. Criminal reports [of cases determined in the High Court, Allahabad], 1937- . [?Allahabad], 1937- .

1291. Criminal rulings of the Allahabad High Court, 1904-34. Allahabad, 1936. 2 v.

1292. Decisions of the Nizam Adawlut, North-Western Provinces, 1851-60. Agra, 1852-61? 9 v.

1293. Oudh criminal cases [decided by the Oudh High Court], 1874-1912. Lucknow, 1929. 1 v.

Rent

1294. Jacob, R.G.F. A reprint of the Rent Act rulings of the Judicial Commissioner of Oudh, 1871-95. Lucknow, 1900. 1 v.

1295. Uttar Pradesh rent control cases [determined in the High Court of Allahabad], 1976- . Allahabad, Dandewal Publishing House, 1976- . 9 v.

Revenue Law

1296. Agnihotri, S.K. Selected revenue decisions [decided upon appeal by the High Court], 1927-36. Allahabad, 1936. 1 v.

1297. Lal, R.N. Selected decisions of the Board of Revenue of the United Provinces of Agra and Oudh, 1934-1944. Allahabad, 1945. 1 v.

1298. Revenue and criminal law journal (of Aligarh) [containing cases decided by the Board of Revenue and by the High Court on appeal], 1915-26. Aligarh, 1915-26. 12 v.

1299. Revenue decisions being full reports of cases decided by the Board of Revenue, Allahabad High Court and Oudh High Court, 1883-? Lucknow, Indian Law Houses, 1928-? 19 v.

1300. Revenue reports [decided by the Board of Revenue], 1880-1913. n.d. 1 v. In Urdu.

1301. Revenue reports [of cases decided in the Allahabad High Court], 1938-40. [Allahabad], c.1945. 3 v.

Reprinted from Allahabad weekly reporter.

1302. Saksena, V.N. Unpublished decisions of the Board of Revenue, 1902-39. Allahabad, 1902-39. 20 v.

1303. Sastry, L.S. Selected decisions of the Board of Revenue of the United Provinces of Agra and Oudh, 1936-41. Allahabad, 1941. 1 v.

1304. Sastry, S.S. and Sinha, K.K. Selected decisions of the Board of Revenue of the United Provinces of Agra and Oudh, 1882-1927. Allahabad, 1928. 1 v.

Previous eds.: 1907, 1913, 1920.

1305. Srivastava, G.S. Selected decisions of the Board of Revenue of the United Provinces of Agra and Oudh, 1933-45. Lucknow, 1946? 1 v.

WEST BENGAL

For publications before 1947 **see** Bengal

See also the following series of no. 977: (Calcutta) 1914-

1306. Calcutta law journal, 1905- . Calcutta, Calcutta Law Journal, 1905- . 127 v.

1307. Calcutta weekly notes [containing decisions of the Calcutta High Court], 1896/97- . Calcutta, Calcutta Weekly Notes, 1896- . 86 v.

Details of a collateral reprint given in no. 985.

1308. Indian law reports: Calcutta series, containing cases determined by the High Court at Calcutta and by the Judicial Committee of the Privy Council on appeal, 1875- . Calcutta, West Bengal Government Press, 1876- . 114 v.

1875-1900 reprinted: Indian decisions (n.s.), Madras, 1912-22; see also nos. 985, 994, 1011, 1015, 1016, 1018.

Privy Council appeals ceased in 1949. Federal Court of India appeals included from 1946.

IRELAND

From the Union Act of 1801 to 1922, the whole of Ireland was part of the United Kingdom. In 1949 the Republic of Ireland left the Commonwealth leaving Northern Ireland as part of the United Kingdom.

See also Northern Ireland for reports from 1922 **and** nos. 316, 392, 531, 532, 687, 747, 758, 760, 860

1309. Crawford, G. and Dix, E.S. Abridged notes of cases argued and determined in the several courts of law and equity of Ireland. With some decisions at Nisi Prius and on the circuits, 1837-38. Dublin, 1939. 1 v.

Microfilm: Dobbs Ferry, Oceana.

1310. [Glascock's reports on all the courts] Glascock, W. Miscellaneous reports of cases argued and determined in the Courts of King's Bench, Common Pleas, & Exchequer, in Ireland, 1831-32. Dublin, 1832, 1 v.

Microfilm: Dobbs Ferry, Oceana.

v. 1 only published.

1311. Irish Chancery reports, being a series of reports of cases argued and determined in the High Court of Chancery and the Rolls Court, in Ireland, 1850-66. Dublin, 1852-67. 17 v.

Reprinted: Abingdon, Professional Books, 1976; Microfilm: Dobbs Ferry, Oceana.

Subtitle varies in v. 6-8.

1312. Irish common law reports. Reports of cases argued and determined in the Courts of Queen's Bench, Common Pleas, Exchequer, Exchequer Chamber, and Court of Criminal Appeal, 1849-66. Dublin, 1852-67. 17 v.

Reprinted: Abingdon, Professional Books, 1976; Microfilm: Dobbs Ferry, Oceana.

1313. Irish equity reports (third series of 'The law recorder'), particularly of points of practice, argued and determined in the High Court of Chancery, the Rolls Court, and the Equity Exchequer, in Ireland, 1838-50. Dublin, 1838-52. 13 v.

Reprinted: Abingdon, Professional Books, 1976; Microfilm: Dobbs Ferry, Oceana.

Title varies: v. 2- no mention of The law recorder.

1314. Irish jurist reports. Containing reports of cases decided in the several courts of equity and common law [with a digest of the cases reported in the first ten vols. of the Irish law reports, in the Jurist for the year ending Michaelmas, 1894; and an index to the cases in equity, reported in the Jurist during the same period], 1849-55. Dublin, 1849-55. 7 v.

Issued with the Irish jurist, separately paged.

1315. Irish jurist reports. New series, 1855-66. Dublin, 1856-66. 11 v.

v. 1 new series also called Volume VIII. Issued with the Irish jurist, New series, separately paged.

1316. The Irish jurist reports of cases decided by the Supreme Court of Justice, the Court of Criminal Appeal, the High Court of Justice (including the Court of the Irish Land Commission), the Chief Justice, and the Circuit Court of justice, of the Irish Free State and by the Court of Appeal (and on appeal thereon from the House of Lords), the Court of Criminal Appeal, the several divisions of the High Court of Justice and the Lord Chief Justice, of Northern Ireland, 1933-66. Dublin, 1935-65. 31 v.

Title varies: v. 2-3 The Irish jurist reports of cases heard and decided by the several courts of Justice in the Irish Free State and in Northern Ireland; v. 4 - The Irish jurist reports of cases heard and decided by the several courts of justice of Ireland. Issued with The Irish jurist but separately paginated.

1317. Irish law reports (third series of 'The law recorder'), particularly points of practice, argued and determined in the Courts of Queen's Bench, Common Pleas, and Exchequer, in Ireland, 1838-50. Dublin, 1839-52. 13 v.

Reprinted: Abingdon, Professional Books, 1976; Microfilm: Dobbs Ferry, Oceana.

Data base: LEXIS 1950- .

Title varies: v. 2- no mention of The law recorder.

1318. Irish law reports monthly, 1980- . Dublin, Round Hall Press, 1981- . 2 v.

Data base: LEXIS 1981- .

Unnumbered back vols. also issued covering earlier unreported cases.

1319. Irish law times reports, 1867-1980. Dublin, 1867-1980. 110 v.

Data base: LEXIS 1950-80.

Published as part of Irish law times and solicitors journal. From v. 4 paginated separately. Subtitle varies.

1320. The Irish petty sessions journal. A monthly paper for magistrates, clerks of petty sessions, solicitors and the Royal Irish Constabulary, 1893-1901. Pettigo, 1893-1901. 8 v.

Microfilm: Dobbs Ferry, Oceana.

1321. The Irish reports, published under the control of the Incorporated Council of Law Reporting for Ireland: containing reports of cases argued and determined in the Court of Appeal, the High Court of Justice, the Court of Bankruptcy, in Ireland, and the Irish Land Commission, 1894- . Dublin, The Incorporated Council of Law Reporting for Ireland, 1894- . 121 v.

Data base: LEXIS 1950- .

Reprinted: as Irish law reports. Annotated reprint, 1894-1912. Edinburgh and London, 1913-15; 1894-1974. Abingdon, Professional Books, 1976.

Subtitle and courts covered vary.

1322. [Irish reports. Common law] The Irish reports, published under the control of the Council of Law Reporting in Ireland: containing reports of cases argued and determined in the superior courts in Ireland. Common law series, 1866-78. Dublin, 1867-78. 11 v.

Reprinted: Abingdon, Professional Books, 1976; Microfilm: Dobbs Ferry, Oceana.

1323. Irish weekly reports, 1895-1902. Dublin, 1895-1902. 8 v.

Microfilm: Dobbs Ferry, Oceana.

Title varies: v. 6 Irish weekly law reports and journal; v. 7-8 Irish law journal and reports. v. 7-8 also called v. 1-2 new series. v. 8; pts. 1-3 only published.

1324. The law recorder, containing reports of cases and proceedings in the courts of law and equity, etc. at Dublin and elsewhere, 1827-32. Dublin, 1928-32. 4 v.

Microfilm: Dobbs Ferry, Oceana.

1325. The law recorder, containing reports of select cases and decisions, chiefly on points of practice, in the courts of equity and common law, 1833-38. Dublin, [1833-38]. 6 v.

Microfilm: Dobbs Ferry, Oceana.

v. 1 also called v. 5 new series.

1326. [Law reports, Ireland, (4th series)] The law reports (Ireland), published under the control of the Council of Law Reporting in Ireland: containing reports of cases argued and determined in the Court of Appeal, the High Court of Justice and the Court of Bankruptcy, in Ireland, 1873-93. Dublin, 1879-93. 32 v.

Microfilm: Dobbs Ferry, Oceana.

1327. Legal reporter, 1840-43. Dublin, 1840-43. 3 v.

In v. 3 nos. 1-26 only issued.

1328. The new Irish jurist and local government review. Reports. Being a complete guide to the case law in the Irish courts, 1901-05. Dublin, 1901-05. 5 v.

Microfilm: Dobbs Ferry, Oceana.

Subtitle varies: v. 2 - Reports of cases and decisions in all the Irish courts.

1329. No Entry.

1330. Student law reporter: extracted from Irish law reports monthly, 1982- . Dublin, Round Hall Press, 1983- . 1 v.

SPECIFIC COURTS

Appeals

1331. [Ridgeway's appeal cases] Ridgeway, W. Reports of cases upon appeals and writs of error in the High Court of Parliament in Ireland since the restoration of the appellate jurisdiction, 1784-96. Dublin, 1795-98. 3 v.

Microfilm: Dobbs Ferry, Oceana.

Chancery

1332. Ball, T. and Beatty, F. Reports of cases argued and determined in the High Court of Chancery in Ireland, during the time of Lord Chancellor Manners. 2nd ed., 1807-14. London, 1823-24. 2 v.

Microfilm: Dobbs Ferry, Oceana.

Other eds.: London, 1813-24; Dublin, 1821-24; Philadelphia 1839 (in 1 v.).

1333. Beatty, F. Reports of cases argued and determined in the High Court of Chancery in Ireland, during the time of Lord Chancellor Hart, with a few in the time of Lord Chancellor Manners, 1813-30. Dublin, 1847. 1 v.

Microfilm: Dobbs Ferry, Oceana.

1334. Connor, H. and Lawson, J.A. Reports of cases argued and determined in the High Court of Chancery, during the time of Lord Chancellor Sugden, 1841-43. Dublin, 1824-44. 2 v.

Microfilm: Dobbs Ferry, Oceana.

1335. Drury, W.B. Reports of cases argued and determined in the High Court of Chancery, during the time of Lord Chancellor Sugden, 1843-44. Dublin, 1851. 1 v.

Microfilm: Dobbs Ferry, Oceana.

1336. Drury, W.B. Select cases argued and determined in the High Court of Chancery, during the time of Lord Chancellor Napier, 1858-59. Dublin, 1860. 1 v.

Microfilm: Dobbs Ferry, Oceana.

1337. Drury, W.B. and Walsh, F.W. Reports of cases argued and determined in the High Court of Chancery, during the time of Lord Chancellor Plunket, 1837-41. Dublin, 1839-42. 2 v.

Microfilm: Dobbs Ferry, Oceana.

1338. Drury, W.B. and Warren, R.R. Reports of cases argued and determined in the High Court of Chancery during the time of Lord Chancellor Sugden, 1841-43. Dublin, 1843-44. 4 v.

Microfilm: Dobbs Ferry, Oceana.

1338A. Finlay, J. Digest and index of all the Irish reported cases in law and equity ... and also of the reported cases in ecclestiastical and criminal law, together with a variety of original cases, from authentic sources, containing many of the judgments of Lord Lifford, 1769-71. Dublin 1830.

The Digest section contains cases from 1615-1829.

1339. Howard, G.E. The rules and practice of the High Court of Chancery in Ireland, with the several statutes relative thereto. As also, several adjudged cases thereon, 1619-1771. Dublin, 1772. 1 v.

Microfilm: Dobbs Ferry, Oceana.

Supplement, 1775 including cases decided in 1775.

1340. [Irish reports. Equity series] The Irish reports, published under the control of the Council of Law Reporting in Ireland: containing reports of cases argued and determined in the superior courts in Ireland. Equity series, 1866-78. Dublin, 1867-78. 11 v.

Reprinted: Abingdon, Professional Books, 1976. Microfilm: Dobbs Ferry, Oceana.

1341. Jones, T. and La Touche, E.D. Reports of cases argued and determined in the High Court of Chancery during the time of Lord Chancellor Sugden, 1844-46. Dublin, 1846-49. 3 v.

Microfilm: Dobbs Ferry, Oceana.

1342. Lloyd, B.C. and Goold, F. Reports of cases argued and determined in the High Court of Chancery in Ireland, during the time of Lord Chancellor Sugden, 1835. London, Dublin, 1836. 1 v.

Reprinted: Albany, N.Y., 1865; Microfilm: Dobbs Ferry, Oceana.

1343. Lloyd, B.C. and Goold, F. A selection of cases argued and determined in the High Court of Chancery in Ireland, during the time of Lord Chancellor Plunket, 1834-36. Dublin, 1839. 1 v.

Microfilm: Dobbs Ferry, Oceana.

1344. Molloy, P. Reports of cases argued and determined in the High Court of Chancery in Ireland, during the time of Lord Chancellor Hart, 1827-31. Dublin; London, 1832. 3 v.

v. 3: pt. 1 only published.

1345. Schoales, J. and Lefroy, T. Reports of cases argued and determined in the High Court of Chancery, in Ireland, during the time of Lord Redesdale, 1802-07. London; Dublin, 1806-10. 2 v.

Reprinted: New York, 1808-11; London & Dublin, 1806-21. Microfilm: Dobbs Ferry, Oceana.

1346. [Wallis' Chancery] Wallis, J. and Lyne, J. Reports of select cases argued and determined in the High Court of Chancery in Ireland, principally in the time of Lord Lifford; together with some cases determined in the other superior courts during the same period. Edited from the original notes of the late John Wallis, Esq., K.C. by James Lyne, Esq. Barrister-at-Law, 1766-91. Dublin, 1839. 1 v.

Microfilm: Dobbs Ferry, Oceana.

Circuit Cases

1347. [Cases on the six circuits] Reports of cases argued and determined on six circuits in Ireland: taken during the assizes, 1841-43. Dublin, 1843. 1 v.

Microfilm: Dobbs Ferry, Oceana.

Title includes the names of the 12 reporters.

1348. Crawford, G. and Dix, E.S. Reports of cases argued and ruled on the circuits, in Ireland, together with cases decided at the Nisi Prius sittings, and the courts of criminal jurisdiction at Dublin, 1839-46. Dublin, 1841-47. 3 v.

Microfilm: Dobbs Ferry, Oceana.

1349. Rules and orders of the common law judges, and reserved cases, 1860-64. Dublin, 1865.

Microfilm: Dobbs Ferry, Oceana.

Common Pleas

1350. Smythe, H. Reports of cases argued and determined in the Courts of Common Pleas and Exchequer Chamber in Ireland, 1839-40. Dublin, 1840. 1 v.

Microfilm: Dobbs Ferry, Oceana.

v. 1 only published.

Exchequer

1351. Hayes, E. Reports of cases argued and determined in the Court of Exchequer in Ireland, 1817, 1830-32. Dublin, 1837. 1 v.

Microfilm: Dobbs Ferry, Oceana.

Only one case from 1817.

1352. Hayes, E. and Jones, T. Reports of cases argued and determined in the Court of Exchequer, in Ireland, 1832-34. Dublin, 1843. 1 v.

Microfilm: Dobbs Ferry, Oceana.

1353. Howard, G.E. A treatise on the rules and practice of the equity side of the Exchequer in Ireland; ... Also several adjudged cases on the practice in Courts of Equity, both in England and Ireland, ... 1651?-1759. Dublin, 1760. 2 v.

2nd ed.: Dublin, 1793-92? 2 v. in 1.

1354. Jones, T. Reports of cases argued and determined in the Court of Exchequer, in Ireland, 1834-38. Dublin, 1838-47. 2 v.

Microfilm: Dobbs Ferry, Oceana.

Continuation of: Jones and Carey. Reports in Exchequer.

1355. Jones, T. and Carey, H. Reports of cases argued and determined in the Court of Exchequer in Ireland, 1838-39. Dublin, 1840. 1 v.

Microfilm: Dobbs Ferry, Oceana.

Continuation of: Jones. Reports in Exchequer.

1356. Longfield, R. and Townsend, J.F. Reports of cases argued and determined in the Court of Exchequer in Ireland, 1841-42. Dublin, 1843. 1 v.

Microfilm: Dobbs Ferry, Oceana.

King's/Queen's Bench

1357. Alcock, J.C. and Napier, J. Reports of cases argued and determined in the Courts of King's Bench and Exchequer Chamber in Ireland, 1831-33. Dublin, 1834. 1 v.

Microfilm: Dobbs Ferry, Oceana.

1358. Batty, E. Reports of cases argued and determined in the Court of King's Bench in Ireland, 1825-26. Dublin, 1828. 1 v.

Microfilm: Dobbs Ferry, Oceana.

1359. Cooke, J.R. and Alcock, J.C. Reports of cases argued and determined in the court of King's Bench in Ireland, 1833-34. Dublin, 1835. 1 v.

Microfilm: Dobbs Ferry, Oceana.

Pt. 1 only published.

1360. [Davies' King's Bench] Davies, Sir J. A report of cases and matters in law, resolved and adjudged in the King's Courts in Ireland, collected and digested by Sir John Davies, Knight ... Now first translated into English, [1604-1612]. Dublin, 1762. 1 v.

Reprinted: English reports; Microfilm: Dobbs Ferry, Oceana.

Previous eds.: (in Anglo French): Dublin, 1615; London 1628; London, 1674; Dublin, 1677.

1361. Fox, M.C. and Smith, T.B.C. Reports of cases argued and determined in the Court of King's Bench and Court of Error, 1822-24. Dublin, 1825. 2 v.

Microfilm: Dobbs Ferry, Oceana.

1362. Hudson, W.E. and Brooke, J. Reports of cases argued and determined in the Courts of King's Bench and Exchequer Chamber in Ireland, 1827-31. Dublin, 1829-46. 2 v.

Microfilm: Dobbs Ferry, Oceana.

1363. Jebb, N. and Bourke, R. Reports of cases argued and determined in the Court of Queen's Bench, in Ireland, 1841-42. Dublin, 1843.

Microfilm: Dobbs Ferry, Oceana.

1364. Jebb, R. and Symes, A.R. Reports of cases argued and determined in the courts of Queen's Bench and Exchequer Chamber in Ireland, with tables of the names of the cases and the principal matters, 1838-41. Dublin; London, 1840-42. 2 v.

Microfilm: Dobbs Ferry, Oceana.

1365. Ridgeway, W., Lapp, W. and Schoales, J. Irish term reports; or, reports of cases determined in the King's Courts, Dublin, 1793-95. Dublin, 1796. 1 v.

Microfilm: Dobbs Ferry, Oceana.

v. 1 only published.

1366. Smith, T.B.C. and Batty, E. Reports of cases argued and determined in the Court of King's Bench in Ireland, 1824-25. Dublin, 1830. 1 v.

Microfilm: Dobbs Ferry, Oceana.

1367. [Vernon and Scriven's King's Bench] Vernon, G.W. and Scriven, J.B. Irish reports; or, reports of cases determined in the King's Courts, Dublin; with select cases in the House of Lords in Ireland, 1786-88. Dublin, 1790. 1 v.

Microfilm: Dobbs Ferry, Oceana.

v. 1 only published.

Nisi Prius

1368. Armstrong, R., Macartney, J. and Ogle, J.C. Reports of cases, civil and criminal, argued and determined at Nisi Prius and the Commission in Dublin, respectively, 1840-42. Dublin, 1843. 1 v.

Microfilm: Dobbs Ferry, Oceana.

1369. Blackham, J., Dundas, W.J. and Osborne, R.W. Reports of practice and Nisi Prius cases (including registry and civil bill appeals) decided in the Superior Courts in Dublin, 1846-48. Dublin, 1849. 1 v.

Microfilm: Dobbs Ferry, Oceana.

1370. Select cases at Nisi Prius. Reports of trials in Dublin in Easter term and the ensuing sittings: to be continued at succeeding terms, assizes, etc. by different reporters, 1802. Dublin, 1802. 1 v.

Pt. 1 only published.

Rolls Court

1371. Flanagan, S.W. and Kelly, C. Reports of cases in Chancery, argued and determined in the Rolls Court, during the time of the Right Hon. Sir Michael O'Loghlen, Bart., Master of the Rolls, 1840-42. Dublin, 1843. 1 v.

Microfilm: Dobbs Ferry, Oceana.

1372. Hogan, W. Reports of cases argued and determined in the Rolls Court in Ireland, during the time of the Right Hon. Sir William McMahon, Bart., Master of the Rolls, 1816-34. Dublin, 1828-38. 2 v.

Microfilm: Dobbs Ferry, Oceana.

1373. Sausse, M.R. and Scully, V. Reports of cases in Chancery argued and determined in the Rolls Court during the time of the Rt. Hon. Sir Michael O'Loghlen, Bart., Master of the Rolls; and the case of Ogle v. Ogle, decided in the Court of Exchequer and Exchequer Chamber, 1837-40. Dublin, 1841. 1 v.

Microfilm: Dobbs Ferry, Oceana.

SUBJECT REPORTS

Criminal Law

1374. Armstrong, J.S. A report of trials under a Special Commission for the County of Clare. Held at Ennis, 1848. Dublin, 1848. 1 v.

1375. Armstrong, J.S. A report of trials under a Special Commission for the County of Limerick. Held at Limerick, 1848. Dublin, 1848. 1 v.

1376. Brett, J.P. Grand Jury law: decisions on the Grand Jury Act (6 & 7 Will. IV. c.116) and Acts amending same: with recent statutes. Laws and practice as to obtaining compensation for maiming, malicious injuries, and malicious injuries (unlawful assemblies): and rights of taking materials ... Notes of all decisions reported since 1884, with notes of numerous unreported decisions and judgments. 2nd ed., 1884-94. Dublin, 1895. 1 v.

Microfilm: Dobbs Ferry, Oceana.

1st ed.: Dublin 1894.

1377. Brewster, A. A report of seven trials at the Clonmel Summer Assizes of MDCCXXXIX, including those which arose out of the occurrences at Borrisokane, 1829. Dublin, 1830. 1 v.

Data base: LEXIS 1950-83.

1378. Chamney, W.G. 'The Fenian conspiracy'. Report of the trials of Thomas F. Burke and others, for high treason, and treason-felony at the Special Commission, Dublin, held at the Court House, Green Street, Dublin, commencing 8th April, 1867. Dublin, 1869. 1 v.

1379. Frewen, G.L. Judgements of the Court of Criminal Appeal, 1924/78- Dublin, Incorporated Council of Law Reporting for Ireland, 1983- . 1 v.

1379A. Harrington, T. Diary of coercion, being a list of the cases tried under the Criminal Law and Procedure Act (1887-89). Dublin, 1888-90. 3 pts.

1380. Jebb, R. Cases, chiefly relating to the criminal and presentment law, reserved for consideration and decided by the twelve judges of Ireland, 1822-40. Dublin, 1841. 1 v.

Reprinted: Philadelphia, 1842; Microfilm: Dobbs Ferry, Oceana.

1381. Judgements of the Superior Courts in Ireland and in cases under the Criminal Law and Procedure (Ireland) Act, 1887, and others, 1882-1903. Dublin, 1903. 1 v.

Microfilm: Dobbs Ferry, Oceana.

Previous eds.: 1889, 1890. Also known as: Judgements under the Criminal Law and Procedure (Ireland) Act.

1382. MacNevin, T. The leading state trials in Ireland, 1794-1803. Dublin, 1844. 1 v.

1383. Millin, S.S. A digest of the reported decisions of the superior courts relating to petty sessions in Ireland, 1875-98. Dublin, 1898. 1 v.

Microfilm: Dobbs Ferry, Oceana.

Contains 17 unreported decisions.

1384. Mongan, J. A report of trials before the Right Hon. The Lord Chief Justice and the Hon. Baron Sir Wm. C. Smith, Bart., at the Special Commission at Maryborough, 1832. Dublin, 1832. 1 v.

1385. Reports of proceedings of the Special Commission (1867), for the County and City of Cork, and the County and City of Limerick, in cases of high treason and treason felony, and of trials for treason felony, at the summer assizes of the same year, for the Counties of Clare and Kerry, 1867. Dublin, 1871. 1 v.

Also known as: Fenian trials.

1386. Ridgeway, W. A report of the proceedings in cases of high treason at a court of oyer and terminer, held at the new Sessions House, under a Special Commission, 1803. Dublin, 1803. 1 v.

1386A. Ridgeway, W. A report of the proceedings in cases of high treason at a Special Commission of oyer and terminer held in and for the County and City of Dublin, July 1798, 3rd edition. Dublin, 1798.

Contains the trials of H. and J. Sheares, J. M'Cann, M-W Byrne, O. Bond.

Ecclesiastical Law

1387. [Bernard's church cases] Bernard, W.L. The Irish Church Acts, 1869 & 1872 ... together with reports of leading cases ... , [4th ed.], 1870-75. Dublin, 1876. 1 v.

Microfilm: Dobbs Ferry, Oceana.

1st ed.: Dublin, London, 1871; 2nd ed. Dublin, London, 1871; 3rd ed. Dublin, London, 1873.

1388. Erck, J.C. An account of the ecclesiastical establishment subsisting in Ireland; as also an ecclesiastical register of the names of the dignitaries and parochial clergy, and of the parishes and their respective patrons ... with appendixes, containing amongst other things, several cases of 'quare impedit'. 1608-1825. Dublin, 1830. 1 v.

Previous eds.: did not contain cases. Also known as Erck's Ecclesiastical.

1388A. Howard, G.E. Several special cases on the laws against the further growth of popery in Ireland, 1720-73. Dublin, 1775.

Also known as: Howard's popery cases.

1389. Milward, C.R. Reports of cases argued and determined in the Court of Prerogative in Ireland, and in the Consistory Court of Dublin, during the time of the late Right Hon. John Radcliff, 1819-42. Dublin, 1847. 1 v.

Microfilm: Dobbs Ferry, Oceana.

Family Law

1390. Roberts, J. Divorce bills in the imperial parliament, 1816-1905. Dublin, 1906. 1 v.

Microfilm: Dobbs Ferry, Oceana.

Has a section containing abstracts of cases not published elsewhere.

1391. [Smythe and Bourke's marriage cases] Smythe, H. and Bourke, R. The Queen v. Milles, and the Queen v. Carroll. Report of two cases upon the marriage law of Ireland, argued and determined in the Court of Queen's Bench, in Ireland, 1842. Dublin, London, 1842.

Microfilm: Dobbs Ferry, Oceana.

Fisheries

1392. Conner, H.D. and Farren, E.C. The Fisheries (IR.) Acts 1842-1901 being the statutes relating to salmon, trout, pollan, eel, oyster, and other fisheries in Ireland, with notes of cases decided under the several statutes, 1842-1908. Dublin, 1908. 1 v.

Previous ed.: 1892.

1393. Fisheries Commission appeals, 1861-1906. Dublin, 1861-1906.

Individual cases paged separately.

Industrial Law

1394. Decisions of the Employment Appeals Tribunal under the Maternity Protection of Employees Act, 1981. Dublin, Employment Appeals Tribunal, 1981- .

Typescript.

1395. Decisions of the Employment Appeals Tribunal under the Minimum Notice and Terms of Employment Act, 1973. Dublin, Employment Appeals Tribunal, 1973- .

Typescript.

1396. Decisions of the Employment Appeals Tribunals under the Redundancy Payments Acts, 1967-69. 1967- . Dublin, Employment Appeals Tribunal, 1967- .

Typescript.

1397. Recommendations of the Labour Court, 1946- . Dublin, Labour Court, 1946- .

1398. Shillman, B. Irish workmen's compensation cases, 1934-38. Dublin; London, 1939. 1 v.

v. 1 only published.

1399. [Unfair dismissals cases] Decisions of the Employment Appeals Tribunal under the Unfair Dismissals Act, 1977. 1977- . Dublin, Employment Appeals Tribunal, 1977- .

Typescript. Important decisions for 1977-78 and for 1979 published by the Stationery Office, 1980-83.

Land Law

1400. Brunskill, G.F. Recent judicial decisions affecting the law of landlord and tenant. Reported for the Irish Land Agents Association, 1891-95. Dublin, [1892-95]. 6 v.

Microfilm: Dobbs Ferry, Oceana.

1401. [Donnell's land cases] Donnell, R. Reports of one hundred and ninety cases in the Irish Land courts; with preliminary tenant-right chapters. A new edition, greatly enlarged, of tenant-right chapters and reports, 1871-76. Dublin, 1876. 1 v.

Microfilm: Dobbs Ferry, Oceana.

Previous ed.: 1873. Also known as: Donnell's Land Act reports.

1402. Finlay, J. A treatise on the law of renewals in respect to leases for lives renewable for ever in Ireland, with the cases and decisions thereon, including an extensive report of the important and heretofore unpublished case of Fitzsimon v. Burton; also the cases in respect to the renewals of ecclesiastical leases in Ireland, 1722-1826. Dublin, 1829. 1 v.

1403. Four land cases reprinted from the Irish reports, at the request of the Irish Land Commission, by the Incorporated Council of Law Reporting for Ireland, 1898-99. Dublin, 1900. 1 v.

1404. Greer, E. Irish Land Acts: one hundred and ninety reports of leading cases decided in the House of Lords, the Supreme Court of Judicature, the Court for Land Cases Reserved, Courts of Assize, the Courts of the Irish Land Commission, County Courts, and Sub-Commissions, 1872-97. Dublin, 1897. 1 v.

Appendix ... containing sixty of the most recent decisions under the Land Law (Ireland) Act, 1896, 1897-98. Dublin, 1898.

1405. Hughes, H.S.J. Select cases in registration in Ireland with an appendix of statutes, rules, and order, 1894-1915. Dublin, 1916. 1 v.

1406. Irish land acts. Monthly law reports of leading cases. Edited by Edward Greer, 1897-1903. Dublin, 1899-1903. 5 v.

Microfilm: Dobbs Ferry, Oceana.

1407. The Irish land reports. This publication contains full and revised reports of all the important current cases bearing on the relation of landlord and tenant decided either by the Superior Courts, the Chief Land Commission, the County Courts, or the Sub-Commission Courts, 1895-1920. Dublin, 1897-1920. 25 v.

1408. Lyne, J. A treatise on leases for lives, renewable for ever, 1716-1833. Dublin, 1837. 1 v.

Second part of this work (paged in Roman numerals) contains cases only.

1409. MacCarthy, J.H. Leading cases in land purchase law, 1887-92. Dublin, 1892. 1 v.

Microfilm: Dobbs Ferry, Oceana.

1410. MacDevitt, E.O. Land cases: being a collection of decisions under the Irish Land Acts since the passing of the Land Law (Ireland) Act, 1887, with other cases now reported for the first time, and a general index, 1882-84. Dublin, 1884. 1 v.

Microfilm: Dobbs Ferry, Oceana.

1411. Maxwell, T.H. Irish land purchase cases 1904-1911 being a verbatim reprint of all cases dealing with land purchase reported in The Irish reports and in The Irish law times reports ... together with some cases heretofore unreported. Compiled for the Irish Land Commission, 1904-11. London, H.M.S.O., 1912. 1 v.

1412. Roche, C.R., Dillon, L. and Kehoe, D. Reports of cases decided by the Irish Land Commission, 1881-82. Dublin, 1882. 1 v.

Microfilm: Dobbs Ferry, Oceana.

At head of title: The Irish Land Commission reports.

Local Government

1413. Irish local government orders and legal decisions. This publication contains all statutes, orders, rules and regulations and all important legal decisions bearing on the subject of local government in Ireland, 1899-1920. Dublin, 1902-20. 17 v.

Edit. by H.M. Fitzgibbon and others.

Mercantile Law

See no. 827

Parliament

See no. 860.

Practice

See also no. 873

1414. Irish practice decisions, of the Supreme Court of Appeal, the High Court of Justice, the county courts, and the Recorder's courts, 1906-09. Dublin, 1909. 1 v.

1415. Reported cases on costs, 1867-91. Dublin, 1892. 1 v.

Microfilm: Dobbs Ferry, Oceana.

Registration Cases

1416. Alcock, J.C. Registry cases reserved for consideration and decided by the twelve Judges of Ireland, 1832-41. Dublin, 1837-41. 3 v.

Microfilm: Dobbs Ferry, Oceana.

1417. Cleary, A.P. Registration cases. Being a supplement to the franchises and the registration of parliamentary voters in Ireland, 1886-87. Dublin, 1887. 1 v.

Microfilm: Dobbs Ferry, Oceana.

A pamphlet containing two cases.

1418. Fitzgibbon, H.M. Irish registration appeal cases, 1894. Dublin, 1895. 1 v.

Microfilm: Dobbs Ferry, Oceana.

1419. Harrington, T. Parliamentary registration cases. Being a digest of each of the cases decided on appeal from the revision courts held in Ireland and England, 1889. Dublin, 1890. 1 v.

1420. Irish reports. Registry appeals in the Court of Exchequer Chamber and appeals in the Court for Land Cases Reserved, 1868-76. Dublin, 1886. 1 v.

Microfilm: Dobbs Ferry, Oceana.

1421. Lawson, W. Notes of decisions under the Representation of the People Acts and The Registration Acts, 1885-1914. Dublin, London, 1894-1914. 4 v.

Microfilm: Dobbs Ferry, Oceana.

1422. Welsh, T. Registry cases comprising all the published, and many of the recent unpublished, decisions in Ireland, respecting the registration of voters, under the Irish Reform Act, and 10 Geo. IV C.8; with an appendix containing in full, the above statutes and the provisions of all the Stamp Acts relating to instruments required to be produced at registry, 1830-40. Dublin, 1845. 1 v.

Microfilm: Dobbs Ferry, Oceana.

Previous ed.: 1838. Limited to sittings at the 1838 Sligo Spring Assizes.

Revenue Law

1423. Cantwell, J. A treatise on tolls and customs. 2nd ed. with notes and additions by W.C. McDermott, 1596-1829. Dublin, 1829. 1 v.

Previous ed. Dublin, 1817.

Contains an appendix of cases, six of which are not reported elsewhere.

1424. [Irish tax cases] Reports of Irish tax cases, printed under the directions of the Revenue Commissioners and by permission of the Incorporated Council of the Law Reporting for Ireland, 1922- . Dublin, Stationery Office, 1923- . 3 v. to 1964.

Subsequently issued as leaflets.

Social Security

1425. [National health insurance appeals] Reports of decisions on appeals and applications under Section 67 of the National Insurance Act, 1911 and Section 27 of the National Insurance Act, 1913, 1913-16. Dublin, 1916. 1 v.

Transport

1426. Duffy, C.G. A chapter of accidents being a concise epitome of all the reported decisions on road accident cases in the Irish courts, 1901-41. Dublin, 1942. 1 v.

ISLE OF MAN

1427. Farrant, R.D. Digest of Manx cases, heard and decided, 1927-47. Douglas, 1948. 1 v.

1428. Manx law bulletin, 1982-83- . Douglas, Attorney General's Chambers, 1983- .

1429. Manx law reports, 1981/83- . Oxford, Law Reports International, 1985- .

Volumes are published retrospectively and it is planned to take the series back to 1884.

J A M A I C A

See also no. 1862

1430. Clarke, A.J. Supreme Court of Judicature of Jamaica judgments, with a digest of the same, 1917-32. Kingston, 1936. 1 v.

1431. The Gleaner law reports: cases determined in the Court of Appeal, 1963-68. Kingston, 1963-68. 6 v.

1432. Grant, J. Notes of cases adjudged in Jamaica, 1774-1787. Edinburgh, 1787. 1 v.

1432A. Jamaica law reports [new series] Supreme Court of Judicature ... cases determined in the Circuit Court [Nisi Prius] and ... the Court of Appeal, [1905-June 1906]. Kingston, 1905-06. 2 v.

1433. Jamaica law reports [old series], 1855-76. Kingston, 1873-78. 2 v.

1434. The Jamaica law reports: decisions of the Supreme Court being decisions of single judges, the Full Court and the Court of Appeal in all jurisdictions, 1933- . London, Butterworths, 1935- . 15 v.

Subtitle varies.

1435. Judah, A. and Swan, R. Cases argued and decided in the Supreme Court of Judicature, Jamaica, June Term, 2 Vict., 1839. Spanish Town, 1839. 1 v.

1436. Macdougall, W.C. Reports of cases argued and determined in the Supreme Court and of cases at Nisi Prius in the Supreme and Assize Courts, Jamaica, 1835-38. Spanish Town, 1840. 1 v.

1437. Morris, (?) Reports of cases, 1836-44. [Kingston], 1843/44. 1 v.

1438. Mumford, W. Reports of cases argued and determined in the Supreme Court and Court of Assize for the island of Jamaica in October Term, 2 Vict., 1838/39. Kingston, 1839. 1 v.

1439. Ogilvie, C.M. Judgments of the Supreme Court on Appeals from the Resident Magistrate's Courts, 1917-23. Kingston, 1923. 1 v.

1440. Stephens, J.E.R. Supreme Court decisions of Jamaica and Privy Council decisions, 1774-1923. London, 1924. 2 v.

K E N Y A

To 1905 called East Africa Protectorate

See also nos. 2, 3, 4

1441. [East Africa law reports] East Africa Protectorate law reports, containing cases determined by the High Court at Mombasa ... the Appeal Court at Zanzibar and ... the Privy Council, 1897-1915. Nairobi, 190618. 7 v.

Compiled by R.W. Hamilton. Continued by: Kenya law reports which continues the volume numbering. v. 1-2 published in London.

1442. Kenya High Court digest, 1971-73. Nairobi, University of Nairobi Faculty of Law, 1971-73. 2 v.

1443. [Kenya law reports] Colony and Protectorate of Kenya. Law reports containing cases determined by the Supreme Court, Kenya ... the Court of Appeal for Eastern Africa and ... the Privy Council, 1919/21-1956. Nairobi, 1919-61. 21 v.

Continuation of: East Africa law reports, and continues volume numbering. Compiled by R.W. Hamilton and others. Title varies: v. 8-9 Law reports of East Africa; v. 10 Law reports of Kenya.

1444. Kenya law reports, 1976- . [Nairobi], East Africa Publishing House, [1981]- . 3 v.

SUBJECT REPORTS

Mercantile Law

See no.1

K I R I B A T I

To 1975 called Gilbert Islands

1445. Gilbert Islands law reports, 1977-78. [Tarawa], [1979-80]. 2 v.

Continued by: Kiribati law reports. In mimeographed form. Appended to v. 1 is a 'digest of cases and appeals, heard by the High Court in the Gilbert Island, in some years prior to 1977'.

1446. Kiribati law reports, 1979- . [Tarawa], [Attorney-General's Chambers], [1981]- . 1 v.

Continuation of: Gilbert Islands law reports. In mimegraphed form.

L E S O T H O

To 1966 called Basutoland

See also nos. 5, 6

1447. Judgment in the case of Chief C.B. Griffith v. A.M.S. Griffith, Chieftainess. In the High Court of Basutoland, delivered ... March 30, 1943. Maseru, 1943. 1 v.

1448. The Lesotho law reports, 1967/70- . Maseru, Government Printer, 1976- . 6 v.

Continuation, in part, of: High Commission Territories law reports.

SUBJECT REPORTS

Mercantile Law

See no. 1

M A L A W I

To 1964 called Nyasaland

See also Rhodesia and Nyasaland

1449. African law reports. Malawi series, 1923/60-1971/72. Zomba, 1962-74. 6 v.

Continued by: Malawi law reports. Also known as: Malawi law reports. v. 1-5 published in Dobbs Ferry.

1450. Malawi law reports, 1973. Zomba, 1979. 1 pt.

Continuation of: African law reports. Malawi series. v. 7, pt. 1 only published.

1451. Nyasaland Protectorate. Law reports, containing judicial circular issued by the High Court of Nyasaland and cases determined by the High Court of Nyasaland, the Court of Appeal for Eastern Africa and the Rhodesia and Nyasaland Court of Appeal, 1922-1946/52. Zomba, 1925-54. 6 v.

Subtitle varies: Also known as: Nyasaland law reports.

SUBJECT REPORTS

Mercantile Law

See no. 1

M A L A Y S I A

From 1896 to 1946 the Federated Malay States: to 1948 the Malayan Union; to 1963 the Federation of Malaya; from 1963 as Malaysia, comprising Malaya, Sabah, Sarawak and, till 1965, Singapore.

1452. [Federated Malay States law reports] F.M.S. reports, 1899-1905. Singapore, 1906. 1 v.

Reprinted: Dobbs Ferry, Oceana, 1970.

Published as an appendix to the Straits Settlements law reports (old series) v. 9.

1453. [F.M.S. law reports] The law reports of the Federated Malay States, 1906-41. Kuala Lumpur, 1922-47. 16 v.

Continued by: Malayan Union law reports. Vols. 1-7 cover 1906-31, the unnumbered volumes covering 1931-41 form a new series which includes some reports from the unfederated states of Johore and Kedah.

1454. Malayan cases: being a collection of old and important cases which are still law, 1909- . Singapore, Malayan Law Journal, 1939- . 4 v.

Subtitle varies, v. 2: 'being a collection of important cases hitherto unreported'. Preface to v. 1: '... important decisions which have for some reason been omitted from the Straits Settlements law reports or the F.M.S. law reports.'

1455. Malayan law journal, 1932-42; 1946- . Singapore, Malayan Law Journal, 1932-42; 1946- . 50 v. Some judgments in Malay from 1982.

Reprinted: Publisher, 1960- .

Includes selected decisions of the Supreme Court of Sarawak, North Borneo and Brunei from Oct. 1954 and decisions of the High Court of Borneo from 1963. Originally a journal but from 1954 almost entirely law reports.

1456. Malayan law reports, 1950-54. Kuala Lumpur. 1951-[54]. 5 v.

Continuation of: Malayan Union law reports. Title varies: v. 1 Law reports of the Federation of Malaya. v. 1-3 also contain law reports from Singpore. Suppl. to v. 3, published 1956.

1457. [Malayan Union law reports] Law reports of the Malayan Union, 1946-47. Kuala Lumpur, 1948-50. 2 v.

Continuation of: F.M.S. law reports. Continued by: Malayan law reports.

SUBJECT REPORTS

Constitutional Law

1458. Constitutional law cases from Malaysia and Singapore, 1958-70. Singapore, Malayan Law Journal, 1971. 1 v.

2nd edition published 1976 extended coverage to 1973.

Public International Law

1459. Public international law cases from Malaysia and Singapore. 1813-1970. Singapore, Singapore University Press, 1974. 1 v.

JOHORE

Until 1946, one of the unfederated Malay States. Now part of Malaysia

See also no. 1453.

1460. [Johore law reports] Law reports of the state of Johore: cases determined by the Supreme Court of the State of Johore in its original and appellate jurisdiction civil and criminal, 1915/37-40. Singapore, 1939-41. 2 v.

SABAH

To 1963 called North Borneo

See also no. 1463

1461. North Borneo law reports, 1935-39. [Kota Kinabalu], 1935-39. 1 v.

Published irregularly as supplements to the British North Borneo gazette.

SUBJECT REPORTS

Customary Law

1462. Cases on native customary law in Sabah, 1953-72. Sabah, 1973. 1 v.

SARAWAK

1463. Sarawak, North Borneo and Brunei Supreme Court reports, 1952-63. Kuching, Sarawak, [1954?]-[1964]. 1952-63. 7 v.

Continuation, in part, of Supreme Court of Sarawak. Reports of decisions.

1464. Supreme Court of Sarawak. Reports of decisions, 1928-41; 1946-51. Kuching, Sarawak, 1928-39; [1947]-1953. 9 v.

Reprinted: Government Printer, 1955 as Sarawak Supreme Court reports.

Continued by: Sarawak, North Borneo and Brunei Supreme Court reports. Title varies: 1946-49 Supreme Court reports; 1950-51 Sarawak law reports.

STRAITS SETTLEMENTS

1826-1946 Malacca, Penang and Singapore united to form the Incorporated

Settlements, better known as the above.

See also no. 1452

1465. Magistrates' appeal cases, 1884-93. Penang, [c.1895]. 1 v.

1466. Norton-Kyshe, J.W. Cases heard and determined in Her Majesty's Supreme Court of the Straits, 1808-90. Singapore, 1885-90. 4 v.

1467. Quarterly notes of cases decided in the Supreme Court of the Straits Settlements, 1926-27. Singapore, 1926-27. 1 v.

1468. Straits law journal and reporter: cases decided in the Straits Settlements and Siam, 1888-92. Singapore, 1888-92. 5 v.

The reports in v. 5 are in a separately paginated section entitled: Straits law reports, new series.

1469. Straits law reports: being a report of cases decided in the Supreme Court of the Straits Settlements, Penang, Singpore and Malacca; also a few judgments of the Indian and English cases, 1827-77. Penang, 1877. 1 v.

A Straits law reports, new series, appeared in v. 5 of the Straits law journal and reporter.

1470. Straits Settlements law reports, [new series], 1926-42. Singapore, 1927-50. 16 v.

1471. Straits Settlements law reports, [old series], 1867-1922. Singapore, [1893]-1931. 15 v.

Reprinted: Dobbs Ferry, Oceana, 1970.

v. 9, 1905 contains as an appendix: F.M.S. reports, v. 1, 1899-1905. Cases in the Judicial Commissioner's Court appeared as a supplement to v. 6.

SUBJECT REPORTS

Customary Law

1472. A selection of oriental cases decided in the Supreme Courts of the Straits Settlements, 1842-69. Pinang, 1869. 1 v.

Reprinted: London, Sweet & Maxwell, 1911.

Preface: 'a repertorium pointing out the most important exceptions

1472 *MALAYSIA*

that have been engrafted on the law in favour of our Chinese, Mahometan, Hindoo and other native population.'

MALTA

1473. Collezione di decisioni criminali intorno a questioni di diritto emanate dal 10 Guigno 1854 dalle Corte Criminale di S.M. in Malta e di decisioni civili e commerciali emanate dal 1mo Gennaro 1858 dalle Corti Superioro della stessa Isola, 1854-1934. Malta, 1858-1948. 28 v. In Italian.

Continued by: Kollezzjoni ta'decizjonijet tal-grati superjuri ta' Malta. Title varies: v. 2-15: Collezione di decisioni dei Tribunali Superiori dell'Isola di Malta; v. 16-28: Collezione di decisioni delle Corti Superiori dell'isola di Malta. Contains Supreme Court decisions in respect of criminal, civil and commercial causes.

1474. Collezione di decisioni dei Tribunali, 1839-42. Malta, 1840-44. 4 v. In Italian.

1475. Decisioni scelte delle Corti Superiori, 1847-49. [Malta], 1850. 1 v. In Italian.

1476. Kollezzjoni ta'decizjonijet tal-grati superjuri ta'Malta, 1934- . Malta, Department of Information, 1950- . 11 v. In Maltese.

Continuation of: Collezione di decisioni criminali intorno [etc.]. Vol. numbering continues that of no. 1473.

1477. Repertorio di decisioni sceltes del Supremo Magistrato di giustezea di Malta, 1713-1838. Malta, 1841. 1 v. In Italian.

MAURITIUS

1478. Mauritius reports, 1861- . Mauritius, Government Printer, 1861- . 119 v.

Reprinted: v. 1, 2 London; Edinburgh; Paris; 1863, 1866, as 2nd eds.

Title varies 1861-1926; contains reports of civil cases on appeal from the Seychelles to 1976. Also known as: Mauritius decisions.

1479. Recueil de decisions judiciaires de l'Isle Maurice: reports of cases argued and determined before the courts of Mauritius, compiled and edited by R. Bruzard, 1842-45. Mauritius, 1845. 1 v. Most judgments in French.

Selected cases reprinted in: Digest of reported criminal jurisprudence.

This work contains reprints of cases from Revue judiciaire de l'Isle Maurice.

1480. Revue judiciaire de l'Isle Maurice: reports of cases argued and determined in the Court of Appeal and other courts, 1843-45. Mauritius, [1843-45]. 1 v. Most judgments in French.

Reprinted in: Recueil de decisions judiciaires de l'Isle Maurice.

Pts. 1-24 by R. Bruzaud; pts. 25-7 by N. Savy.

SUBJECT REPORTS

Criminal Law

1481. Digest of reported criminal jurisprudence of the Supreme Court of Mauritius, compiled and edited by W. Greene, 1842-83. Port Louis, 1884. 1 v.

Contains reprints of Selected cases from Recueil de decisions judiciaires de l'Isle Maurice, and Reports of assize cases.

N E W   Z E A L A N D

See also nos. 24, 100

1482. Colonial law journal, being a selection of reports and cases argued in the Supreme Court of New Zealand, 1865-75. Dunedin, 1875. 1 v.

Reports separately paged.

1483. [Court of Appeal reports] Reports of cases determined by the Court of Appeal of New Zealand, 1867-77. Wellington, 1872-77. 3 v.

Also known as: New Zealand Court of Appeal reports; Johnston's reports.

1484. The gazette law reports, 1898-1953. Christchurch, n.d.-1953. 55 v.

From 1953 incorporated in New Zealand law reports.

1485. Macassey, J. Reports of cases argued and determined in the Supreme Court of New Zealand, Southern District: Province of Otago. Otago and Southland District, and an appeal to the Court of Appeal of New Zealand, 1861-72. Dunedin, 1873. 1 v.

1486. Magistrates' Court decisions, 1939-79. Wellington, 1940-80. 14 v.

Continued by: New Zealand District Court reports. From 1953 incorporated Magistrates' Court reports. Title varies: v. 1-9 New Zealand law journal Magistrates' Court decisions.

1487. Magistrates' Court reports, 1906-53. Christchurch, 1906-53. 48 v.

Title varies: v. 1-4 District Court and Magistrates' Court reports. From 1953 incorporated in New Zealand law journal Magistrates' Court decisions.

1488. New Zealand District Court reports, 1980- . Wellington, Butterworths of New Zealand, 1893- .

Continuation of: Magistrates' Court decisions.

1489. [New Zealand jurist, new series] The New Zealand jurist reports: comprising reports of cases in the Supreme Court of New Zealand and in the Court of Appeal of New Zealand, 1875-79. Dunedin, 1876-79. 4 v.

1489A. New Zealand jurist. Reports of cases argued and determined in the Supreme Court of New Zealand and on appeal to the Court of Appeal, 1873-75. Dunedin, 1874-75. 2 v.

Continued by: New Zealand jurist, n.s. Contains appendix of important cases previously decided.

1489B. New Zealand law reports. Cases determined by the Court of Appeal of New Zealand, 1883- . Wellington, Butterworths, 1883- . 112 v.

Data base: LEXIS 1970- .

Subtitle and coverage varies between 1916-81. Includes Privy Council cases, 1933-78; 1981- , and Supreme Court cases, 1940-80.

1490. New Zealand Privy Council cases, being appeals from the New Zealand courts determined by the Judicial Committee of the Privy Council, 1840-1932. Wellington, 1938. 1 v.

1491. Ollivier, F.M., Bell, H.D. and Fitz-gerald, W. Reports of cases decided in the Court of Appeal and the Supreme Court of New Zealand, 1878-80. Wellington, [1890], 1 v.

SUBJECT REPORTS

Administrative Law

1492. New Zealand adminstrative reports, 1976- . Wellington, Butterworths of New Zealand, 1980- . 2 v.

Contains selected decisions from a wide range of adminstrative tribunals.

Criminal Law

1493. Criminal reports of New Zealand, 1983- . Wellington, Brooker and Friend, 1983- . [looseleaf] 1 v.

Family Law

1494. Family reports of New Zealand, 1983- . Wellington, Brooker and Friend, 1984- . [looseleaf] 1 v.

1495. Matrimonial Property Act cases, 1977/78- . Wellington, New Zealand Council of Law Reporting, 1978- . 5 v.

1496. New Zealand family law reports, 1981- . Wellington, Butterworths of New Zealand, 1983- . 1 v.

Industrial Law

1497. [Arbitration Court judgments] Judgments, etc. ... of the Arbitration Court of New Zealand made under the Industrial Relations Act, 1976- . Wellington, Department of Labour, 1978- . 12 v.

1976-80 court called Industrial Court.

1498. [Book of awards] Awards, recommendations, agreements, etc. made under the Industrial Conciliation and Arbitration Act, 1894- . Wellington, Department of Labour, 1901- . 82 v.

1499. New Zealand workers' compensation cases, 1901-40. Wellington, 1903-46. 39 v.

Title varies: v. 1 Decisions of the Court of Arbitration under 'The Workers' Compensation for Accidents Act, 1900', v. 2-8 Decisions under the Workers Compensation for Accidents Act.

Land Law

See also no. 1504

1500. New Zealand conveyancing and property reports, 1959- . Wellington, Butterworths of New Zealand, 1983- .

1501. New Zealand town planning appeals, 1956- . Wellington, Butterworths of New Zealand, 1961- . 8 v.

Title varies: v. 1-3 Town and country planning appeals.

Local Government

1502. Butterworth's New Zealand local government reports, 1935/36. Wellington, 1935-72. 14 v.

Also known as: New Zealand local government reports.

Maori Law

1503. Fenton, F.D. Important judgments delivered in the Compensation Court and Native Land Court, 1866-79. Auckland, 1879. 1 v.

1504. Tai Whati; judicial decisions affecting Maoris and Maori land, 1958/83- . Wellington, Department of Maori Affairs, 1984- . 1 v.

Mercantile Law

See also no. 27

1505. New Zealand company law cases, 1981- . Auckland, CCH (New Zealand), 1984- . 1 v.

Cases first issued in loose-leaf form in New Zealand Company Secretary's Manual.

Revenue Law

See also nos. 39-40, 42

1506. New Zealand Taxation Board of Review decisions, 1961-74. Wellington, 1963-74. 5 v.

Continued by: Tax reports (New Zealand).

1507. New Zealand tax cases, 1973- . Auckland, CCH (New Zealand), 1974- . 4 v.

v. 1 published by CCH Australia.

1508. Tax reports (New Zealand), 1974/76- . Wellington, Butterworths of New Zealand, 1976- . 4 v.

Continuation of: New Zealand Taxation Board of Review decisions.

Tort

1509. New Zealand accident compensation reports, 1981-84. Wellington, 1981-84. 1 v.

Transport

1510. Butterworths road transport licensing appeals, 1953-74. Wellington, 1958- . n.d. 6 v.

Continuation of: Transport appeal decisions, N.Z. v. 6: pt. 1 only published.

1511. Transport appeal decisions, N.Z., 1942/48-1949/52. Te Awamutu, n.d. 2 v.

Continued by: Butterworths road transport licensing appeals. Title varies: v. 2 Transport licensing appeal decisions, N.Z.

N I G E R I A

The country was divided into regions in 1951, into states in 1967 and further re-organised in 1976. Some law reports continued their former coverage regardless of administrative changes.

See also no. 7

1512. The all Nigeria law reports, 1961- . Lagos, National Committee on Law Reporting, 1962- . 20 v.

1961-70 reprinted: London, Sweet & Maxwell, 1982.

1513. Colony and Protectorate of Nigeria. Appeals to and from the West African Court of Appeal, 1938. Lagos, 1938. 1 v.

1514. Federation of Nigeria law reports, 1976- . St. Peter's Port, Guernsey, Heritage Publications, 1981- . 9 v.

1976-84 published in Ibadan.

1515. Judgments of the Supreme Court of Nigeria, 1972- . Lagos, Supreme Court, 1972- . 12 v.

Title varies: 1976- Reserved judgments ...

1516. The law reports of Nigeria, 1980- . Lagos, Butterworths (Nigeria), 1980- . 3 v.

1517. Nigeria Court of Appeal reports, 1977- . Lagos, MIJ Publishers, 1985- .

1518. Nigeria law reports, 1881/1911-55. Lagos, 1915-57. 21 v.

Reprinted: London, Eyre & Spottiswoode, 1958.

1519. Nigerian monthly law reports, 1964-76. Ibadan, 1964-76. 13 v.

1520. Nigerian weekly law reports, 1985- . Lagos, Nigerian Law Publications, 1985- .

1521. Renner, P.A. Reports, notes of cases and proceedings and judgments in appeals, etc. ... relating to the Gold Coast Colony and Nigeria ... and a few decisions given by Her Majesty's Judicial Committee of the Privy Council affecting the aforesaid Colony, 1861-1914. London, 1915. 1 v.

Also known as: Nigeria courts reports.

1522. Reports of certain judgments of the Supreme Court, Vice-Admiralty Court and Full Court of Appeal, 1884-92. Lagos, 1884-92. 1 v.

1523. Reserved judgments of the Federal Court of Appeal, 1977-78. Lagos, 1977-78. 2 v.

1524. Selected judgments of the Federal Supreme Court of Nigeria, 1956-60. Lagos, 1958-64. 5 v.

1525. Supreme Court of Nigeria law reports, 1983- . Lagos, Nigerian Law Publications, 1984- .

1526. University of Ife (Nigeria) law reports, 1971-74. Ile-Ife, 1970-76. 4 v.

SUBJECT REPORTS

Constitutional Law

1527. Nigerian constitutional law reports, 1981- . Lagos, Nigerian Law Publications, 1981- . 3 v.

Criminal Law

1528. The Nigerian criminal reports, 1980- . Oxford, African Law Reports, 1981- . 2 v.

Industrial Law

1529. National Industrial Court law reports, 1978/79- . Lagos, 1981- . 2 v.

Mercantile Law

See also no. 1

1530. Nigerian commercial law reports, 1969- . Oxford, Law Reports International, 1975- .

This series is made up of material reprinted from the African law reports (commercial series) with added cases.

Revenue Law

1531. Federal Revenue Court law reports, 1973-74- . Ibadan, Sketch Publishing Company, 1980- . 4 v.

BENDEL STATE

1960-1976 called Midwestern State

1532. Midwestern State of Nigeria law reports, 1964-70. Benin City. 1964-79. 5 v.

Title varies: 1964 Midwestern Nigeria law reports.

1533. Selected judgments of the High Court of Bendel State, 1976- . Benin-City, High Court of Bendel State, 1976- . 5 v.

EAST CENTRAL STATE

Until 1967, part of the Eastern Region. In 1976 split into Anambra and Imo states

1534. Law reports of East-Central State of Nigeria, 1970/71-76. Enugu, 1972-81. 6 v.

EASTERN REGION

From 1967, divided into East Central, Rivers and South Eastern States

1535. Law reports of the Eastern Region of the Federation of Nigeria, including hitherto unreported cases previously decided in the Supreme Court of Nigeria, 1956-65. Enugu, 1956-71. 10 v.

IMO STATE

1967-76 part of East-Central State

1536. Imo State law reports, 1977- . Ibadan, Evans Brothers (Nigeria), n.d. 3 v.

LAGOS STATE

1537. High Court of Lagos State selected judgments, 1967- . Lagos, High Court Law Library, 1972- . 19 v.

1538. Law reports of High Court of Lagos State, 1957-67. Lagos, 1959-70. 11 v.

Title varies: 1957-62 Law reports of the High Court of the Federal Territory of Lagos.

SUBJECT REPORTS

Land Law

1539. Land registration cases (Lagos-State), 1940-57. Lagos, [1976]. 1 v.

NORTHERN REGION

1540. Case notes on Northern Nigeria, 1961-63. Kaduna, 1961-64.

Continued by: Sharia law reports.

1541. Law reports of Northern Nigeria, 1955/56-69. Kaduna, 1955-69. 14 v.

1542. Selected cases from the area courts of the Province of Benue, Northern Nigeria, 1963-67. Zaria, 1968. 1 v.

SUBJECT REPORTS

Criminal Law

1543. Some cases on criminal procedure and evidence in the northern states of Nigeria, 1968. Zaria, 1968. 2 v.

Islamic Law

1544. Sharia law reports, 1980- . Zaria, Ahmadu Bello University, Centre for Islamic Legal Studies and Institute of Administration, 1980- .

Continuation of: Case notes on Northern Nigeria.

OGUN STATE

1967-1976 part of Western State

1545. Selected judgments of the Ogun State High Court, 1976- . Abeokuta, Ogun State Government, 1977- . 2 v.

ONDO STATE

1967-1976 part of Western State

1546. Selected judgments of the Ondo State High Court of Justice, 1976/80- . Akure, High Court of Justice, 1976/80- . 1 v.

OYO STATE

1967-1976 part of Western State

1547. Selected judgments of the High Court of Oyo State of Nigeria, 1976- . Ibadan, High Court of Justice, 1977- . 5 v.

PLATEAU STATE

1548. Plateau law reports, 1980- . Enugu, Fourth Dimension Publishing, 1980- . 2 v.

RIVERS STATE

Until 1967, part of the Eastern Region

1549. Law reports of Rivers State of Nigeria, 1970/72- . Port Harcourt, Ministry of Justice, 1973- . 4 v.

WESTERN STATE

Until 1967, called Western Region. In 1976 split into Ogun, Ondo and Oyo States.

1550. Selected judgments of the High Court of Western State, 1974- . Ibadan, Government Printer, 1974- . 2 v.

1551. Selected judgments of the Western State Court of Appeal, 1967/68- . Ibadan, 1968- . 3 v.

Title varies: 1967/68-71 Judgements ...

N O R T H E R N I R E L A N D

For reports before 1922 **see** Ireland

See also no. 1316

1552. Northern Ireland law reports bulletin of judgments delivered in the Superior Courts in Northern Ireland, 1970- . Belfast, Incorporated Council of Law Reporting for Northern Ireland, 1970. 13 v.

Title varies: 1970-74 Northern Ireland monthly reports. Also known as: 'Bluebooks'.

1553. The Northern Ireland law reports containing reports of cases argued and determined in the High Court of Justice and on appeal therefrom in the Court of Appeal in Northern Ireland, 1925- . Belfast, Incorporated Council of Law Reporting for Northern Ireland, 1925. 58 v.

SUBJECT REPORTS

Industrial Law

1554. Industrial Court, Northern Ireland. Numbered decisions, 1963- . Belfast, H.M.S.O., 1963- .

1555. Industrial tribunals. Reports of decisions [of the Industrial Tribunals on appeals and references] under the Contracts of Employment and Redundancy Payments Act (Northern Ireland) 1965, 1966-78. Belfast, 1966-78.

From 1981 selected decisions appear in the Bulletin of Northern Ireland law.

Land Law

1556. Lands Tribunal and Compensation Act (N.I.), 1964. [Decisions] in the matter of appeal[s] against valuation for rating purposes, 1965- . Belfast, Lands Tribunal Office, 1965- .

Typescript.

1557. Lands Tribunal and Compensation Act (N.I.), 1964. Decisions in the matter of the Business Tenancies Act (N.I.), 1964, 1965- . Belfast, Lands Tribunal Office, 1965- .

Typescript.

1558. Lands Tribunal and Compensation Act (N.I.) 1964. [Land development appeals], 1965- . Belfast, Lands Tribunal Office, 1965- .

Typescript.

Social Security

1559. Reported decisions of the Commissioners under the Family Allowances, National Insurance and Industrial Injuries Acts (Northern

Ireland) and the Social Security Acts (Northern Ireland), 1961-77. Belfast, H.M.S.O., 1978. 1 v.

Continuation of: Reported decisions of the Umpire under the Family Allowances, National Insurance and Industrial Injuries Acts (N.I.) 1948-61. Continued by: [Reported] decisions of the Commissioners under the National Insurance ... Acts.

1560. [Reported] decisions of the Commissioners under the National Insurance ... Family Allowances ... Social Security ... Act(s), 1973- . Belfast, Department of Health and Social Services, 1973- .

Issued in various parts according to benefit concerned. Continuation of: Reported decisions of the Umpire under the ... Acts.

1561. Reported decisions of the Umpire under the Family Allowances, National Insurance and Industrial Injuries Acts (Northern Ireland), 1948-61. Belfast, H.M.S.O., 1963. 1 v.

Continued by: Reported decisions of the Commissioners under the ... Acts.

1562. Selected decisions given by the Umpire for Northern Ireland respecting claims to benefit [under the Unemployment Insurance Acts], 1922-30. Belfast, H.M.S.O., 1931. 1 v.

P A K I S T A N

Formerly part of British India. Created in August 1947 and, geographically divided, known as West Pakistan and, till 1971, East Pakistan (now Bangladesh). In 1972 Pakistan left the Commonwealth

See also the following series on no. 977: (Lahore) 1914-50; (Peshawar) 1914-50; (Dacca) 1949-55.

1563. All Pakistan legal decisions, 1949- . Lahore, c. 1950- . 36 v.

Covers all the major courts, national and provincial; includes Dakka High Court reports, 1949 v. 1 - 1957 v. 4, and East Pakistan High Court reports (Dacca), 1958 v. 3 to 1971 v. 3.

1564. All Pakistan legal decisions. Selected Privy Council cases, 1947/51. Lahore, c. 1953. 1 v.

Issued as a complementary unnumbered vol. to All Pakistan legal decisions.

1565. The Federal Court reports: containing cases determined by the Federal Court of Pakistan, 1950/51-56. Karachi, c.1952-57. 6 v. in 8.

Continued by: Pakistan Supreme Court reports.

1566. Karachi law reports, 1960- . [Karachi], 1960- .

A journal incorporating judgments of the Supreme Court, Federal Shariat, Peshawar and Baluchistan High Courts, all tribunals and courts of foreign jurisdiction.

1567. The Karachi weekly law reports: a weekly publication containing important judgments of the High Court of West Pakistan, Karachi Bench, Karachi, 1960- . Karachi, 1960- . c.25 v.

Continuation of: Pakistan law reports: Karachi series.

1568. Law reports. Karachi series, containing cases determined by the Chief Court of Sind, the Federal Court of Pakistan and on appeal from all High Courts in India and Pakistan by the Privy Council, 1948-50. Karachi, 1948-50. 3 v.

Continuation of: Indian law reports, Karachi series (the last two parts of the 1947 vol. dropping the title 'Indian'); continued by Pakistan law reports, Karachi series; 1949 vol. has corrigenda altering title to 'Pakistan law reports', Karachi series but 1950 vol. t/p repeats 1948 vol. title.

1569. National law reporter, c.1978- . c.1978- .

Includes reports of civil and criminal cases in the major courts of Pakistan together with a separate section covering High Courts and the Supreme Court.

1570. Pakistan law reports: Karachi series, 1951-59. Karachi. 1951-59. 7 v.

Continuation of: Law reports, Karachi series. Continued by: Karachi law reports.

1571. Pakistan law reports, Lahore. Cases determined by the High Court of Judicature, Lahore, the Federal Court of Pakistan and Privy Council on appeal from the Lahore High Court, 1948-55. Lahore, c. 1949-56. 9 v.

Continuation of: Indian law reports: Lahore series. Continued by: Pakistan law reports, West Pakistan. 1951 v. 4 is wrongly numbered v. 26 on t/p.

1572. Pakistan law reports, Lahore series. Cases determined by the Lahore High Court, v. 2, July 1970- . Lahore, July 1970- .

Continuation of: Pakistan law reports, West Pakistan.

1573. Pakistan law reports, West Pakistan. Cases determined by the High Court of West Pakistan and by the Supreme Court of Pakistan on appeal of the High Courts of West and East Pakistan, 1956 - v. 1, June 1970. Lahore, 1956-June 1970. c. 30 v.

Continuation of: Pakistan law reports, Lahore. Continued by: Pakistan law reports, Lahore series. 2 vols issued p.a. on average. 1957 v. 1 is incorrectly subtitled 'Lahore series' on t/p, and 1959 v. 2 is incorrectly subtitled 'West Pakistan series'.

1574. Pakistan Supreme Court reports: containing cases determined by the Supreme Court of Pakistan, 1956-70. Karachi, 1958-70. 13 v.

Continuation of: Federal Court reports.

SUBJECT REPORTS

Criminal Law

1575. Pakistan criminal law journal, 1949- . 1949- . c. 36 v.

Contains reports of criminal cases in the High Courts and Supreme Court.

Industrial Law

1576. Pakistan labour cases, edited by M. Shafi; 1957/58- . Lahore, Pakistan Labour Cases, 1959- . 21 v.

Islamic Law

1577. Shariat decisions, being judgments and orders [of] the Supreme Court of Pakistan, c. 1978- . c. 1978- . c.6 v.

Revenue Law

1578. Pakistan tax decisions, 1959- . Lahore, Pakistan Tax Decisions, c. 1960- . 41 v.

To 1974, v. 1 case law, v. 2 Appellate tribunals and statutes.

P A L E S T I N E

Mandated by the League of Nations to Great Britain 1923-1948. Territory now divided between Israel and Jordan

1579. Annotated law reports, 1937-47. Tel Aviv, [1938-48], 14 v.

Incorporated Current law reports from 1943. Title varies: 1937-43 Annotated Supreme Court judgements.

1580. Collection of judgments of the courts of Palestine, 1919-33, including civil and criminal judgments of the Privy Council, Court of Appeal, High Court, Special Tribunal, District Court, Land Court, Criminal Courts, 1919-36. Tel Aviv, 1935-38. 9 v.

1581. Collection of judgments of the District and Land Courts of Haifa, 1935-42. Haifa, 1942. 1 v.

In mimeograph form.

1582. Current law reports, 1937-42. Tel Aviv, c.1937-43. 11 v.

Vol. 1 was issued in mimeographed form; a second edition, revised, was printed. From 1943 incorporated with the Annotated law reports.

1583. Haifa law reports, 1945-47. Haifa, c.1945-47. 6 v.

In mimeograph form.

1584. Law reports of the District Court of Tel Aviv, 1937-42. Tel Aviv, 1938-42. 5 v.

Continued by: Selected cases of the District Courts of Palestine.

1585. [Palestine law reports] The law reports of Palestine, 1920/33-47. Jerusalem, 1934-48. 14 v.

1586. Selected cases of the District Courts of Palestine, 1943-48. Tel Aviv, 1943-48. 6 v.

Continuation of: Law reports of the District Court of Tel Aviv.

SUBJECT REPORTS

Revenue Law

1587. Palestine income tax cases, 1935-45. Tel Aviv, 1945. 1 v.

Edited by A.M. Apelbom and B. Bravde.

PAPUA NEW GUINEA

1588. Papua New Guinea law reports: cases determined in the Supreme Court of Justice, and in the National Court of Justice, 1960- . Sydney, Law Book Company, 1963- . 16 v.

RHODESIA AND NYASALAND

A Federation consisting of Northern and Southern Rhodesia and Nyasaland (now Zambia, Zimbabwe and Malawi) from 1953-1963

1589. Rhodesia and Nyasaland Court of Appeal law reports, 1947-52. Salisbury, 1948-53. 1 v.

Continuation of: Rhodesian Court of Appeal law reports.

1590. Rhodesia and Nyasaland law reports, 1956-63. Salisbury, 1956-64. 8 v.

Continuation of and continued by separate series for each territory.

1591. [Rhodesian Court of Appeal law reports] Decisions of the Rhodesian Court of Appeal, 1939-46. Salisbury, 1940-47. 3 v.

Continued by: Rhodesia and Nyasaland Court of Appeals Law Reports. The Court heard appeals from the High Court of Northern Rhodesia and the High Court of Southern Rhodesia.

S T. L U C I A

See no. 1863

S T. V I N C E N T

See no. 1863.

S C O T L A N D

See also nos. 316, 531, 534, 747, 758, 760, 803, 822, 894, 897

1592. Scots law times, 1893- . Edinburgh, W. Green, 1894- . 103 v.

Incorporates: Scottish law reporter from 1925. Contains a news sections and reports of cases in the House of Lords, Court of Session and Court of Justiciary, and separately paginated reports as follows: Sheriff Court reports, 1922- ; poor law reports, 1932-41; notes of recent decisions, 1946- ; Lyon Court reports, 1950-60, thereafter irregularly; Scottish Land Court reports, 1964-81; Lands Tribunal for Scotland reports, 1971-81, the latter two reports merging, 1982- .

Data base: LEXIS 1950- .

1593. The Scottish jurist, 1829-1873. Edinburgh, 1928-73. 45 v.

Reprinted: Scots revised reports; Microfilm: Dobbs Ferry, Oceana.

1594. The Scottish law reporter, 1865-1924. Edinburgh, 1866-1924. 61 v.

Incorporated in: Scots law times.

SPECIFIC COURTS

Court of Exchequer

1595. [Exchequer cases] Reports of cases argued and determined in the Court of Exchequer, Scotland, 1840-53. Edinburgh, 1853. 1 v.

Court of Justiciary

1596. Adam, E. Reports of cases before the High Court of Justiciary in Scotland, 1893-1916. Edinburgh, 1895-1919. 7 v.

Microfilm: Dobbs Ferry, Oceana.

1597. Arkley, P. Reports of cases before the High Court and Circuit Courts of Justiciary in Scotland, 1846-48. Edinburgh, 1849. 1 v.

Microfilm: Dobbs Ferry, Oceana.

1598. Broun, A. Reports of cases before the High Court and Circuit Courts of Justiciary in Scotland, 1842-45. Edinburgh, 1844-46. 2 v.

Microfilm: Dobbs Ferry, Oceana.

1599. Couper, C.T. Reports of cases before the High Court and Circuit Courts of Justiciary in Scotland, 1868-85. Edinburgh, 1871-87. 5 v.

Microfilm: Dobbs Ferry, Oceana.

1600. Irvine, A.F. Reports of cases before the High Court and Circuit Courts of Justiciary in Scotland, 1852-67. Edinburgh, 1855-68. 5 v.

Microfilm: Dobbs Ferry, Oceana.

1601. [Justiciary cases] Cases decided in the High Court of Justiciary, 1916- . Edinburgh, W. Green, 1920- . 66 v.

From 1916, although Justiciary cases may be separately bound (in volumes covering several years), they are the same reports as appear in Session Cases. Also known as: Session cases (J.C.).

1602. MacLaurin, J. Arguments and decisions in remarkable cases before the High Court of Justiciary and other supreme courts in Scotland, 1670-1773. Edinburgh, 1774. 1 v.

Microfilm: Dobbs Ferry, Oceana.

1603. Shaw, J. Reports of cases before the High Court and Circuit Courts of Justiciary in Scotland, 1848-52. Edinburgh, 1853. 1 v.

Microfilm: Dobbs Ferry, Oceana.

1604. Shaw, P. Cases decided in the Court of Justiciary, 1819-31. Edinburgh, 1831. 1 v.

Microfilm: Dobbs Ferry, Oceana.

1605. Swinton, A. Reports of cases before the High Court and Circuit Courts of Justiciary in Scotland, 1835-41. Edinburgh, 1838-42. 2 v.

Microfilm: Dobbs Ferry, Oceana.

1606. Syme, D. Reports of proceedings in the High Court of Justiciary, 1826-29. Edinburgh, 1829. 1 v.

Microfilm: Dobbs Ferry, Oceana.

1607. White, J.C. Reports of cases before the High Court and Circuit Courts of Justiciary in Scotland, 1885-93. Edinburgh, 1888-93. 3 v.

Microfilm: Dobbs Ferry, Oceana.

Court of Parliament

1608. [Acta Dominorum Auditorum] The acts of the Lords Auditors of causes and complaints, 1466-94. [Edinburgh], 1839. 1 v.

Edited by T. Thomson. Contains the judicial proceedings of the Parliament of Scotland.

1609. Acta Dominorum Concilii: the acts of the Lords of Council in civil cases, 1478-1503. Edinburgh, 1839-1943. 3 v.

v. 1: T. Thomson; v. 2: G. Neilson and H. Paton; v. 3: T.A. Crawford. (Stair Society v. 8).

1610. Hannay, R.K. The acts of the Lords of Council in public affairs, 1501-54. Edinburgh, 1932. 1 v.

Court of Session

1611. Bell, R. Cases decided in the Court of Session, 1790-92. Edinburgh, 1794. 1 v.

Microfilm: Dobbs Ferry, Oceana.

1612. Bell, R. Cases decided in the Court of Session, 1794-95, collected by appointment of the Society of Clerks to the Signet, Edinburgh, 1796. 1 v.

Microfilm: Dobbs Ferry, Oceana.

1613. Bell, S.S Dictionary of the decisions of the Court of Session, 1808-33. Edinburgh, 1841-42. 2 v.

Microfilm: Dobbs Ferry, Oceana.

1614. Bruce, A. The decisions of the Lords of Council and Session in most cases of importance ... , 1714-15. Edinburgh, 1720. 1 v.

Microfilm: Dobbs Ferry, Oceana.

This volume of Bruce (1714-1715) is often bound with Remarkable decisions of the Court of Session Vol. 1 (1716-1728) by Henry Home, Lord Kames, and is known as 'Bruce and Home's Decisions'.

1615. [Clerk Hame] Hame, A. Decisions of the Court of Session, 1735-44. Edinburgh, 1757. 1 v.

Microfilm: Dobbs Ferry, Oceana.

1616. Dalrymple, H. Decisions of the Court of Session, 1698-1718. Edinburgh, 1758. 1 v.

Microfilm: Dobbs Ferry, Oceana.

1617. Dirleton, Lord. The decisions of the Lords of Council and Session in most cases of importance ... , 1665-77. Edinburgh, 1698. 1 v.

Microfilm: Dobbs Ferry, Oceana.

Bound with 'Some doubts and questions in the law especially of Scotland', known as Dirleton's Doubts.

1618. Dunlop, A. Cases decided in the Court of Session, 1838-62. Edinburgh, 1839-62. 24 v.

Reprinted: Scots revised reports.

From v. 10 (1847-48) cases from the Teind Court and Court of Exchequer are included. From v. 13 (1850-51) House of Lords cases are added with separate pagination and index. Continuation of: Shaw's Session cases. Continued by: Macpherson's Session cases. Also known as: Session cases, 2nd. series.

1619. Durie, Lord. The decisions of the Lords of Council and Session, 1621-42. Edinburgh, 1690. 1 v.

Microfilm: Dobbs Ferry, Oceana.

Also known as: Gibson's decisions.

1620. Edgar, J. The decisions of the Court of Session, 1724-25. Edinburgh, 1742. 1 v.

Microfilm: Dobbs Ferry, Oceana.

Sometimes bound with Falconer's reports v. 1 and known as Edgar and Falconer.

1621. Elchies, Lord. Decisions of the Court of Session ... collected and digested into the form of a dictionary, 1733-54. Edinburgh, 1813. 2 v.

Microfilm: Dobbs Ferry, Oceana.

Edited from the original manuscript by W.M. Morison. v. 1 (reports of cases) forms Appendix 2 of Morison's Dictionary. v. 2 consists of Lord Elchies' notes on the cases reported by him.

1622. [English judges] The decisions of the English judges during the usurpation, 1655-1661. Edinburgh, 1762. 1 v.

Microfilm: Dobbs Ferry, Oceana.

1623. [Faculty collection (new series)] Decisions of the first and second divisions of the Court of Session, 1808-25. Edinburgh, 1811-28. 7 v.

Reprinted: Scots revised reports; Microfilm: Dobbs Ferry, Oceana.

Continuation of: [Faculty collection (o.s.)]. Also known as: Faculty of Advocate reports (n.s.). Vols. contain abstracts of cases appealed to the House of Lords, and owing to binding variants sets may contain more than the vols. stated. Some vols. appear in more than one edition.

1624. [Faculty collection (old series)] Decisions of the Court of Session, 1752-1808. Edinburgh, 1760-1810. 14 v.

Microfilm: Dobbs Ferry, Oceana.

Continued by: [Faculty collection (n.s.)] Also known as: Old faculty reports; Faculty of Advocates reports; Faculty decisions. Volumes contain a note of cases appealed to the House of Lords. v. 3 has bound in 'Decisions of the Court of Session ... 1716-17 ... by Mr. A. Bruce' not previously published. Volumes and sets vary in their make-up but generally have 'Decisions' and the date on the spine. Owing to binding variants a set may contain more than the vols. stated.

1625. [Faculty decisions] Decision of the Court of Session, 1825-41. Edinburgh, 1826-41. 16 v.

Microfilm: Dobbs Ferry, Oceana.

Also known as: Faculty of Advocates reports, octavo series.

1626. Falconer, D. The decisions of the Court of Session, 1744-51. Edinburgh, 1874-53. 2 v.

Microfilm: Dobbs Ferry, Oceana.

Sometimes bound with Edgar's decisions and known as Edgar and Falconer.

1627. Forbes, W. A journal of the Session containing the decisions of the Lords of Council and Session, 1705-13. Edinburgh, 1763. 1 v.

Microfilm: Dobbs Ferry, Oceana.

Previous ed.: 1714.

1628. Fountainhill, Lord. The decisions of the Lords of Council and Session, 1678-1712. Edinburgh, 1759-61. 2 v.

Microfilm: Dobbs Ferry, Oceana.

1629. Fraser, H.J.E. Cases decided in the Court of Session, Court of Justiciary and House of Lords, 1898-1906. Edinburgh, 1899-1906. 8 v.

Continuation of: Rettie's Session cases. Continued by: Session cases, n.s. Also known as: Session cases, 5th series. The three sections are separately paginated and indexed.

1630. [Gilmour and Falconer] A collection of decisions of the Lords of Council and Session, 1661/66; 1681/86. Edinburgh, 1701. 1 v.

Microfilm: Dobbs Ferry, Oceana.

Pt. 1: Sir R. Gilmour; pt. 2: Sir D. Falconer.

1632. Halkerston, P. A compendium or general abridgment of the Faculty Collection of Decisions of the Lords of Council and Session, 1752-1817. Edinburgh, 1819. 1 v.

Microfilm: Dobbs Ferry, Oceana.

1633. Harcarse, Lord. Decisions of the Court of Session, 1681-91. Edinburgh, 1757. 1 v.

Microfilm: Dobbs Ferry, Oceana.

1634. Hume, D. Decisions of the Court of Session, 1781-1822. Edinburgh, 1839. 1 v.

In dictionary form.

Microfilm: Dobbs Ferry, Oceana.

1635. Kames, Lord. Remarkable decisions of the Court of Session, 1716-52. Edinburgh, 1728-66. 2 v.

Microfilm: Dobbs Ferry, Oceana.

v. 1 (1716-28) is often bound with Bruce's Decisions and known as Bruce and Home's Decisions.

1636. Kames, Lord. Select decisions of the Court of Session, 1752-68. Edinburgh, 1780. 1 v.

Microfilm: Dobbs Ferry, Oceana.

1637. Kilkerran, Lord. Decisions of the Court of Session, collected and digested into the form of a dictionary, 1738-52. Edinburgh, 1775. 1 v.

Microfilm: Dobbs Ferry, Oceana.

1638. Macfarlane, R. Reports of jury trials in the Court of Session, 1838-39. Edinburgh, 1841. 1 v.

1639. Mackenzie, Sir G. Pleadings in some remarkable cases before the Supreme Courts of Scotland, since the year 1661, to which the decisions are subjoyn'd, 1661-71. Edinburgh, 1672. 1 v.

Reprinted: 1673, 1704.

1640. Macpherson, N. Cases decided in the Court of Session, Teind Court and House of Lords, 1862-73. Edinburgh, 1863-73. 11 v.

Reprinted: Scots revised reports.

Continuation of: Dunlop's Session cases. Continued by: Rettie's Session cases. Also known as: Session cases, 3rd series.

1641. Rettie, M. Cases decided in the Court of Session, Court of Justiciary and House of Lords, 1873-98. Edinburgh, 1874-98. 25 v.

Continuation of: Macpherson's Session cases. Continued by: Fraser's Session cases. Also known as: Session cases, 4th series. Incorporated Scottish jurist. The three sections are separately paginated and indexed.

1642. Scots revised reports, 1707-1873. Edinburgh, 1898-1909. 45 v. Reissue of selected decisions.

1643. [Session cases (new series)] Cases decided in the Court of Session, and also in the Court of Justiciary and House of Lords, 1906/07- . Edinburgh, T. & T. Clark, 1907- . 82 v.

Data base: LEXIS 1950- .

Continuation of: Fraser, H.J.E. Session cases. Published for the Faculty of Advocates until 1957/58 when the Scottish Council for Law Reporting assumed responsibility.

1644. [Session notes] Notes of cases decided in the Court of Session and also in the Court of Justiciary and House of Lords, 1925-48. Edinburgh, 1925-48. 24 v.

1948 v.: 2 pts. only. Frequently superseded by full reports in Session cases.

1645. Shaw, P. Cases decided in the Court of Session, 1821-38. Edinburgh, 1822-38. 16 v.

Reprinted: Scots revised reports.

A second edition, 'new and enlarged', of the first five volumes was printed in 1834. Continued by: Dunlop's Session cases. Also known as: Session cases.

1646. Stair, Lord. The decisions of the Lords of Council and Session, 1661-81. Edinburgh, 1683. 2 v.

Microfilm: Dobbs Ferry, Oceana.

Court of Session Collaterals

1647. Brown, M.P. General synopsis of the decisions of the Court of Session, -1827. Edinburgh, 1829. 4 v.

Microfilm: Dobbs Ferry, Oceana.

This digest, by M.P. Brown, contains all the cases in Morison's Dictionary, including its additional volumes, as well as those in Brown's Supplement, various other printed reports, and some cases from m.s. reports. It also includes cases decided in the House of Lords.

1648. Brown, M.P. Supplement to the Dictionary of Decisions of the Court of Session, 1620-1794. Edinburgh, 1826. 5 v.

Microfilm: Dobbs Ferry, Oceana.

Contains cases, printed and manuscript reports, which were omitted from Morison's Dictionary.

1649. Buchanan, W. Reports of certain remarkable cases in the Court of Session, and trials in the High Court of Justiciary, 1806-13. Edinburgh, 1813. 1 v.

Microfilm: Dobbs Ferry, Oceana.

1650. Deas, G. and Anderson, J. Cases decided in the Court of Session, Jury Court and High Court of Justiciary, 1829-32. Edinburgh, 1829-33. 5 v.

Microfilm: Dobbs Ferry, Oceana.

1651. Kames, Lord and Woodhouslee, Lord. The decisions in the Court of Session ... in the form of a dictionary, 1540-1796. Edinburgh, 1741-1804. 5 v.

Microfilm: Dobbs Ferry, Oceana.

v. 1, 2 (1741): H. Home, Lord Kames, 2nd ed. 1791; v. 3, 4 (1797): A.F. Tytler, Lord Woodhouslee; v. 5 suppl. to v. 3, 4 (1804): T. McGrugar: Tait's Index (1823) states (1) v. 3, 4 superseded a single vol. issued 20 years earlier which was incorporated in v. 3, 4, (2) another ed. of v. 1, 2 was issued in 5 vols. in 1774, the editor being unknown. Also known as: The Folio Dictionary.

1652. Morison, W.M. Decisions of the Court of Session digested in the form of a dictionary, 1540-1816. Edinburgh, 1801-[1817]. 38 in 19 v.

Reprinted: Scots revised reports; Microfilm: Dobbs Ferry, Oceana.

Originally issued in 38 v., (1801-07), usually bound in 19 v. Supplementary material added as follows: A synopsis or digest of reported cases, either bound separately as v. 20 & 21, 1804, or bound in the relevant vols. of the main work; a 'supplemental volume', v. 22, 1815, which includes additional cases and House of Lords judgments; two appendices: Appendix I (cases to 1808), 1810, usually bound in the main work, each title following the corresponding title of the dictionary; Appendix II, cases reported by Lord Elchies, normally separately bound in 2 v. and so treated (see no. 1621); a continuation entitled 'Synopsis of ... decisions of the Court of Session', in 2 v. (1808-16), 1814- n.d., the second being incomplete, sometimes bound as v. 23 & 24 of the dictionary; and an index to the whole, issued 1816. Also known as: Morison's Dictionary. See also: Brown's Supplement (no. 1648).

1653. Stuart, R., Milne, J.S. and Peddie, W. Reports of cases decided in the Court of Session, Teind Court, Court of Exchequer, Court of Justiciary and in the House of Lords, 1851-53. Edinburgh, 1852-53. 2 v.

House of Lords

1654. [Bell's appeal cases] Bell, S.S. Cases decided in the House of Lords on appeal from the courts of Scotland, 1842-50. Edinburgh, 1843-52. 7 v.

Reprinted: Scots revised reports; Microfilm: Dobbs Ferry, Oceana.

1655. Maclean, C.H. and Robinson, G. Cases decided by the House of Lords on appeal and writs of error, 1839. London, 1840. 1 v.

Reprinted: English reports, Scots revised reports; Microfilm: Dobbs Ferry, Oceana.

1656. MacQueen, J.F. Reports of Scotch appeals and writs of error together with peerage, divorce and practice cases in the House of Lords, 1851-65. Edinburgh, 1855-66. 4 v.

Reprinted: Scots revised reports; Microfilm: Dobbs Ferry, Oceana.

1657. Paterson, J. Reports of Scotch appeals in the House of Lords, 1851-73. Edinburgh, 1879-95. 2 v.

Microfilm: Dobbs Ferry, Oceana.

The reports were originally published in the Scottish jurist.

1658. Paton, S. Reports of cases decided in the House of Lords, upon appeal from Scotland, 1726-1821. Edinburgh, 1849-56. 6 v.

Reprinted: Scots revised reports; Microfilm: Dobbs Ferry, Oceana.

v. 1 edited by, and sometimes known as, Craigie, Stewart and Paton.

1659. Robertson, D. Reports of cases on appeal from Scotland, decided in the House of Peers, 1707-27. London, 1807. 1 v.

Reprinted: Scots revised reports; Microfilm: Dobbs Ferry, Oceana.

1660. Robinson, G. Cases decided in the House of Lords on appeal from the courts of Scotland, 1840-41. Edinburgh, 1840-42. 2 v.

Reprinted: Scots revised reports; Microfilm: Dobbs Ferry, Oceana.

1661. Shaw, P. Cases decided in the House of Lords on appeal from the courts of Scotland, 1821-24. Edinburgh, 1826-28. 2 v.

Reprinted: Scots revised reports; Microfilm: Dobbs Ferry, Oceana.

1662. Shaw, P. and Maclean, C.H. Cases decided in the House of Lords on appeal from the courts of Scotland, 1835-38. Edinburgh, 1836-39. 3 v.

Reprinted: Scots revised reports; Microfilm: Dobbs Ferry, Oceana.

1663. Wilson, J. and Shaw, P. Cases decided in the House of Lords on appeal from the courts of Scotland, 1825-35. Edinburgh, 1829-39. 7 v.

Reprinted: Scots revised reports; Microfilm: Dobbs Ferry, Oceana.

Additional reporters: v. 6 C.H. Maclean, W.R. Courtenay; v. 7 C.H. Maclean.

Lyon Court

See no. 1592

Privy Council

1664. Register of the Privy Council of Scotland, 1545-1625. Edinburgh, 1877-98. 14 v.

1665. Register of the Privy Council of Scotland, 1625-1660. Edinburgh, 1899-1908. 8 v.

1666. Register of the Privy Council of Scotland, 1661- . Edinburgh, H.M.S.O., 1908- . 16 v.

The Scottish Record Office still hope to complete the series although no volumes have been issued since v. 16 in 1970.

Sheriff Court

1667. [Dundee] Law chronicle, 1856-58. Dundee, 1856-60. 3 v.

1668. Guthrie, W. Select cases decided in the Sheriff Courts of Scotland, 1861-92. Edinburgh, 1879-94. 2 v.

Microfilm: Dobbs Ferry, Oceana.

v. 2 called 2nd series.

1669. Scots law times: Sheriff Court reports, 1922- . Edinburgh, W. Green, 1923- . 60 v.

Data base: LEXIS 1950- .

1670. Scottish law journal and Sheriff Court record, 1858-61. Glasgow, 1859-61. 3 v.

Microfilm: Dobbs Ferry, Oceana.

Continued by: Scottish law magazine and Sheriff Court reporter.

1671. Scottish law magazine and Sheriff Court reporter, 1861-67. Glasgow, 1862-67. 6 v.

Continuation of: Scottish law journal and Sheriff Court record.

1672. Scottish law review and Sheriff Court reports, 1885-1963. Glasgow, 1885-1963. 79 v.

The reports are separately paginated and have their own title page, index and digest.

Teind Court

1673. Shaw, P. and others. Cases decided in the Court of Teinds, 1821-31. Edinburgh, 1831. 1 v.

Microfilm: Dobbs Ferry, Oceana.

SUBJECT REPORTS

Agriculture

1674. Anderson, S. Decisions in the Court of Session in cases connected with the agriculture of Scotland, 1800-83. Edinburgh, 1883. 1 v.

Microfilm: Dobbs Ferry, Oceana.

Previous ed.: 1878.

1675. Connell, I. Leading decisions under the Agricultural Holdings (Scotland) Act, 1908, 1908-15. Edinburgh, 1916. 1 v.

Criminal Law

1676. Murray, J. Reports of cases tried in the Jury Court, 1816-30. Edinburgh, 1818-31. 5 v.

Microfilm: Dobbs Ferry, Oceana.

1677. Scottish criminal case reports, 1981- . Edinburgh, Law Society of Scotland, 1982- . 2 v.

Data base: LEXIS.

Ecclesiastical Law

1678. Fergusson, J. Reports of some recent decisions by the Consistorial Court of Scotland in actions of divorce, 1811-17. Edinburgh, 1817-23. 1 v.

Microfilm: Dobbs Ferry, Oceana.

Also printed as an appendix to Treatise on the present state of the consistorial law in Scotland by J. Fergusson, 1829, which includes three later cases.

1679. Leading ecclesiastical cases decided in the Court of Session, 1849-74. Edinburgh, 1878. 1 v.

Microfilm: Dobbs Ferry, Oceana.

1680. [St. Andrews] Liber officialis Sancti Andree. Curie Metropolitane Sancti Andree in Scotia sententiarum in causis consistorialibus que extant, 1512-54. Edinburgh, 1845. 1 v. In Latin.

Collected by J.H. Forbes, Lord Medwyn, for the Abbotsford Club (Abbotsford Club publication no. 25), from remaining records of the Episcopal Courts of Scotland. His selection contains all cases of marriage, divorce and legitimacy.

Land Law

1681. Cases on appeal under the Land Valuation Acts determined by the judges, 1858-79. [Edinburgh], 1859-80. 1 v.

Continued by: Cases on appeals under the Land Valuation Acts, n.s.

1682. Cases on appeals under the Land Valuation Acts determined by the judges, new series, 1880-1970. Edinburgh, 1881-1971.

Continuation of: Cases on appeals under the Land Valuation Acts. From 1881 cases issued in individual parts, from 1967 in annual vols.

1683. The Lands Tribunal for Scotland reports, 1971- . Edinburgh, W. Green, 1971- . 11 v.

Published as separate section of Scots law times. From 1982 merged with Scottish Land Court reports to form a single section.

1684. Ross, G. Leading cases in the law of Scotland: land rights, 1638-1849. Edinburgh, 1849-51. 3 v.

Microfilm: Dobbs Ferry, Oceana.

1685. Scottish Land Courts reports, 1912-63. Glasgow, 1913-1963. 51 v.

Published as supplement to the Scottish law review. Continued as separate section of the Scots law times from 1964. In both instances may be separately bound. From 1982 the Scottish Land Court reports were merged with the Lands Tribunal for Scotland reports to form a single section of Scots law times.

Mercantile Law

See nos. 827, 839

Parliament

1686. Wight, A. An inquiry into the rise and progress of parliament, chiefly in Scotland ... with a supplement including the cases at large to the present period, 1806. Edinburgh, 1806. 2 v.

Previous ed. 1784.

Revenue Law

1687. Walker, A. De-rating appeals in Scotland under the Rating and Valuation (Apportionment) Act 1928, decided by the Lands Valuation Appeal Court, 1929-30. Edinburgh, 1930. 1 v.

Social Security

See also no. 1592

1688. Hay, W. Decisions on the poor law of Scotland in the Court of Session, and awards by arbitration, 2nd ed., 1711-1865. Edinburgh, 1865. 1 v.

Microfilm: Dobbs Ferry, Oceana.

1st ed. 1859.

Succession

1689. Duncan, J.M. Digest of entail cases ... and the judgments of the court, 1726-1855. Edinburgh, 1856. 1 v.

Tort

1690. Borthwick, J. A treatise on the law of libel and slander as applied in Scotland ... with an appendix containing reports of several cases respecting defamation, 1748-1825. Edinburgh, 1826. 1 v.

Microfilm: Dobbs Ferry, Oceana.

1691. Hay, W. Decisions of the supreme courts of England and Scotland on the liability of proprietors, masters and servants, for reparation of injuries arising from accidents and the negligence of parties, 1798-1860. Edinburgh, 1860. 1 v.

S E Y C H E L L E S

See also nos. 4, 1478

1692. Bourke, P.J. Digest of decisions of the Supreme Court of the Seychelles, 1903-33 and references to appeals from district courts, 1870-1902. Seychelles, 1934. 1 v.

Compiled from court records.

1693. Seychelles Court of Appeal reports, 1965-76. London, 1965-76. 1 v.

1694. Seychelles law reports, 1936/55- . Seychelles, Government Printer, [1982]0 . 6 v.

1695. Seychelles law reports: decisions of the Supreme Court of Seychelles, 1921-23. Victoria, Seychelles, Government Printing Office, [1924]. 1 v.

SUBJECT REPORTS

Mercantile Law

See no. 1

S I E R R A L E O N E

See also nos. 7, 8

1696. African law reports. Sierra Leone series, 1920/36-72/73. Oxford, 1969-77. 9 v.

1950/56-68/69 published Dobbs Ferry, Oceana. Also known as: Sierra Leone law reports.

1697. Sierra Leone law recorder: being a report of decisions of the Supreme and circuit courts on appeal from decisions by the Police

Magistrate of Freetown and the District Commissioners of the Colony and Protectorate, 1922/31-1935/45. Freetown, 1931-50. 3 v.

1698. Sierra Leone law reports being a selection from the cases decided in the full court of the Colony of Sierra Leone, 1912-24. London, 1925. 1 v.

1699. The Sierra Leone law reports: cases decided by the Supreme Court and on appeal therefrom in the Court of Appeal and the Judicial Committee of the Privy Council, 1960/61-63. London, 1966. 3 v.

SUBJECT REPORTS

Mercantile Law

See no. 1

S I N G A P O R E

To 1946, part of the Straits Settlements; a crown colony 1946; joined the Federation of Malaysia 1963; became an independent sovereign state 1965

See also no. 1456

1700. Singapore law reports, 1946-49; 1953-56. Singapore, 1950-51, 1954-57. 8 v.

SUBJECT REPORTS

Constitutional Law

See no. 1459

Public International Law

See no. 1458

SOLOMON ISLANDS

Until 1974 called British Solomon Islands

1701. Solomon Islands law reports, 1980- . [Honiara], High Court of the Solomon Islands, [1983]- . 1 v.

In mimeograph form.

SOMALI REPUBLIC

Formed in 1960 by the merger of British Somaliland and Somalia

1702. Somalia law reports, 1961-65. Mogadiscio, c.1964-67, 2 v.

In mimeograph form.

SUBJECT REPORTS

Mercantile Law

See no. 1

SOUTH AFRICA

In 1951 South Africa left the Commonwealth

1703. All South Africa law reports, 1947. Durban, Butterworths, 1947. 1 v.

Merged with South African law reports, 1948.

1704. [Appellate Division reports] Decisions of the Supreme Court of South Africa (Appellate Division), 1910-46. Cape Town, 1911-47. 38 v.

Reprinted: Johannesburg, Digma Publications, 1973; Microfiche: Cape Town, Juta.

Continued by: South African law reports.

1705. Buchanan, D.M. Cases decided in the Appellate Division of the Supreme Court of South Africa, 1910-12. Grahamstown, 1910-13. 2 v.

Vols. numbered 4 and 5 in continuation of: Buchanan, J. and Buchanan, E.J. Cases decided in the Court of Appeal of the Cape of Good Hope. Cases from that Court additionally included in v. 4, pt. 1.

1706. Prentice Hall weekly legal service, 1923- . Durban, Prentice Hall, 1923- . 121 v. Some judgments in Afrikaans.

1707. The South African law reports, 1947- . Cape Town, Juta, 1947- 140 v. Some judgments in Afrikaans.

Continuation of: Appellate Division reports, Cape Provincial Division reports, Eastern Districts' Local Division reports, Griqualand West Local Division reports, Orange Free State Provincial Division reports; South West Africa High Court reports; Transvaal Provincial Division reports; Witwatersrand Local Division reports.

Absorbed All South Africa law reports, 1948. Includes Zimbabwean decisions.

1708. South African law reports: translation of Afrikaans passages in reported cases, 1969-80. Cape Town, Juta, 1970-80. 11 v.

SUBJECT REPORTS

Customary Law

1709. [Appeal Court of Commissioners' Courts reports] Reports of the Appeal Courts for Commissioners' Courts. Verslae van die Appelhowe vir Kommissarishowe, 1952- . Pretoria, Government Printer, 1952- . Some judgments in Afrikaans.

Name of Courts varies: 1952-62 Native Appeal Courts; 1962-71 Bantu Appeal Courts. Preceded by separate series for each Division. North-Eastern, Central, Southern.

1710. Decisions of the Native Appeal and Divorce Court (Transvaal and Natal), 1929-48. Cape Town, 1930-49. 20 v.

Continued by: Selected decisions of the Native Appeal Court (North-Eastern Division).

1711. Decisions of the Native Appeal Court (Central Division), 1948-51. Pretoria, 1948-52. 1 v.

Continuation of: Native Appeal Court reports (Cape and Orange Free State). Continued by: Appeal Court for Commissioners' Courts reports.

1712. [Native Appeal Court reports (Cape and Orange Free State)] Selection of cases decided in the Native Appeal and Divorce Court (Cape and Orange Free State Division), 1929-48. Cape Town, 1930-48. 20 v.

Continuation of: Reports of cases decided in the Native Appeal Courts of the Transkeian Territories. Continued by: Decisions of the Native Appeal Court (Central Division) and (Southern Division).

1713. Selected decisions of the Native Appeal Court (North-Eastern Division), 1948-51. Pretoria, 1952. 1 v.

Continuation of: Decisions of the Native Appeal and Divorce Court (Transvaal and Natal). Continued by: Appeal Court for Commissioners' Courts reports.

Industrial Law

1714. Industrial law reports; including decisions of the Supreme Court of South Africa and the Industrial Court, 1980- . Cape Town, Juta, 1980- . 5 v.

Published as part of Industrial law journal.

Intellectual Property

1715. Burrell's patent law reports, 1953- . Cape Town, Juta, 1981-.

1716. [Patent law reports] Patent journal, 1961- . Pretoria, Government Printer, 1961- . 23 v.

Maritime Law

1717. [Prize Court reports] Cases decided in the Prize Court of South Africa, 1914-1918. Cape Town, [1925]. 1 v.

Revenue Law

1718. South African tax cases, 1921- . Cape Town, Juta, 1926- . 46 v. Some judgments in Afrikaans.

Includes Zimbabwean cases.

Tort

1719. Rhyn, G. van. Collected decisions on motor collisions. Bloemfontein, [1937]. 1 v.

Water Law

1720. Hall, C.G. Decisions of the Water Courts of the Union of South Africa, 1921-28. Cape Town, 1928. 1 v.

Continuation of: Krummeck. Water Courts decisions. Continued by: Watermeyer. Water Courts decisions.

1721. Krummeck, C.T. Decisions of the Water Courts of the Union of South Africa, 1913-21. Cape Town, 1922. 1 v.

Continued by: Hall. Water Courts decisions.

1722. Vos, W.J. Beslissings van die Waterhowe van Suid-Afrika. Decisions of the Water Courts of South Africa, 1947-69. Cape Town, 1971. 1 v.

Continuation of: Watermeyer. Water Courts decisions.

1723. Watermeyer, H.E.P. Decisions of the Water Courts of the Union of South Africa, 1928/36-1936/46. Cape Town, 1937-47. 2 v.

Continuation of: Hall. Water Courts decisions. Continued by: Vos. Water Courts decisions.

BOPHUTHATSWANA

1724. Bophuthatswana law reports, 1977- . Mafeking, Via Afrika, 1981- .

CAPE PROVINCE

Until 1910, a British colony called Cape Colony; Cape of Good Hope

1725. Buchanan, E.J. Cases decided in the Supreme Court of the Cape of Good Hope, 1873-79. Cape Town, 1874-94. 7 v. in 5.

Reprinted: Cape Town, 1889-94; Johannesburg, Digma Publications, 1973. Microfiche: Cape Town, Juta.

The first vol. is erroneously numbered vol. 3.

1726. Buchanan, J. Cases decided in the Supreme Court of the Cape of Good Hope, 1868-70. Cape Town, 1869-71. 3 v. in 1.

Reprinted: Johannesburg, Digma Publications, 1973; Microfiche: Cape Town, Juta.

1727. Buchanan, J. and Buchanan, E.J. Cases decided in the Court of Appeal of the Cape of Good Hope, 1880-1909. Cape Town, 1905-13. 3 v.

Reprinted: Johannesburg, Digma Publications, 1973; Microfiche: Cape Town, Juta.

There are no cases for 1887-1903 when the Court was abolished. Continued by: Buchanan, D.M. Cases decided in the Appellate Division of S.A.

1728. [Cape Provincial Division reports] Decisions of the Supreme Court of South Africa (Cape of Good Hope Provincial Division), 1910-46. Cape Town, 1911-47. 36 v.

Reprinted: Johannesburg, Digma Publications; 1973; Microfiche: Cape Town, Juta.

Continuation of: Supreme Court reports; Continued by: South African law reports.

1729. 'Cape Times' law reports; a record of every matter disposed of in the Supreme Court, 1891-1910. Cape Town, 1891-1910. 20 v.

1730. Commercial Advertiser reports, 1855. 1 v.

Reprinted from the South African commercial advertiser & Cape Town mail.

1731. [Eastern Districts' Court reports] Cases decided in the Eastern Districts' Court of the Cape of Good Hope, 1880-1910. Cape Town. 1881-88. 24 v.

Reprinted: Johannesburg, Digma Publications, 1973; Microfiche: Cape Town, Juta.

Continued by: Eastern Districts' Local Division reports.

1732. [Eastern Districts' Local Division reports] Cases decided in the Eastern Districts' Local Division (Supreme Court of South Africa), 1910-46. Cape Town, 1911-47. 36 v.

Reprinted: Johannesburg, Digma Publications, 1973; Microfiche: Cape Town, Juta,

Continuation of: Eastern Districts' Court reports; Continued by: South African law reports.

1733. Foord, A.J. Cases decided in the Supreme Court of the Cape of Good Hope, 1880. Cape Town, 1903. 1 v.

Reprinted: Johannesburg, Digma Publications, 1973; Microfiche: Cape Town, Juta.

Previous ed.: 1887.

1734. [Griqualand West High Court reports] Reports of cases decided in the High Court of Griqualand, 1882-1910. Cape Town, 1884-1911. 10 v.

Reprinted: Johannesburg, Digma Publications, 1973.

Continued as: Griqualand West Local Division reports. Also known as: Griqualand reports.

1735. [Griqualand West Local Division reports] Reports of cases decided in the Supreme Court of South Africa (Griqualand West Local Division), 1910-46. Cape Town, 36 v.

Reprinted: Johannesburg, Digma Publications, 1973; Microfiche: Cape Town, Juta.

Continuation of: Griqualand West High Court reports; Continued by: South African law reports.

1736. [Juta's daily reporter] Decisions of the Cape Provincial Division of the Supreme Court of South Africa (and decisions of the Appellate Division when sitting in Cape Town), 1915-25. Cape Town, 1915-25. 11 v.

Cases reprinted from the Cape Times.

1737. Menzies, W. Cases decided in the Supreme Court of the Cape of Good Hope, 1828-49. Cape Town, 1903. 3 v.

Reprinted: Johannesburg, Digma Publications, 1973: Microfiche: Cape Town, Juta.

Previous ed.: 1868-82.

1738. [Monthly law reporter] Decisions of the Supreme Court of South Africa (Eastern Districts Local Division), 1915-25. Grahamstown, 1915-25. 9 v.

Reprinted: Johannesburg, Digma Publications, 1973.

1739. Roscoe, E.R. Cases decided in the Supreme Court of the Cape of Good Hope, 1861-67; 1871-72; 1877-78. Cape Town, 1885. 3 v.

Reprinted: Johannesburg, Digma Publications, 1973; Microfiche: Cape Town, Juta.

1740. Russell, G.F. and W.H. Stuart. Juta's cases decided in the Court of Appeal of the Cape of Good Hope, Oct. 1909-May 1910. Cape Town, 1910. 1 v.

1741. Searle, M.W. Cases decided in the Supreme Court of the Cape of Good Hope, 1850-67. Cape Town, 1884-94. 5 v.

Reprinted: Johannesburg, Digma Publications, 1973; Microfiche: Cape Town, Juta.

1742. [Supreme Court reports] Cases decided in the Supreme Court of the Cape of Good Hope, 1880-1910. Cape Town, 1882-1910. 27 v.

Reprinted: Johannesburg, Digma Publications, 1973; Microfiche: Cape Town, Juta.

Continued by: Cape Provincial Division reports. Also known as: Juta's Supreme Court reports; Supreme Court cases.

1743. Watermeyer, E.B. Cases decided in the Supreme Court of the Cape of Good Hope, 1857. Cape Town, 1883. 1 v.

Reprinted: Johannesburg, Digma Publications, 1973; Microfiche: Cape Town, Juta.

1744. The weekly reporter, 1912-14. Cape Town, 1912-14. 3 v.

Cases reprinted from the South African news. Also known as: Juta's weekly reporter.

NATAL

Before 1910, a British colony

1745. Natal law reports, 1873-78. Pietermaritzburg, 1881. 6 v.

Reprinted: Johannesburg, Digma Publications, 1973; Microfiche: Cape Town, Juta.

Also known as: Finnemore and Dulcken. An intermediate series, published between Old Series (1870-72) and so-called New Series (1879-). v. 1: R.I. Finnemore; v. 206; A.C. Dulcken.

1746. Natal law reports [new series] Cases decided in the Natal Provincial Division of the Supreme Court of South Africa, 1910-32. Cape Town, 1910-33. 23 v.

Reprinted: Johannesburg, Digma Publications, 1973; Microfiche: Cape Town, Juta.

Continuation of: Natal law reports [n.s.] Supreme Court. Continued by: Natal Provincial Division reports.

1747. Natal law reports [new series]. Supreme Court, 1879-1909. Pietermaritzburg, 1902-10. 30 v.

Reprinted: Johannesburg, Digma Publications, 1973.

Continuation of: Natal law reports [o.s.]. Continued by: Natal law reports [n.s.]. Cases decided in the Natal Provincial Division.

1748. Natal law reports [old series], 1867-72. Pietermaritzburg, 1881. 6 v.

Edited by W.B. Morcam.

1749. [Natal Provincial Division reports] Cases decided in the Natal Provincial Division of the Supreme Court of South Africa, 1933-46. Cape Town, 1934-47. 15 v.

Reprinted: Johannesburg, Digma Publications, 1973; Microfiche: Cape Town, Juta.

Continuation of: Natal law reports [n.s.]. Continued by: South African law reports.

1750. Phipson, T. Supreme Court reports, Natal, 1855-59. Pietermaritzburg, 1859. 1 v.

SUBJECT REPORTS

Criminal Law

1751. Cases in the Court of the Special Commission for Zululand, Nov. 1888-April 1889. London, 1889. 1 v.

Contains five cases of High treason and four of murder.

Customary Law

1752. Decisions of the Native High Court, 1899-1929. Pietermaritzburg, 1900-29. 31 v.

Title varies: Reports of decisions ...; Province of Natal. Reports ...

ORANGE FREE STATE

Until 1900 an independent republic. 1900-10 a British colony called Orange River Colony

1753. Gregorowski, R. Zaken Beslist in het Hoog Gerechtshof van den Oranje Vrijstaat, 1883-87. Philippolis, 1886-93. 2 v. In Dutch.

Reprinted: Johannesburg, Digma Publications, 1973; Microfiche: Cape Town, Juta.

1754. [Orange Free State High Court reports] Reports of cases decided in the High Court of the Orange Free State, 1874-78. Philippolis, 1879, 1 v.

Reprinted: Johannesburg, Digma Publications, 1973; Microfiche: Cape Town, Juta.

Compiled by A.P. de Villiers.

1755. [Orange Free State Provincial Division reports] Decisions of the Supreme Court of South Africa (Orange Free State Provincial Division), 1910-46. Cape Town, 1912-47. 37 v.

Reprinted: Johannesburg, Digma Publications, 1973; Microfiche: Cape Town, Juta.

Continuation of: Orange River Colony law reports; Continued as: South African law reports.

1756. [Orange River Colony law reports] Reports of cases decided in the High Court, 1903-09. Grahamstown, 1904-10. 7 v.

Reprinted: Johannesburg, Digma Publications, 1973; Microfiche: Cape Town, Juta.

Continued as: Orange Free State Provincial Division reports.

1757. Zaken Beslisd in het Hooge Gerechtshof van den Oranjevrijstaat, 1879-83. Bloemfontein, 1880-83. 5 v. In Dutch.

Reprinted: Johannesburg, Digma Publications, 1973.

Spelling in title varies.

SUBJECT REPORTS

Criminal Law

1758. Remarks of the judges of the High Court [of the Orange River Colony] in dealing with cases on review and appeal during the years 1903 to Sept. 30, 1906. Bloemfontein, n.d. 1 v.

1759. Remarks of the judges of the High Court [of the Orange River Colony] in quashing and altering sentences of resident magistrates and special Justices of the Peace up to 30 June 1904. Bloemfontein, n.d. 3 v.

SOUTH WEST AFRICA

Prior to 1920 a German possession mandated to South Africa in 1915

1760. The law reports of South Africa. South West Africa. Decisions of the High Court of South West Africa, 1920-45. Cape Town, 1921-46. 26 v.

Reprinted: Johannesburg, Digma Publications, 1973.

Continued by: South African law reports.

TRANSKEI

SUBJECT REPORTS

Customary Law

1761. Decisions of the Native Appeal Court (Southern Division), 1948-51. Pretoria, 1948-52. 1 v.

Continuation of: Native Appeal Court reports (Cape and Orange Free State). Continued by: Appeal Court for Commissioners' Courts reports.

1762. Reports of cases decided in the Native Appeal Courts of the Transkeian Territories, 1894-1929. Cape Province, 1910-30. 6 v.

Continued as: Native Appeal Court reports (Cape and Orange Free State).

1763. Warner, W.E. Reports of all important cases heard in Native Territories, Appeal Court sitting in Umtata and Butterworth from the date of its establishment to 1907. Butterwoth, 1907. 1 v.

TRANSVAAL

Until 1877 and 1881-1900 an independent republic called the South African Republic; 1877-81 and 1900-1910 a British colony called Transvaal

1764. Duxbury, W.S. Complete record of all cases decided in the High Court of Justice of the South African Republic, May-June, 1895. Johannesburg, 1895. 1 v.

1765. Hertzog, J.B.M. Cases decided in the High Court of the South African Republic, 1893. London, 1903. 1 v.

English translation of no. 1766. Translated by J.W.S. Leonard. Sometimes referred to as Supreme Court cases, S.A.R. v. 5.

1766. Hertzog, J.B.M. Rapporten van zaken in het Hoog Gerechtshof der Z.A.R. beslist, 1893. Leiden, 1897. In Dutch.

For English translation see no. 1765.

1767. Kotze, J.G. Cases decided in the High Court of the Transvaal Colony, 1877-81. London & Pretoria, 1912. 1 v.

Reprinted: Johannesburg, Digma Publications, 1973; Microfiche: Cape Town, Juta.

Cases during the British occupation, 1877-81. Previous eds.: 1885, 1896.

1768. Kotze, J.G. Zaken in het Hooggerechtshof der Z.A.R. beslist, 1881-84. Pretoria, 1893. In Dutch.

For English translation see v. 1 of no. 1772.

1769. [Leader law reports] Cases decided in the Supreme Court of the Transvaal and Witwatersrand High Court, 1909-10. Johannesburg, 1909-10. 2 v.

Cases reprinted from the Transvaal Leader [a Johannesburg newspaper].

1770. The official reports of the High Court of the South African Republic, translated into English, 1894-99. London, 1903-12. 6 v.

Reprinted: Johannesburg, Digma Publications, 1973; Microfiche: Cape Town, Juta.

English translation of no. 1771. v. 1-4 published in Cape Town.

1771. Officieele rapporten van het Hooggerechtshof der Z.A.R. Republic, 1894-99. Pretoria, 1893-1912. 4 v. In Dutch.

For English translation see no. 1770.

1772. [Supreme Court cases, S.A.R.] Reports of cases decided in the Supreme Court of the South African Republic (Transvaal), 1881-92. Durban, 1894-1903. 4 v.

Reprinted: Johannesburg, Digma Publications, 1973; Microfiche: Cape Town, Juta.

V. 1 is an English translation of no. 1768. v. 1: J.G. Kotze; v. 2: J.G. Kotze and S.H. Barber; v. 3-4: S.H. Barber and W.A. Macfadyen. For v. 5 see no. 1765.

1773. [Transvaal Provincial Division decisions] Cases decided in the Transvaal Provincial Division (Supreme Court of South Africa), 1910-46. Cape Town, 1911-47. 37 v.

Reprinted: Johannesburg, Digma Publications, 1973; Microfiche: Cape Town, Juta.

Continuation of: Transvaal Supreme Court reports; Continued by: South African law reports.

1774. [Transvaal Supreme Court reports] Reports of cases decided in the Supreme Court, 1902-09. Grahamstown, 1903-10. 9 v.

Reprinted: Johannesburg, Digma Publications, 1973; Microfiche: Cape Town, Juta.

Continued by: Transvaal Provincial Division decisions.

1775. [Witwatersrand High Court reports] Reports of cases decided in the Witwatersrand High Court, 1902-1909. Grahamstown, 1903-10. 9 v.

Reprinted: Johannesburg, Digma Publications, 1973; Microfiche: Cape Town, Juta.

Continued by: Witwatersrand Local Division reports.

1776. [Witwatersrand Local Division reports] Cases decided in the Witwatersrand Local Division, 1910-46. Cape Town, 1911-46. 37 v.

Reprinted: Johannesburg, Digma Publications, 1973; Microfiche: Cape Town, Juta.

Continuation of: Witwatersrand High Court reports; Continued by: South African law reports.

SPECIALISED SUBJECTS

Mining

1777. Barber, S.H. Transvaal gold law, translation into English of Law No. 15 of 1898, together with reports of cases decided ..., 1898-1904. Cape Town, 1904. 1 v.

S O U T H   Y E M E N

1839-1967, part of the territory known as Aden, a British Protectorate

See also nos. 3, 4

1778. Law reports of Aden: containing cases determined by the Supreme Court of the Colony of Aden, 1937-60. Aden, 1955-64. 4 v.

S R I   L A N K A

To 1972 called Ceylon

1779. Balasingham, K. Reports of cases decided by the Supreme Court of Ceylon, Court of Vice Admiralty of Ceylon and His Majesty's Privy Council on appeals from Ceylon, 1904-10. Colombo, 1904-11. 5 v.

There is a supplement to v. 2. v. 1 has some earlier cases from 1887 onwards.

1780. Beven, E. and Mills, A. Legal miscellany: containing decisions of Supreme Court, sitting in appeal, 1820-67. Colombo, 1864-67. 1 v.

Two eds. of pt. 1 issued 1864.

1781. Browne, K.G.D. Reports of cases decided in the Supreme and other courts of Ceylon, 1872-1902. Colombo, [1900-03]. 3 v.

1782. Ceylon law journal; embodying reports and notes of cases decided by the Supreme Court of Ceylon, and in appeal by His Majesty, the King, in His Privy Council, 1936-48. Colombo, 1936-48. 9 v.

1783. Ceylon law recorder: legal miscellany and law reports. new series, 1960-62. Kolte, 1960-[62]. 2 v. Some judgments in Sinhalese.

Law reports in ordinary pagination, other matter paginated as preliminaries. Continuation of: Ceylon law recorder: monthly legal miscellany and law report.

1784. Ceylon law recorder: monthly legal miscellany and law report, 1918-46. Kolte. 1919-46. 22 v.

Originally published in Colombo. Title varies: some vols, including v. 7-14, new series. Continued by: Ceylon law recorder: legal miscellany and law reports, new series.

1785. Ceylon law reports: being reports of cases decided in the Supreme Court of Ceylon, 1887-97. Colombo, 1892-97. 3 v.

Editors: v. 1 T.E. De Sampayo and J. Van Langenberg; v. 2 H.L. Wendt and T.E. De Sampayo; v. 3 H.L. Wendt, T.E. De Sampayo and F.M. De Saram.

1786. Ceylon law weekly: containing cases decided by the Supreme Court of Ceylon, and His Majesty the King in the Privy Council on appeal from the Supreme Court of Ceylon, 1931-72. Colombo, 1931-72. 81 v. Some judgments in Sinhalese and Tamil.

Editor: v. 1 H.H. Basnayake.

1787. Ceylon weekly reporter, 1915-20. n.d. 8 v.

1788. Conderlag, W.M. and Peiris. Reports, 1843-52.

1789. Creasy, H. Ceylon reports: judgments of the Supreme Court between 1859 and 1870; with comments and notes of English and other cases by Sir Edward Creasy, 1859-70. London, 1876. 1 v.

1790. Crowther, J. Decisions in the Supreme Court sitting in appeal, 1863. Colombo, [1869], 1 v.

1791. Current law reports of Ceylon being reports of law cases heard by the Supreme Court and by the Privy Council on appeal from Ceylon. [Edited by] F.A. Hayley, 1909-10. Colombo, [1909-10]. 2 v.

1792. De Witt, A.L. and Weeresinghe, G.E.C. Appeal Court reports, 1905-10. Colombo, 1907-[10]. 5 v.

Some cases from 1903.

1793. [Examiner reports] Ceylon Examiner reports: judgments of the Supreme Court of Ceylon, 1896-98. Colombo, 1896-98. 1 v.

1794. Grenier, Sir J.C.S. Appeal reports for 1872 being reports of cases argued and determined in the Supreme Court of Ceylon sitting in appeal, 1872-74. Colombo, 1872-74. 3 v.

1795. Jayewardene, A. St. V. and De Alwis, L.H. Court of Appeal cases of Ceylon: being reports of cases decided by the Supreme Court of Ceylon in its original and appellate jurisdiction and sitting as a colonial court of Admiralty and by His Majesty's Privy Council on appeal from Ceylon, 1911-16. Colombo, [1912-16]. 4 v.

Editors from v. 3: A. St. V. Jayewardene, L.H. De Alwis, J. Joseph and E.G.P. Jayetileke.

1796. Joseph, A.O. and Bevan, E. Digest of decisions of the Supreme Court, 1859. Colombo, 1863. 1 v.

The appendix contains Privy Council judgment in the case of Charles Hargraves Ledward, 1860. Some cases are reported in extenso.

1797. Leader law reports, 1907-12. [n.d.]. 6 v.

1798. Leembruggen, G.H.P. and Asirvatham, R.N. Supreme Court decisions in appeal, 1905-07. Colombo, 1906-08. 3 v.

1799. Lorenz, C.A. Appeal reports being reports of cases argued and determined in the Supreme Court of Ceylon sitting in appeal, 1856-59. Colombo, 1860-71. 3 v.

A revised edition in 2 v. covering 1856-57, with obsolete cases reduced to summaries only, was published in 1939-40.

1800. Matara cases: being a collection hitherto unpublished decisions by the Supreme Court of Ceylon, on appeal from the District Court of Matara, 1891-1914. Colombo, 1911-15. 2 v.

Edited by O.L. De Kretser.

1801. Modern law reports, embodying cases decided by the Supreme Court of the Republic of Sri Lanka, 1975- . Colombo, C.L. Perera, 1975- . Some judgments in Sinhalese.

1802. Morgan, O.W.C. Legal miscellany, 1852-53. 1859. 1 v.

1803. Murray, A. Cases heard and determined in appeal by the Supreme Court of the Island of Ceylon, 1846-47. Colombo, 1848. 1 v.

1804. New law reports of cases decided by the Supreme Court of Ceylon, the Court of Vice-Admiralty in the Island, and Her Majesty the Queen in Her Privy Council on appeal from the Supreme Court of the Island, 1894-1978. Colombo, 1896-[1981]. 79 v.

Reprinted: v. 1-3, 1929-53.

Includes some earlier cases, including one 1874 case. v. 79 was published in two separately paginated sections. Number 18 of v. 79 II published in 1981, numbers 19-21 undated. Continuation of: Supreme Court Circular. Continued by: Sri Lanka law reports.

1805. Notes of cases decided by the Supreme Court of Ceylon, 1911-16. Colombo, 1914-18. 6 v.

Edited by K. Balasingham.

1806. Rajarathnam, S. Revised reports of Ceylon cases. Tellippalai, 1922. 1 v.

1807. Ramanathan, P. Judgments of the Supreme Court of Judicature and of the High Court of Appeal of the Island of Ceylon, 1820-33. Colombo, 1877. 1 v.

1808. Ramanathan, P. Reports of cases heard and determined by the Supreme Court of Ceylon, 1877. Colombo, 1878. 1 v.

1809. Ramanathan, P. Reports of important cases heard and determined by the Supreme Court of Ceylon, 1843-55. Colombo, 1884. 1 v.

1810. Ramanathan, P. Reports of important cases heard and determined by the Supreme Court of Ceylon, 1860-68. Colombo, 1880-81. 2 v.

An appendix to v. 1 contains cases during the period by the Judicial Committee of the Privy Council on appeal from the Supreme Court of Ceylon.

1811. Ramanathan, P. Reports of important cases heard and determined by the Supreme Court of Ceylon, 1872, 1875-76. Colombo, 1890, 1 v.

1812. Revised reports of Ceylon: being a re-publication of all such cases of the Supreme Court of the Island of Ceylon reported from the year 1820 as are still of practical utility, with notes, 1820-42. Jaffna, n.d. 1 v.

1813. Sri Lanka law reports, 1978- . Colombo, Ministry of Justice, 1978- . 8 v. Sinhalese and English.

Continuation of: New law reports. Published in collaboration with the Bar Association of Sri Lanka. Published in two volumes each year, one for the Court of Appeal, one for the Supreme Court.

1814. Supreme Court circular: containing reports of cases decided and of orders and minutes issued by the Supreme Court, 1878-91. Colombo, 1879-92. 9 v.

Issued as a supplement to the Ceylon Government Gazette. Superseded by: New Law reports.

1815. [Supreme Court decisions] Important decisions by the Supreme Court of the Island of Ceylon. Edited by G. Koch, 1899. Colombo, [1900]. 1 v.

1816. [Supreme Court judgments] Judgments and other decisions and directions of the Supreme Court of the Island of Ceylon from the promulgation of the New Charter, 1st October, 1833 to March 1836, arranged according to the respective subjects of them. Edited by Sir Charles Marshall, 1833-36. Paris, 1839. 1 v.

1817. Supreme Court reports, being reports of cases decided by the Supreme Court of Ceylon, 1892-94. Colombo, 1893-96. 3 v.

v. 1 includes several earlier cases. Editors: v. 1 W. Pereira and C.M. Fernando; v. 2 C.M. Fernando, H.A. Loos and H.A. Jayewardene; v. 3 H.A. Loos and H.A. Jayewardene.

1818. [Tambyah, I.] Reports of cases decided in the Supreme Court of Ceylon, Court of Admiralty, and Privy Council, 1899-1911. Colombo, 1899-1912. 7 v.

Before 1899 included in Ceylon law review, subsequently paginated with their own title page. Some earlier cases included. no. 1819 published with v. 7.

1819. Tambyah, I. and Sansoni, W. Appeal cases of Ceylon, 1911. Colombo, 1912. 1 v.

Issued as a separately paginated volume in Ceylon law review with volume 7 of Reports of cases ... edited by I. Tambyah, which also appeared as a separately paginated volume.

1820. Times of Ceylon law reports, 1922/23-42; 1950/51. Colombo, 1922-42; 1951. 19 v.

Title varies: From v. 7. New series.

1821. Vanderstraaten, J.W. Decisions of the Supreme Court of Ceylon sitting in appeal, 1869-71. Colombo, [1874]. 1 v.

1822. Weerakoon, E.B. Supreme Court decisions in appeal, 1908-12. Colombo, 1908-12. 7 v.

1823. Wendt, H.L. Reports of cases argued and determined in the Supreme Court of Ceylon, sitting in appeal, 1882-83. Colombo, 1884. 1 v.

1824. Wijeyewardene, E.A.L. Appeal cases, 1913. 1913, 1 v.

SPECIFIC COURTS

Police and Court of Requests

1825. Fernando, G. Decisions of the Supreme Court of appeal from Police Courts and Courts of Requests in Kandy, 1875-76. Kandy, 1878. 1 v.

Several earlier decisions are included.

1826. Neil, L. Courts of Requests: a practical treatise on their constitution and mode of procedure; including a selection of circulars, correspondence and forms and decisions of the Supreme Court on reviews and appeals, 1845-55. Colombo, 1858. 1 v.

1827. [Police Court cases] Handbook of Police Courts, being a digest of orders of Supreme Court in Police Court cases. Edited by W.W. Beling and J.W. Vanderstraaten, 1846-68. Colombo, 1863-69. 2 v.

1828. Solemo, F.C. Decisions of the Supreme Court on appeals from Courts of Requests, 1861-67. Kandy, 1871. 1 v.

SUBJECT REPORTS

Constitutional Law

1829. Decisions of the Constitutional Court of Sri Lanka, 1973- . Colombo, Registry of the Constitutional Court, 1973- .

Criminal Law

1830. Criminal appeal reports containing cases decided by the Supreme Court of Ceylon in the exercise of its criminal appellate jurisdiction, 1914-30. Colombo, [1914]-31. 3 v.

Edited by A.B. Cooray, E.A.L. Wijeyewardene and E.F.N. Gratiaen.

Hindu Law

1831. Decisions on Hindu law. Edited by H.L. Muthukrishna, 1825-50. [n.d.]. 1 v.

Islamic Law

1832. Muslim marriage and divorce law reports: containing cases decided by the Board of Kathis on appeal, and by the Supreme Court of Ceylon on appeal from the Board of Kathris, 1937-39. Colombo, [1939]. 1 v.

Edited by Y.S. Hameed.

1833. Muslim marriage and divorce law reports; containing cases decided by the Board of Quazis, the Supreme Court of Ceylon, and Her Majesty the Queen in Her Privy Council on appeal from the Supreme Court of Ceylon, and articles on marriage and divorce matters, with a digest, 1962-65. Colombo, n.d. 2 v.

Editor-in-chief: M. Markhani.

Kandyan Law

See also no. 1837

1834. Appeal reports: being decisions of the Supreme Court on appeal from the District Court of Kandy, 1833-59. Colombo, 1862. 1 v.

Edited by N.J. Austin.

1835. Beven, E. and Siebel, E.L. Appeal reports, being decisions of the Supreme Court on appeals from the District Court of Kandy, 1859-75. Kandy, 1877. 1 v.

Land Law

1836. Land acquisition cases: reports of decisions of the Supreme Court. Colombo, 1912. 1 v.

1837. Siebel, E.L. Liability of estate owners, and of superintendents; being a collection of important decisions on the subject, by the Supreme Court and the District Court of Kandy. Colombo, [1877]. 1 v.

Practice

1838. Lorenz, C.A. Contributions to a treatise on namptissement; being reports of cases decided by the Supreme Court and the District Court of Colombo, and translations of the titles of Voet and Kersteman on the subject, 1830-56. Colombo, 1856. 1 v.

2nd edition by J.B. Weinman in Peltah, 1881, omitting District Court decisions but adding the latest Supreme Court decisions.

Revenue Law

1839. Ceylon income tax cases, 1933-36. Colombo, 1937-38. 1 v.

Edited by K.S.V. Aiyar.

1840. Nell, L. Tolls: a collection of cases, under the Ordinance no. 9 of 1845, fully reported with the evidence, arguments of counsel, and decisions in appeal, 1845-58. Cotta, 1858. 1 v.

1841. Reports of Ceylon tax cases containing cases decided by the Supreme Court of Ceylon and Her Majesty the Queen in Her Privy Council on appeal from the Supreme Court of Ceylon, 1905-71. Colombo, 1960-74. 3 v.

Title varies: v. 3 Reports of Sri Lanka tax cases. Also known as: Ceylon tax cases; Sri Lanka tax cases. Contents: v. 1 Income tax, excess profits duty and profits tax cases, 1933-60; v. 2 Stamp duty, 1905-60, Estate duty, 1920-60; v. 3 Continuation covering all topics.

Social Security

1842. Sinnacutty, W. Law of maintenance, being a collection of cases on the subject decided in appeal under the Vagrant Ordinance, 1846-76. Jaffna, 1878. 1 v.

S U D A N

1843. Cases in the Court of Appeal and the High Court, 1953-54. Khartoum. 1955. 1 v.

Edited by Justice (R.C.) Stanley-Baker.

1844. Digest of the decisions of the Court of Appeal of the Sudan, 1915-26. Khartoum, 1926. 1 v.

Edited by R.H. Dun and T.N. Francoudi.

1845. Sudan law journal and reports, 1956- . Khartoum, Technical Bureau, Supreme Court, [1959]- . 20 v. From 1970 some judgments in Arabic.

1846. Sudan law reports (civil), 1900- . Khartoum, Sudan Law Project, Faculty of Law, University of Khartoum, 1964- . 7 v.

1900-40 reprinted: Dobbs Ferry, Oceana, 1969, as Sudan law reports: civil cases.

Issued in mimeograph form.

SUBJECT REPORTS

Criminal Law

1847. Court of Criminal Appeal. Law reports, 1949-55. Khartoum, 1954-55. 1 v.

Also known as: The green book.

1848. Sudan law reports: criminal cases, 1900/40- . Khartoum, Sudan Law Project, Faculty of Law, University of Khartoum, 1971- . 1 v.

Issued in mimeograph form.

Mercantile Law

See no. 1.

S W A Z I L A N D

See also nos. 5, 6

1849. The Swaziland law reports, 1963- . Mbabane, Government Printer, 1969- .

Continuation, in part, of: High Commission Territories law reports.

SUBJECT REPORTS

Mercantile Law

See no. 1

T A N Z A N I A

Formed in 1964 by the union of Tanganyika and Zanzibar

See also nos. 3, 4

1850. The law reports of Tanzania, 1973-80. Dar es Salaam, Faculty of Law, University of Dar es Salaam, 1973-80. 8 v.

1851. Tanzania High Court digest, 1967-72. Dar es Salaam, University of Dar es Salaam, Faculty of Law, 1967-72. 6 v.

SUBJECT REPORTS

Mercantile Law

See no. 1

TANGANYIKA

1852. A digest of appeals from local courts, 1930/52-64. Dar es Salaam, 1953-65. 11 v.

1853. Tanganyika law reports of cases determined by the High Court of Tanganyika and upon appeals therefrom by the Court of Appeal for Eastern Africa and the Privy Council, 1921/52-1953/57. Dar es Salaam, 1955-59. 2 v.

Revised and extended reprint of no. 1854.

1854. Tanganyika Territory law reports, 1921/28-1938/47. Dar es Salaam, 1928-47. 5 v.

For reprint see no. 1853.

Originally published as supplements to the Government Gazette.

ZANZIBAR

1855. Zanzibar Protectorate law reports containing cases determined by the High Court for Zanzibar, 1868/1918-1951/56. Zanzibar, 1919-61. 8 v.

v. 1 includes cases on appeal to the High Court of Judicature, Bombay; v. 1-4 includes cases on appeal to the Privy Council; v. 1-6 includes cases on appeal to the Court of Appeal for Eastern Africa. v. 1-3 published in London. Continued by: Eastern Africa law reports.

T O N G A

1856. Tongan law reports: cases decided in the Supreme Court of Tonga, 1908/59- . Nuku'alofa, Government Printer, 1961- . 3 v.

T R I N I D A D   A N D   T O B A G O

See also 1862

1857. [Trinidad and Tobago law reports] Judgments delivered in the Supreme Court, 1893- . Port of Spain, Government Printer, 1913- . 20 v.

v. 1-5 reprinted: Buffalo, William S. Hein, 1968 as Trinidad Supreme Court reports.

v. 8-9, 1940-48, v. 17-18, 1957-65 never published.

1858. Trinidad and Tobago Royal gazette, 1910- . Port of Spain, 1910- .

Since May 1910 includes all printed judgments.

U G A N D A

See also nos. 3, 4

1859. The Uganda law reports, containing cases determined by the High Court of Uganda, and by the Court of Appeal for Eastern Africa, on appeal from the Court, 1904/10-73. Kampala, 1910-73. 11 v.

v. 1-7 published in Entebbe; v. 8 published in Oxford. Continued by: East African law reports. Title varies: v. 1-6 Uganda Protectorate law reports.

SUBJECT REPORTS

Customary Law

1860. Customary law reports: being a digest of decisions on customary law made by the principal court of His Highness the Kabaka of Buganda?, 1940/55-58. Kampala, 1960, 1957. 2 v. Some judgments in Luganda?

Mercantile Law

See no. 1

W E S T I N D I E S

See also entries under individual islands: Bahamas, Barbardos, Belize, Bermuda, Guyana, Jamaica, Trinidad and Tobago

1861. No Entry

1862. West Indian reports, 1958/59- . London, Butterworths, 1960- 29 v.

1862 WEST INDIES

Includes decisions from the Bahamas, Barbados, Belize, Bermuda, Eastern Caribbean States, Guyana, Jamaica and Trinidad and Tobago.

WINDWARD ISLANDS

From 1885-1959, the Islands had an independent constitutional identity

1863. Greaves, Sir W.H. Reports of judgments of the Windward Islands Court of Appeal, 1866-1904. Barbardos, 1905. 1 v.

Covers appeals from Barbados, Grenada, St. Lucia and St. Vincent.

W E S T E R N S A M O A

1864. Western Samoa law reports, 1921-29; 1960-69. Apia, Attorney-General's Office, c. 1980- . 2 v.

In mimeograph form. Published irregularly.

Z A M B I A

To 1964 called Northern Rhodesia

See also Rhodesia and Nyasaland

1865. [Northern Rhodesia law reports] Law reports of Northern Rhodesia, 1931/37-55/58. Lusaka. 6 v.

Reprinted: Revised ed. v. 1-4, Lusaka, 1962.

Continued by: Rhodesia and Nyasaland law reports.

1866. Zambia law reports, containing selected judgments of the Court of Appeal for Zambia, the Supreme Court of Zambia, the High Court for Zambia and Magistrates' Courts, 1963/64- . Lusaka, Council of Law Reporting, 1976- . 19 v.

Title varies: v. 1 Zambia and Northern Rhodesian law reports.

SUBJECT REPORTS

Mercantile Law

See no. 1

Z I M B A B W E

To 1964 called Southern Rhodesia. To 1980 called Rhodesia.

See also Rhodesia and Nyasaland **and** nos. 1707, 1718

1867. The Rhodesian law reports, 1964-79. Salisbury, 1965-80. 17 v.

Continuation, in part, of: Rhodesia and Nyasaland law reports. Continued by: Zimbabwe law reports.

1868. [Southern Rhodesia law reports] Decisions of the High Court of Southern Rhodesia, 1911-55. Salisbury, 1911-56. 46 v.

To 1914 published in Cape Town. Continued in part by: Rhodesia and Nyasaland law reports. Also known as: Juta's reports of the High Court of Southern Rhodesia.

1869. Zimbabwe law reports, 1980- . Harare, Government Printer, 1981- 4 v.

Continuation of Rhodesian law reports.

SUBJECT REPORTS

Criminal Law

1870. Cases [i.e. criminal cases] reviewed by the Chief Native Commissioner, 1928/32-1958. Salisbury, 1928-58. 4 v.

Published with no. 1871.

Customary Law

1871. [Native Appeal Court reports] Reports of cases in the Native Appeal Court, 1928-62. Salisbury, 1928-63. 6 v.

Reprinted in 1 v. Salisbury, Government Printer, [1975?].

Continued by: Reports and decisions of the Court of Appeal for African civil cases. No. 1870 published with this 1928-58.

1872. Reports and decisions of the Court of Appeal for African civil cases, 1963-79. Salisbury, 1964-80. 16 v.

Continuation of: Native Appeal Court reports.

Mercantile Law

See no. 1

Revenue Law

See no. 1718

T I T L E   I N D E X

References are to item numbers. Where the jurisdiction is not apparent from the title, this has been included in square brackets. The following abbreviations have been used.

Aust	Australia
B.Col	British Columbia
Bel	Belize
Beng	Bengal
Bot	Botswana
Can	Canada
Cape	Cape Province, South Africa
E&W	England & Wales
Guer	Guernsey
Guj	Gujarat
Guy	Guyana
HCT	High Commission Territories, Southern Africa
HK	Hong Kong
Ir	Ireland
J&K	Jammu & Kashmir
Jam	Jamaica
Jers	Jersey
Karn	Karnataka
Ker	Kerala
Kiri	Kiribati
L.Burma	Lower Burma
Les	Lesotho
Mad.Pra	Madhya Pradesh
Mah	Maharashtra
Mal	Malaysia
Man	Manitoba
Maur	Mauritius
NSW	New South Wales
NWT	North West Territory, Australia
NZ	New Zealand
New Br	New Brunswick
Newf	Newfoundland
Nig	Nigeria
Nov.Sc	Nova Scotia
OFS	Orange Free State
Ont	Ontario
Ori	Orissa
Pak	Pakistan
Pal	Palestine
Pun	Punjab
Queb	Quebec
Qld	Queensland

Raj	Rajasthan
S.Afr	South Africa
Sar	Sarawak
Sco	Scotland
Sri L	Sri Lanka
Tam.Nad	Tamil Nadu
Tang	Tanganyika
Transk	Transkei
Tvl	Transvaal
UP	Uttar Pradesh
Ugan	Uganda
Vic	Victoria
W.Aust	Western Australia
W.Beng	West Bengal
Zam	Zambia
Zim	Zimbabwe

SUBJECT INDEX

References are to item numbers.

INDEX OF JURISDICTIONS

References are to page numbers